A LYRICIST IS BORN

A Memoir of Consistency, Patience, and Perserverance

A LYRICIST IS BORN

A Memoir of Consistency, Patience, and Perserverance

MANLEY PETIT

ARPress
45 Dan Road Suite 15
Canton MA 02021

Hotline: 1(888) 821-0229
Fax: 1(508) 545-7580

Ordering Information:

Quantity sales. Special discounts are available on quantity purchases by corporations, associations, and others. For details, contact the publisher at the address above.
Printed in the United States of America.

ISBN-13:	Paperback	979-8-89676-421-2
	eBook	979-8-89676-422-9

Library of Congress Control Number: 2025911335

To my son Marcell, better known as MJ,

Never forget the bedtime stories that taught you about consistency, patience, and perseverance. Apply these three principles to whatever you decide to pursue in life, and you will become a shooting star. Trust me, the old man knows!

Love,

Daddy

Table Of Contents

Introduction... Prelude
Album I:.. Who Am I?
Album II:... The School Supplies
Album III: .... In The Poem Of My Mind
Album IV: ....The French Philosophers
Album V:.. Would You Like To Dance?
Album VI: .... Who's Calling?
Album VII:...The Soundtrack Of My Life
Album VIII: ....The New Ending Of My Life
Album IX: .... Seize The Moment
Album X: ....Happiness
Album XI: ....Peaceful
Album XII:..Consistency
Album XIII: ....Patience
Album XIV: .... Perseverance
Outroduction ....Epilogue
Song Credits... I Gave Myself Credit

PRELUDE

Life is nothing but music in my eardrums. Wait! Let me repeat: life is nothing but music in my eardrums. Life is nothing but words, sounds, and music in my eardrums. My dream of becoming a lyricist was not listed in the soundtrack of so-called life, as my only dream as a kid was becoming a dentist. But I would constantly play with the idea of being a lyrical wizard lyricist in my head, over and over, just like a broken record.

Then again, I would fold the idea just like a deck of cards, because being a lyricist was not inherited in my family's characteristics. Me, a lyricist? That was more than doubtful. Who, me? I would smirk, but the thought was tempting and appealing, as writing had always been a hobby as long as I could remember holding a number two pencil or a pen. Writing became a gifted passion, in every sense of the word.

Because, for the record, I've got soul—but I was not blessed with a soulful voice like those legends: John Legend, Leon Bridges, Michael Kiwanuka, Juke Ross, Sam Cooke, Whitney Houston, Aretha Franklin, Alicia Keys, Adele, Norah Jones, Amy Winehouse, Macy Gray, Jhene Aiko, Erykah Badu and Marvin Gaye in front of the microphone. Nonetheless, having and holding a pen in my right hand to express my feelings and emotions was always, and will always be, my microphone, as I could make words sing melodies. As the great rapper, Nas raps, *"All I need is One Mic,"* I would sing to myself, *"All I need is One Pen."*

Furthermore, I have never performed on stage in front of thousands of fans singing every word of my songs or lyrics, I never sold out venues, never toured the world. Nevertheless, all the pages, napkins, sticky notes, notepads, and notebook I have ever written on have always—and will always—be my die-hard fans, as they follow me wherever I go, much like a "Stan,"a term coined by one of my favorite lyricists, Eminem.

I have never been in a recording studio where composers, producers, musicians, and songwriters joined forces to make beautiful music and hit records. However, the basement on 112 Methuen Street symbolizes the recording studio I never had. It was finished, furnished, and equipped just like a studio, as I fantasized this lifestyle of being a lyricist. I treated that basement like a regular studio, focusing solely on creating lyrics—nothing else mattered. It allowed me to block out all the nuisance and noise. It was soundproof, just like a real studio. My pain, my struggle, my hard work, and my tears are cemented down in that cellar.

That is where I wrote my first lines. That is where I found the oxygen to breathe fresh air and manifest the life I always wanted to live—the place where I elevated to become the man I am today because I honed my craft there, I used to remind myself: when you come from the bottom—in my case, the basement—the only way to go is upstairs. So I worked my behind off, fearlessly elevating my skills and taking the elevator of life, hoping that one day my name would stand among the great songwriters and lyricists. And perhaps, one day, I could look back, count my blessings, and appreciate all the grace I've received along the way—before I fade.

What was the inspiration for this book? Well, I never thought about writing a book—let alone a book on song lyrics—but one day, January 4, 2022, to be exact, I asked myself, *"What are you going to do with all these lyrics?"* At the time, I had penned hundreds of song lyrics: the majority were finished, some incomplete, and others still waiting to be transcribed from sticky notes into a formal Word document. It dawned on me—I cannot take them with me when the heavens above call my name and number. I needed to do something, something that would keep them alive for years to come, even when I am gone, because they cannot be sprinkled on my casket like fine dirt.

So, in that moment, it became a moment of clarity—it was evident that writing a book would sum up a vast panoply of song lyrics and pieces of work. Subsequently, let this book be a gift not only to my brilliant son, Marcell, but also to dreamers around the world. There you have it—that's my story, and I'm sticking to it.

This book is based on song lyrics. As a result, I chose to use musical verbiage throughout to align with its purpose. Over the years, writing lyrics as a hobby to purge ideas and keep my mind occupied and sane, I have always felt that every chapter of my life represents an album—literally. Thus, the word *"Album"* will be used in lieu of chapter to describe each part of this book. Consequently, every album contains a track list; each track or song lyric I ever penned uniquely portrays a distinctive event in my life and tells a specific story. Whether it was good or bad, beautiful or ugly, each song lyric deep down mirrors my life.

So, without further ado, welcome to my listening party of "A Lyricist is Born" Volume I. I hope you enjoy every chapter and event, —or should I say, every album and track—as much as I have.

Last but not least, don't forget to press "Play." Somehow, someway, if you don't get the message, please hit rewind—oops, I mean flip the page.

ALBUM I
WHO AM I?

I am a property of April as I was born on Thursday, April 8, 1982, in Port-Au-Prince, Haiti and raised in a small town called Croix-Des-Missions, locally referred to as Damien. My childhood home was situated in a neighborhood known as *Lakou Kokoye,* which translates to *The Coconut Neighborhood* in English. It was vastly surrounded and encircled by tall, short, and curved coconut trees, with scattered trees such as palm, plantain, banana, mango, and lime, along with ravines, ponds, unpaved corridors, gardens (*jardins*), huts, and concrete houses. From my fenced front yard, looking out, I saw a surviving world—a world where everyone was trying to feed their families, make ends meet to meet their unmet needs and take actions into their own hands, as they could not rely on anyone to provide even the most basic necessities of life.

As such, there were plenty of street vendors and merchants selling everything under the sun to survive:

- Breakfast: spaghetti, hot chocolate, coffee
- Lunch: rice and legumes, rice and beans, sodas, fried fish stew, soup, chicken with sauce, griot (fried goat and plantains), and *pikliz* (similar to coleslaw, but spicy hot)
- Dinner: ice cubes, cooked corn, and many more delicious edibles

One of the things I loved—and still crave to this day—is *Akra*, also known as Malanga fritters: crunchy appetizers served with *pikliz*. That was my heaven on earth as a youngster. I would suck my teeth, trying to rescue every leftover piece of *akra*, saying, *li gou anpil*—in other words, so delicious.

Alternatively, some merchants chose different marketable paths, selling loosies or single cigarettes, gasoline, tools, charcoal, liquors, and beer.

You would also hear shoe shiners ringing their super loud solid brass hand call bells, hoping to attract customers who need their footwear polished and cleaned.

As you navigate towards Damien, you will find a catholic church, L'eglise de Croix-Des-Missions, within easy walking distance of my house and situated in the intersection, not too far from the overpopulated Marche Public (or grocery market). As you pass the market, you will see a variety of local stores in the alley, owned mainly by local owners. Further along, you will notice a bridge and a river—*La Rivière Grise*—always overflowing its banks due to its disastrous design and unfunded preventive maintenance and architecture. It was common for the bridge to be impassable after one raindrop causing major flooding in the area. Yet, pedestrians, taxi drivers, and bus drivers were bold enough to traverse calmly without any sense of emergency or precaution.

Damien is well-known for its agriculture, including corn and rice fields and tropical fruits and flowers. The Ministry of Agriculture *(Ministère de l'Agriculture)* is located across the street from the house where I grew up. Almost every Sunday, my family and I would visit and tour the facility.

Speaking of family members, let me formally introduce my parents and some relatives, but not all family members. Soon, you will understand, so bear with me as my aging mind crawls on memory lane.

I am the son of Marie-Michelle and Jean Andre. My mother is one of thirteen children. Marie-Michelle, the daughter of Louisiana and Almannor, had thirteen children: six daughters and seven sons. These are the names of those who were born in Louisiana and Almannor: Cristiane, Rose-Marie, Adeline, Marlene, Solange, Marie-Michelle, Wilnaire, Ylrick, Rodrigue, Victor, Wysley, Jocelyn, and Henry, not respectively.

I was told that, back in the day, having enough children to form a soccer team was common—and my family was no exception. There were so many cousins that I could remember their names, but you couldn't pay me to create a family genealogy or family tree to outline how I relate to each one. I am the oldest of three.

My father, Jean Andre, son of Amalia and Edgar, had five children: one daughter and four sons. These are the names of those born to Amalia and Edgar, in order: Martha, Nobert, Thomas, Jean Andre, and Emmanuel.

As a juvenile, it was easier to enumerate my father's siblings in order of birth, as I could accurately name each of his siblings using the fingers of one hand. On the other hand, it was—and still is—challenging to name my mother's sibling based on the eldest to youngest or youngest to eldest on the first attempt for one apparent reason: too many kids to count. To this day, I am not confident about naming them based on age or date of birth. So, I am no longer trying to name my mother's siblings; I can only say that my mother, Marie-Michelle, is the seventh confirmed child.

As families across the Caribbean or West Indies began immigrating abundantly to North America, preferably the United States and Canada, seeking better opportunities, so did my father.

On August 20, 1982, my father permanently moved to Miami, Florida, exactly four months and twelve days after I took my first breath in the delivery room. My father's departure broke up the relationship he once shared with my mother. Since they were never married, legally, no one had to fight for petit Manley's custody or visitation. It was understood that I would be raised by my mother—understandably so. After all, we are a generation of men raised by women.

Years later, my mother birthed two other sons, my half-brothers: Max and Lerby, respectively, the sons of Maxo, my stepfather. Maxo, who fathered Max and Lerby and lived with us for the longest time, whom I thought was my father for the longest time because he was in the household for a lengthy period until he likewise permanently moved to the United States.

If I recall correctly, after Maxo's departure, there was a moment of confusion in my immature mind about who my father really was, as I had not established any physical account, interactions, or father-son relationship with Jean Andre. I often heard murmurs in the household and in Lakou Kokoye that I was Jean Andre's son, not Maxo's, but I never questioned my mother.

I must have been seven or eight years old. When I confirmed Maxo was not my father, as the former TV personality Maury Povich would shout to the audience on his show, "He is not your father." Perhaps it was during my biological father's first return to Haiti when he had moved to the U.S. that I physically saw him, formally introduced myself, and lifted the veil of confusion. Or maybe I figured it out during a paid phone call, as we didn't have smartphones back then. I should have known sooner, but I was too naïve. To my credit, my mother never talked about it. Also, culturally speaking, kids did not dare to question their parents with whys. Why? Why? Why? That was the norm, as it was perceived as impolite and belligerent.

Once I found out the truth, one thing I was still confused about was the love I had for Max and Lerby. Although we have different fathers biologically, the way we bonded growing up was naturally pure, just like oxygen and nitrogen in the atmosphere. We never discussed our differences then; and to this day, we are simply brothers—real *bruhs*—just from another father. I had never used "half-brother" until I moved to the U.S. while learning the differences between family members in my ESL (or English as a Second Language) class.

Then, after my stepfather's departure, my mother never dated anyone, at least to my knowledge. As a result, she was a single mother throughout my adolescence. She was just the most resilient, caring, and loving mother on the planet. Those are the main characteristics that come to mind when describing my beautiful mother.

Not having a domestic partner to help, my mom carried the heavy load of raising three boys; she implemented and sustained some parental structure that was deemed necessary. Part of me felt she made it work based on pure instincts and parental guides that my Grandmother, Louisiana, may have instilled in her. Now that I am older, my appreciation and love for my mother have strengthened as I reminisce how challenging it must have been raising three boys in a fatherless household. I stand corrected; after all, we are a generation of men raised by women, so her parenting greatly impacted me. My colleagues, neighbors, and friends considered me a little nebbish as a kid. I was extremely timid and, at times, coy, which made it very challenging not only to express myself publicly but also to be comfortable in specific environments, especially at schools, summer camps, and any public environment. In retrospect, part of my timidness derived from being the way

I was brought up and sheltered by my mother. Marie-Michelle, whom I love so profoundly and the mother of all mothers in my world, I must admit, was too strict and stern.

I was not allowed to leave the house without adult supervision and was prohibited from exploring and wandering around the island like most kids in my neighborhood.

My friends, even my cousins, if not all my cousins, had a longer leash than mine; mine was shorter than a twelve-inch ruler, as my mother ruled every aspect of my existence. Based on my mother's assessment, I could not join my friends in summer camps or participate in most activities because they were too far from home. Even if I wanted to escape, just hearing my mother's voice echoing, "Li twò lwen!, ou pa ka ale" (it's too far! You cannot go) would have stopped me from any attempts. Most of my daily activities occurred within the surrounding area of Lakou Kokoye, which is approximately five miles from the capital, Port-au-Prince, if mapped using Google Maps.

Although it is located five miles and approximately seventeen minutes from the capital, due to the conditions and infrastructure of the roads—partially paved and mainly unpaved roads—and heavy traffic, it would take hours to get there, so long that you could read the entire Old Testament from cover to cover while traveling to the capital.

As I reflect on those years, days, times, and every second, I realize that my mother may have been one of the reasons I developed some social discomfort by being around people, even those closest to me.

Lakou Kokoye has rumors that I was the neighborhood's kindest and most polite kid. To everyone's eyes, the elders and most adults, I couldn't do no wrong. I was as innocent as they come due to my somber demeanor. I barely said a word, even when I spoke or talked; these two words would frequently come out of my mouth: "Yes, sir or yes, mom."

As I remember, the whole neighborhood admired my politeness and calmness. They thought I was a quiet kid, so they thought, as my mother would always beg to differ.

Surprisingly, being shy and coy had some advantages as well; I was able to get away with murder, so much I could have starred alongside Viola Davis in "How to Get Away with Murder," or even taught her a thing or two about evading consequences.

There are so many instances where my brothers and cousins would get into trouble for being belligerent, disobedient, bullying, or making fun of other kids. Then, our respective parents would call all the kids. We would form a straight line as if we had been accused of the latest crime on the island, but rarely would I hear my name being mentioned in such a punitive act because, to everyone's eyes, I was a maverick who did not go along with my cousins and brothers silly and childish plans, I was always found innocent. For that, I was idolized by most of the parents who would say," I wish my kid would behave in such a manner, just like "Mane, or Manounou" which was my nickname growing up, still is, but only used these days mainly by a few relatives. Being shy and quiet also brought a positive sense of trust; old folks never cared if I hung around or joined their clique because they knew I was well-behaved and mannered. Most impressively, I would keep my mouth shut and their secret safe. I was wise beyond my years not to lose their trust and violate their privacy.

In retrospect, these folks planted and watered the seed of my maturity, philosophy, and sage. Being surrounded by people much older than I shielded me from getting in trouble and interacting with troubled kids in the neighborhood.

More importantly, I became wise beyond my years, and because of that, I could stay humble and grounded, knowing if I ever slipped off, I would be reprimanded accordingly.

I benefited from that now. Although I was not saying much when I was around the more experienced individuals, I was tentatively listening to what they were saying about life; some stories were frightening, to the point that I would have nightmares, but for the most part, their thoughtful conversation was exciting and educational as well. I was taking mental notes as they talked for hours, I mean long hours, from the early morning before the tropical birds began chirping near the hibiscus flowers till sometimes late evening; surprisingly, I never missed my bedtime curfew.

They provided the help I sought, especially not having a father figure as my shadow to watch me take my first step and every step along the way. I cherished those chatters because they bridged that gap, not entirely, but somewhat. Because I looked up to these folks, their opinion mattered, whether they knew it or not. They provided a sense of fatherhood during my childhood years.

Among those father figures were Nicko, son of Solange, and Richard, son of Henry.

My two late cousins Nicko and Richard, whom I miss deeply, provided that father figure. Truthfully, I miss them so much that I still tremble whenever my mind travels down memory lane; thinking about them and those memories brings sadness and joy, mainly sadness.

Every second I would spend with Nicko and Richard was time well spent because they made me believe nothing in life was unattainable; I could be a dentist, school principal, poet, or writer at an early age. I cannot confidently say they were believers themselves, but they believed in me. That's all I ever cared about. Although, I didn't get a chance to say a proper goodbye to either one of them before they took their last breath as their death happened unexpectedly and I did not travel to Haiti to attend their burials. Nevertheless, over the years, I have respectfully paid homage, as exemplified in the song "Death & Pain," which I dedicated to them because all I ever wanted was to make them proud; I hope the angels above tell them.

When I was not hanging out with the old folks, I would be in the front yard of my home playing dominoes and checkers under the sixty-foot tall coconut trees, with their long-extended leaves protecting us from crepuscular rays or sun rays. I was not great at either game, but I enjoyed playing checkers amicably because I am a deep thinker who loves to think about the big picture. Thus, I found checkers very appealing; it is a mind game; you have to think strategically before moving any pieces upward on the checkerboard, so your opponent does not foresee your plot.

Moreover, we played soccer all year long—even when Mother Nature poured its heart out on the field, and the field would be muddy and unsafe, even when thunderstorms in the blue sky were forcibly striking the earth; we remained on the field. Although there were times our parents would scream their lungs out or yell for us to come home, we would sojourn somewhere, somewhat safe. Yet, somehow, we always went right back to playing when they weren't looking or were preoccupied.

Lastly, crafting and flying kites was pure joy—especially the process of making them by hand. Small kites were crafted using the stems of coconut trees, while the huge ones were made from bamboo stems.

With all these activities and nuisance with brothers, cousins, and well-circled friends, approved by my mother. You would think I would be the happiest kid in the world, but I was not having the best time of my life, nor was I content because I was falling in love with something else that publicly didn't require any exposure. Something that did not put me in the center stage of attention. I found something that would not expose my shyness or timidness. Something that was beyond what everyone in my neighborhood was enjoying as a hobby, something that was uniquely different from what anyone in my family was interested in. I found these subsequent materials that would forever change the whole narrative and dynamic:

- A dictionary, *Le Petit Larousse*
- A paper mate pen
- A composite notebook

ALBUM II
THE SCHOOL SUPPPLIES

Dictionary

Le Petit Larousse, officially titled Le Petit Larousse Illustré and commonly known simply as Le Petit Larousse, is a French-language encyclopedic dictionary published by Éditions Larousse became a very informative and educative source of information for me during my adolescent years. It was a hardcover containing approximately five hundred white pages encompassing thousands of words, definitions, and synonyms. It was very dense and heavy as a brick. I must have been eight or nine years old when my mother brought it home. I took care of it with great care; I never left it unattended or flipped the pages with dirty hands. I always thoroughly washed my hands at all times.

I obsessively started flipping through pages and looking up words. I don't remember exactly which word I looked up first—perhaps it was "lyric," though I cannot be entirely sure.

But, I would look up words alphabetically as much as possible, so often before bedtime. I usually opened the dictionary and randomly chose any word I had not heard of or used during creative or academic writing.

Some words were so well-defined that I never had to go on a hunt to find their true meaning. Every word is well-defined and easily understood, as described in the short description.

On the other hand, some words would take me on a journey beyond the borders, beyond the walls of my petit bedroom that my two brothers, Max and Lerby, once shared. I would flip through page after page while using one of my fingers as a bookmark to read definition after definition, reference after reference, until I fully comprehended the meaning of the original word I had looked up and bookmarked.

My face would gleam joyfully and excitedly whenever I learned a new word. I demonstrate excitement by utilizing newly discovered words during my creative writing assignments. I did not care if the teachers would be impressed, but part of me hoped the teacher would, to a minimum, take notice of and recognize.

I cannot recall if I ever got such notice or a pat on the back of my tiny head early on. But, I remember the first time I got a nod from my middle school teacher; I was ecstatic; I was smiling from ear to ear; I laughed and smiled so hard. Had I not lost my front teeth two months prior, I would have lost at least one of them, because it had been hanging by a thread of gum. It was a beautiful moment, as I recall. It was unique because it was a personal achievement that was honored privately; it did not attract the attention of a vast audience, and for that, I was pleased.

In conjunction with reading Le Petit Larousse, I started reading books similarly. Although I was never an avid reader, I was more like a slow reader. I found reading to be a memory exercise: deciphering, decoding, and memorizing every word on every sentence and every page for future use. Thus, it would take me years to finish one book or novel.

Consequently, my goal has been to read at least a few books or novels yearly. I learned at a very young age reading and writing are mutually inclusive; that is something that my school teachers at Les Papillons Legers & College Luc Grimard, Port-Au-Prince, Haiti, had instilled in me, which I have carried with me to this day.

So, before my memory fades to black, I would like to thank all the teachers and educators, black, white, or Latinx, especially those teaching in the black communities because if it was not for my middle school teacher who taught me the significance of coupling or combining reading and writing. I would not be writing this book, let alone writing this sentence. So often, in the black communities, we have young black kids serving life sentences, yet they are illiterate and cannot even read a sentence. So, I have the utmost respect for teachers who are constantly impacting these kids' lives academically.

Papermate Pen

My second favorite material, the papermate pen, not any pen, but the one-millimeter (mm) ballpoint stick papermate, which I often referred to as my soulmate. It was special to me because it never lied to me, it solely wrote the truth, and the only truth, always helped me purge my thoughts, always allowed me to get my point across, and always helped me cope with pain.

I have always used it as a weapon to lessen and combat internal pains and daily life struggles. Whenever I could not find a rope to help me cope with this thing, they called life, I would strongly and confidently rely on it for support. I credited that first papermate pen that my mother had placed in the outer pocket of my navy blue JanSport backpack for lighting my writing wick.

It became evident that the pen was a powerful tool.

To this day, I would press downward extremely hard ensuring every letter was clearly legible; with no ambiguity. And so much that I wanted every letter, word, and sentence to be permanently engraved on the piece of paper I was writing on.

I have never been a fan of any pen with blank ink. In fact, I had so much hatred in my heart for the black ink pens, somehow, I would develop writer's block instantly, where my brain would freeze even when there was sunshine. The black ink pen "just did not do it for me." I am not a superstitious individual in the full context of the word, but, in this instance, I became superstitious; the black pen symbolizes darkness. You could call me strange, superstitious, or even weird like Al Yankovic. I would not be humiliated or denigrated and would endorse your opinion. I just knew deep down there was something very uncanny and inexplicable.

However, it was the blue ink paper mate that would make ideas flow through my veins, even a levee would not prevent the overflow of ideas and thoughts that would be circulating in my brain, once I upheld the pen on a piece of paper, most preferably in my Composition notebook. It felt like poetry in motion the moment the tip touched the page. The only thing that mattered was to write—write and write for hours without pause. Then, after a brief break, I would resume, unstoppable. The power of the pen could defeat life's obstacles and break every chain. That is what the Paper Mate means to me.

Notebook

After years of documenting my early creative writing on table napkins and sheets of printing paper, which I would regularly and mistakenly toss in trash cans, and after years of constantly keeping track and archiving every napkin and printer paper I ever wrote on for future use, it became a burden and difficult to locate each scratch paper. Consequently, I had to rely heavily on this book, a composition notebook.

This composition notebook illustrated here is one of the notebooks I have used as a "wanna-be" writer. As the cover states, "Wide Ruled," it has widely ruled my life. Even though the notebook only consisted of blank white pages and wide-ruled lines, as I would start to express myself, I felt like I could rule the world with my pen and wide-ruled notebook.

I am sure that most people would mutter, "It's just a notebook," but as a kid, my views of the notebook were unparalleled to common credos or beliefs. In my fantasized world, it served a different purpose:

1. The wide ruled lines and blank white pages represent uninhabited and bare roads where my ideas or thoughts could travel freely. Even when the journey or roads ahead appeared dicey, I stayed poised and focused because I adhered to the rules and never let anything derail my writing process.
2. It allows me to visit places that I could dream of, places that were less traveled, only traveled by those willing to do whatever necessary to go long distances to chase that dream, and places that only dreamers like myself are permitted to enter and leave a mark.
3. It controlled how I would express myself; as much as I would try to write about a particular topic as a writer, the notebook dictated and controlled how my stories were being told. It became very apparent I wasn't in control when I would start writing; it ruled my destiny as a writer. I had no suspicion; my stories were conveyed based on pure instincts. Every page contained the truth and the ugly in ways I could not eloquently articulate. I was brilliant on every page.

4. It gave me a sense of freedom and structure to express myself freely. I remember the first time I opened the notebook. I had not written down words before; most of my writing had been on printer paper or table napkins. I instantly felt so alive and free to finally have the power to say and speak without any interruptions. Although it was me, myself, a pen, and a notebook, I never felt isolated in any shape or form.

Honestly, it did not matter if my cousins and friends were having the best time of their lives. I was unfazed or unbothered as long as I had those materials in my possessions, which was all the time, I was content. It became my second true best friend; I trusted it, just like I trusted the pen. I was always excited when I began composing a sentence, so much excitement and joy that one would think I had been given a new toy. Even the ice cream truck circling down the block or neighborhood wouldn't have gotten my attention; my focus was on point, just like an arrow.

And I felt as though I was hanging out with a confidant friend; I would tell all my secrets, the naked truth and the ugly, knowing all my secrets were in a vault somewhere, as long as I kept them in a secured place, where no one in the world would find them.

In retrospect, I didn't know how much power words have. It was significant, but in terms of impacting someone's life, I had not fully understood the magnitude of a word. The freedom to express myself on those blank pages slowly started to unsilence me. It was the genesis of my voice.

ALBUM III
IN THE POEM OF MY MIND

Poetry

"But art is not simply works of art; it is the spirit that knows Beauty, that has music in its being and the color of sunsets in its handkerchiefs; that can dance on a flaming world and make the world dance, too." —W. E. B. Du Bois

During my adolescent years, as I matured and journeyed through life, I became an eager reader, not in the complete sense of the word, but adequately reading books, newspapers, literature, and magazines. I would go to the local library, leaving no bookshelves untouched and no pages unflipped. It was a hobby that I added to my repertoire, not initially knowing how it would contribute to my writing down the literary road or line. Consequently, the more I read, the more poems I wrote; I sought poetry to ameliorate and craft my writing skills, and thus, the knack for writing, yet again, strongly intensified.

Moreover, in the summer of 1995, I was finding and discovering who I was and who I could be as a "wanna-be" writer. My focus was abruptly interrupted when I met my first crush, Patricia Emmeline Desir, with whom I had a huge crush. She was as beautiful as the morning breeze if my memory serves me well. Her profile and beauty are vividly and forever embedded in my mind, which was well-annotated in the first love poem I had penned. A part of me wanted to tell her about the poems or at least recite one to her, but just the thought of it terrified me and crushed my heart. I was so terrified that I would hide the notebook under my pillow so that no one would discover my secret crush; it was a clandestine affair.

Over the following months, I must have written hundreds of poems, hoping she would get the message one day. After months, months of hiding my feelings, I was able to approach her and hand her all the poems that I had written for her. Although, at the time, she was in a committed relationship, she nicely refused to accept them. I felt rejected, however, she suggested that we could be friends; nothing more nothing less. I accepted and respected her boundaries and requirements, but deep down, I wanted more, more than a friendship. I had never been a quitter, so I was unbothered by her unpleasant first rejection. So, I did what I do best; I grabbed my pen and paper, went to work, and wrote her more poems.

Miraculously, one day, she had let me borrow one of her books to study because my mom had not purchased mine. After I was done with it, I intentionally inserted a letter in the form of a poem as a bookmark before returning the book to her. I gave it to her, and she replied thank you. As she was running late for class, she didn't inspect it. It took her a few days to realize and ascertain that I had placed a letter in one of the pages.

The day she did find it, she cursed me out in front of all my classmates, as she yelled, "I would never be your girlfriend." I was embarrassed, but in the midst of all it, I kept writing and writing. One day, it was brought to my attention that her boyfriend had left town and moved to the United States, and she was single. A year later, Patricia became my first girlfriend, while admitting that my way with words and the way I used them in a lovable and persuasive manner, in this case, poetry, was mainly the reason she decided to become my girlfriend and that she was sorry for humiliating me the year prior. My self-esteem went through the roof; more importantly, at that moment, I got proof that this writing idea works; it opened people's hardened hearts and changed their hearts, as Patricia did have a change of heart. Once again, someone dear to my heart validated my writing skills. In the years to come, I was painting pictures with words; she was madly in love, and so was I; I was in love with her, but what I loved most was the fact that she understood and saw my vision and dedication from miles away, she saw a writer in me.

Yet again, the more poems I wrote, the more isolated and aloof I became; I became a stranger to my friends and family; I was in my petit world, no pun intended. I don't condone drug addiction, but writing became an addiction; the pen was the needle, which was pretty cool and informally dope. I needed to obsessively write every day, every hour, to be at ease.

It anchored me to the core; I was myself. As I didn't have to please anyone, it gave me a purpose and a self of pride. I had something to look forward to every day, which was sweeter than the island sugar canes.

ALBUM IV
THE FRENCH PHILOSOPHERS

Philosophy

Even though, on January 1, 1804, Haiti became the first black nation to be freed from slavery, proudly so. Six generations later, the scar of slavery still remains and burns as the remnants of slavery can still be traced in our culture, education, and traditions, in every aspect too lengthy for me to annotate in this book thoroughly.

In the mid-90s, during my first year in secondary school (or Segondė in Haitian Creole), which is equivalent to 10th grade in high school, I was introduced to a myriad of French philosophers, poets, and writers during my French literature class. It was undeniably impossible to object to living on an island that was once colonized and ruled by French slave masters and colonizers; the education system was systematically and heavily established and implemented by Frenchmen.

As a result, Haitian teachers and educators were obligated to adopt such a system, teaching and educating Haitians with those same ideologies, rules, and methods that had been established.

I am a byproduct of that generation; I wonder if such an education system still exists since I emigrated from Haiti and immigrated to the United States on Sunday, October 31, 1999.

Nevertheless, it influenced how I saw the world then and how I view it now, figuratively.

Truthfully, all I ever wanted was to follow in the footsteps of my fellow Haitian combatants, who had paved the way for my ancestors' freedom, consequently opening the door for kids like me to even think and dream of being untrammeled writers.

Sadly, those I envied were not Haitian poets or writers; they were of "French" origins. However, they may not have participated in any form of slavery or bigotry against my nation. I naively held them accountable. I felt they were as culpable as their ancestors who enslaved my black and brown people, those same Frenchmen who chained and shackled my ancestors.

More sadly, despite my perpetual animosity, I coveted and admired those French writers and poets; I privily learned and studied their work immensely; in some aspect, I had no choice because they were popularized, chronicled, and glorified on every page and chapter of Haitian literature; it seemed, most notably:

Rene Decarte, Blaise Pascal, Victor Hugo, Jean-Baptiste Poquelin (famously known as Molière)

François-Marie Arouet (better known as Voltaire) and Jean La Fountaine, to enumerate those I truly admired.

These writers embodied everything I wanted to be: brilliant, versatile, and exceptional as it pertains to literature, particularly poetry.

I would read their biographies to fully grasp and comprehend their background, work ethic, and who and what they were as human beings. Yet, I found their level of intellect to be inhumane because their work was extraordinary and marvelous. On the contrary, I was not even an ordinary writer.

These individuals were prolific writers, exceptional philosophers, and poets because they could write in any form of literature. I immensely enjoyed their work, which I valued like a fine art frame. I sensed these writers were crafting and mastering their skills and talents every day, every hour, every minute, and every second.

Their stories were profoundly beautiful and masterful. They wrote stories I could only dream of writing, stories I was too young to challenge or inexperienced to compete with.

Yet I knew that to be great, I had to embrace their greatness—to live and breathe their lifestyle. I must reach for the ladder of greatness and study extremely hard, just like those who have paved the way and cemented themselves in the history books.

Furthermore, I knew their influence had a colossal impact on why I wanted to use words to contribute to the art of literature; perhaps as a poet, a novelist, or a writer, truthfully I had no idea in what specific shape or form all I knew was that I was infatuated with words and I could utilize words; and by using words and converting them to art. Ultimately, I would enter my name into the history books to empower the next kid—Black or Brown—so that they could boldly shout, "I want to be the greatest writer of all time." Even though their work was marvelous, it saddened me deeply. That is one of the reasons I wanted to change the narrative and be part of a change of black and, more importantly, of Haitian history. I wanted to create a blueprint for those aspiring dreamers to follow so they would not have to begin their journey from the bottom of the barrel. That fueled my writing interest ablaze; I did not envision in what specific form of literature or artistry I could contribute; however, I knew one day, one day I would have a voice, the unspoken, the unwritten fire in this quiet and timid kid who grew up silently in Lakou Kokoye, would knock on doors, like heaven doors; doors that had never been knocked on and opened them wide enough; for a wide range of people, including kids all over the globe, who had been uninspired by systematic racism and discrimination, especially here, in this divided states, America.

Consequently, I tried my hardest to emulate the life of those writers by writing tirelessly, by any means necessary. Every second of the day, regardless of whether the idea would not come to fruition, I kept the tip of the pen on the paper. I was determined to endure their blood, sweat, and tears. Moreover, I tried so I could experience the excruciating pain they had to endure to be great because chasing greatness is a sour, unfruitful, and painful process, but its fruit is as delicious as my grandmother's lemonade; once you have a bite of success, you become hungrier and hungrier for more, if you don't believe me ask the legends, they would tell you success is addictive, the craving never ends. It could make you lose everything, I mean everything that you ever loved: relationships, friendships, social life, and even sports life if you are a hard-die fan residing in a city of champions, just like Boston or Beantown.

In the end, would it be worth it? Well, I am not quite sure. I guess I have to keep writing to find out.

ALBUM V
WOULD YOU LIKE TO DANCE?

Music

Where would the world be without music? Without music, the human race would not be able to share cultures, traditions, and views. The power of music enables people of all backgrounds to bridge the gaps between cultures, connecting individuals beyond borders with no boundaries, putting aside our views, even differences, through song lyrics, verse, and bridge. Music can do such a thing, uniting the human race, keeping us young, and making us feel good.

Undoubtedly, the Caribbean islands are universally recognized as one of the top vacation destinations, alluring tourists with its ocean breeze, warm sunshine, and exquisite beaches. As charming as the Caribbean is, if I had to select one thing that truly connects the islands, I would affirm that there is nothing as glamorous as the sounds of music. Music is a lodestone for aspiring musicians of all genres, connecting West Indians locally and the diaspora communities globally.

But, with so many musical sounds, How does one choose a favorite? Where do I even begin?

In retrospect, as a West Indian, I listened to a myriad of music cultivated across the West Indies and the Caribbean—from homegrown Konpa to Rara, Reggae, Soca, Twoubadou, Zouk, Bachata, Merengue, and Salsa. As more family members emigrated overseas, primarily to the U.S., Canada, and France, new musical genres such as Hip-Hop, Rap, Pop, Country, and Soft Rock began to fill our household, our parties, and my ears. Having so many relatives in diaspora communities expanded my musical arsenal and deepened my appreciation for diverse sounds.

As a result, I have never disparaged, and I will never disvalue, any genre simply because each genre has played an instrumental part in my lyrical and musical development. Hence, it's only fair that I elaborate and outline some music genres that have invited me to places, traditions, cultures, and individuals that would normally be beyond my reach.

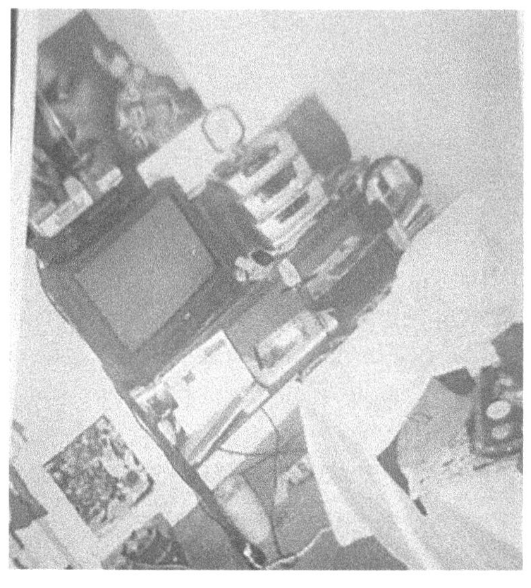

KONPA is homemade, so naturally and culturally, it brings a sense of joy to this place. I love Haiti dearly; Haiti, even more so after I had moved to Lowell, Mass (or Lowell, Massachusetts) in the winter of 1999. It gave me a sense of pride. Don't get me wrong, I have always been proud. However, sharing a valuable part of my inheritance and culture with someone, in this case, Konpa, during a cordial conversation has always been beautiful. As cliche as it may sound, it is true, in a sense, that you never know what you have till it vanishes. I did not see the significance of music in our lives, communities, and households, at least not at the time, until I emigrated to Lowell.

There I was, for the first time in my life, I found myself disconnected with no outlet, distanced from my culture after seventeen years. To make matters worse, there weren't as many Haitians as there are today in Lowell, so to cope, often I would insert one of the Konpa cassette tapes that I had brought with me during my voyage; as soon I would hear the constant pulsating tabou beat in my eardrums; I was moved; instantly reconnecting and reliving once again my adolescent memories through music.

My entire body would be unparalyzed with acute nostalgia for the early years I had spent in Lakou Kokoye listening to those lyrics. It was musical and, more importantly, a cultural reunion as these Konpa songs chronicled the soundtrack of my early life in every aspect; some of those songs I would listen to would bring tears and sadness to my heart as I was staring at the unframed and empty wall of my bedroom adjacent to my sister's bedroom, feeling the loneliness of the dark hours, missing my mother, my brothers, my childhood friends, my childhood home, my neighborhood, Lakou Kokoye, and everything in between seemed so far; thousands of miles away from the edge of my twin bed in my four-by-four closet like bedroom.

As I reminisced about my past life, I evaluated not only the present but also the unknown, the future.

I was terrified of the future, literally and figuratively. But, tapping my feet to those strong regular rhythm tabou beats and singing those lyrics helped me keep my head somewhat outside the clouds and above water, just enough that I could see a bright future on the horizon ahead.

Furthermore, while listening to these songs being played musically through my stereo system, I realized music has a deeper meaning. I recognized that these songs were not solely composed of lines, verses, chorus, bridges, post-chorus, sound, and melodies; instead, these songwriters and artists, more importantly, lyricists, are astute storytellers. Good or bad, their stories resonated and touched me through my core.

I was not just reciting every line and word of a song as you sang along loudly; the feeling I experienced was colossal. Consequently, listening to those marvelous lyrics was magical, as I felt my mind would travel back in time.

The meaning behind these lyrics was extraordinary. It didn't matter how many times I would listen to a particular rhyme, hook, or verse, at least the great songs; it was a perpetual feeling. The lyrics were moving, punchlines punching every organ of my body. Every beat would make my heartbeat skip a beat, at times pinching myself to make sure I was still alive; that is how electrifying those lyrics would make me vibe.

Furthermore, Konpa represents joy and freedom. Joy, in a sense, impacts Haitian culture; it is the positive feeling my body would exhibit as soon as I pressed "Play" on my Walkman; even the sound you would hear after pressing the Play button would bring joy to my heart. That was before we had CD Players, MP3 Players, iPods, tablets, and smartphones. I was never a great Konpa dancer; you would not find me in the middle of the dance floor, nope! I was never the life of the party, but I was the kid attentively listening to the lyrics in the quietest corner I could find. Frequently, there were no quiet spots as West Indian parties are intolerably loud; you could feel the beat pounding to your heart, and whoever was DJing would not skip a beat until everyone was thoroughly soaking wet under the Caribbean sun, having fun. Yet, I was concentrating on learning the process of songwriting.

Some of the great Konpa dancers have mastered “Plogé or Gouyé," which is a dance move where the female and male dancers, figuratively speaking, stay "plugged or connected" to each other until the song is outplayed. It is very intimate, and I would say, knowing what I know now. Once again, I was not into all the grinding or "plogé or gouyé" as we refer to it in Haitian Creole. I was locked into the lyrics; I was plugging, albeit differently; my tiny ears were plugged into the lyrics; they mattered more to me than anything related to a song.

Occasionally, I would go onto the dance floor and break a couple of moves if a friend or a family member insisted I do so if they had found a perfect match for me. However, my moves were internally calculated as I was deciphering the lyrics, studying word selection, line section, and how each line aligns with every dance movement, rhythm, and flow.

Most importantly, Konpa symbolizes freedom as it is Haitian's delicious fruit of its sour journey to freedom; significantly, it is a triumphant weapon used peacefully to commemorate undeniably and unimaginably one of the greatest revolutions of humankind, which presently does not have much to hold on proudly as of late due to perpetual political instability, violence, and poverty. But Konpa fills that void.

It reminds Haitians, even the diasporic populations, not to let anyone who breathes the same air as you break your soul or take your freedom; one must fight bravely, by any means necessary, even when one stumbles, you must fight until you are freed. Then, once you become victorious against those who had chained us, deprived us, and stolen your identities to eradicate your excellence, our prowess, one must shake it off on the dance floor, wiping off all the tears, struggle, bloodstains the Haitians had resiliently sustained, all these messages are embedded in Konpa.Well, if you ever want to get your two left feet wet dancing the Konpa, especially Plogé or Gouyé, with someone special to your heart or whoever, I strongly recommend searching the subsequent artists and musicians on your preferred music app (i.e., Spotify, Tidal, Pandora, iHeartRadio) and add them to your playlist, especially my favorite Konpa songs of all time.

Songs by Carimi: Ayiti (Bang Bang) and Kidnapping

The song titled " Ayiti (Bang Bang)" released in 2001, two years after I had left Haiti, paints a sad and hopeless picture of Haiti, with lyrics:

Intro
F.B.I, C.A.I mé zanmi,
mé zanmi, mé zanmi,
Ho, ho,
F.B.I, C.A.I mé zanmi
mé zanmi, mé zanmi,
Ho, ho,

Verse I
Sa fè de zan'm pa wèl **(Line 1)**
Peyi mwen change koulè **(Line 2)**
Sa fè de zn'm kite'l **(Line 3)**
Figi li make mizè **(Line 4)**
Nou pito fèmen de ge'n **(Line 5)**
Fè samblan sa va change **(Line 6)**
Nou pito fèmen de ge'n **(Line 7)**

In reference to Line 7, *Nou pito fèmen de ge'n*, although I speak Haitian Creole fluently, reading it is not as sharp. You could blame it on Western colonization, as every book I ever read while living in Haiti was in French, so excuse my French, or should I say, excuse my Haitian Creole.

Let's get back to Line 7; while listening to this song, I could conclude the Lead Singer is pointing out that the nation would rather close their eyes and pretend that there's no political instability, violence, and poverty as a survival mechanism. We have become immune to the constant political and economic instability. Cleverly, the term "Bang Bang" is the sound effect of constant gunshots ravaging the cities, from gang bangs, even law enforcers, DEA, and FBI, as hinted in the intro.

Hearing those profound lyrics about the state of violence and bloody streets is still enjoyable to vibe and listen to, as it provides hope to the hopeless. There is beauty in the struggle; there is also joy and happiness. The same lyricist brings you teary eyes and can also make your move with joyful music, as the groove laid down by the drummer and bassist is tough and funky.

In "Kidnapping," Carimi delivered a club banger that transcends borders and cultures. It's a song that one couldn't resist or dare to sit. You had no choice but to find someone to plogé with because the melody and chorus or hook are extraordinary. In my opinion, this song not only cemented their name in Haitian culture but also left a lasting impression on the diaspora communities, making them feel the significance and relevance of the music.

Chorus
Baby cool baby cool now **(Line 1)**
Kite'm lage'm nan carimi **(Line 2)**
Met pase menot nan bra mwen baby cool now **(Line 3)**
Si manman'm pa jan'm kinbe'm konsa **(Line 4)**
Si papa'm pa jan'm kinbe'm **(Line 5)**
Sa fe'm anvi kriye Kidnapping **(Line 6)**

The title is deceiving as it was not intended to foreshadow or project the current state of Haiti, where Kidnapping is prevalent. Still, sadly, that is currently the actual state of Haiti today, in 2023, as Kidnapping is forcing Haitians to sleep with both eyes open, abandoning forsaking their homes in broad daylight and seeking refuge in nearby communities, somewhat safer, to make matters worse kids napping are getting kidnapped, get it?

The true intent of "kidnapping" well is a song about women controlling men; as such, the singer feels like he is being kidnapped because of his girlfriend or partner. He can't go out after 7 PM, cannot go out around 8 PM, he cannot even go out at all, he feels like dying, not literally. In the same song, I did not mention that he is begging his partner to relax or cool off; in other words, he pumps the brakes or loosens. He even says she would lock the front door, even the back door of their house, and unable to find the house key or keys; that is the storyline between Kidnapping is to illustrate how women, not all women, are control freaks they want to know every move of their men, especially when their men are stepping out for a night out. In Lines 4 and 5, the Lead Singer says she is such a control freak that he feels he is being kidnapped. In Line 4 and Line 5, respectively, he sings, "If my mom never treated me, and my dad my father never used to control me in such a manner. Although I have never written any song in my native language, Haitian Creole, I found the lyrics fascinating as they depict a relationship with nature. I studied every song; I heeded the title as well, as it plays an imperative part in attracting the audience or fans to a song.

Songs by Zen Glen: 5 Dwet and Fidel, just to name a few of their songs

In the song titled "Fidel", verse III with lyrics:

Verse III
Sa k pou pran m pou m bliye musik peyi mwen ***(Line 1)***
Sa k ka pran m pou m bliye kulti pa mwen ***(Line 2)***
Ayisyen nou ye ***(Line 3)***
Se Kongo nou ye ***(Line 4)***

These powerful lyrics provided a summary of potential change in Haiti vis-a-vis music and, more importantly, our identity and roots, especially one of my favorite lines: Lines 1 through 4, if not the best part of the song where the Lead Singer chants proudly and faithfully:

Men se Kongo nou ye **(Line 5)**
Se konpa nou jwe **(Line 6)**
Nati Kongo nou ye, nou ye **(Line 7)**

These lyrics further brighten my vision as a lyricist because the message represents something much more profound; lyrically, these words show the significance of Kompa music and remind all Haitians not to forget our African roots, keep playing Konpa music, not change anything, be loyal and proud of who we are. Additionally, these lyrics beautifully, yet sadly illustrate the state of Haiti's identity crisis, at the same time proposing implementation actions required for Haitians to embrace their true identity and embrace the future of Konpa music, as it provides hope to a hopeless nation still wounded with post-revolution syndrome, hoping Konpa is the approved vaccine or the cure to our pains.

Translated version of Line 1, "what would get into me to forget my country's music."
Translated version of Line 2, "what would get into me to forget my country's culture."

We may be Haitians, but more importantly, we are Congonians from Congo, Africa (Kongo in Haitian Creole). As our ancestors were enslaved people from Congo, Africa, we should not forget our history, culture, roots, and music.

These two subsequent lines outlined below, precisely provide the significance of how lyrics are more than words; musicians can use them as a platform to have uncomfortable dialogue, conversations, and debates in communities to communicate to the masses, nonviolently speaking their mind, addressing issues that need to be addressed and resolved, I was sold on the idea that one day, I could have the same impact in my community through writing lyrics—bringing hope to hopeless folks of all ages who look just like me: dark-skinned, with glistening skin and a million-dollar smile. This has always been, and will always be, my mission while listening to these brilliant lyrics—representing us. By "us," I mean Black folks. And if I happen to influence every race, that would be the icing on the cake, because music was never intended to divide us, but to bring everyone together on the dance floor, as the legendary Michael Jackson reminded us in *Black or White.*

Why would we forget who we are? Do not ever forget that we are Haitians. These lyrics further kindled my vision as a writer because it showed the significance and impact written words contribute to our daily lives.

As I wrote this section of the book, I couldn't help but put "Fidel" on repeat in my Spotify playlist titled *Lakay*—which translates to "Home" in English—while singing the hook in **Line 3,** "Ayisyen nou ye," and **Line 4,** "Se Kongo nou ye." These exceptional lines never get old; they hit my soul every time. Even though the song debuted in 1990, when I was just eight years old—a snotty-nosed kid sucking the middle and ring fingers of my right hand—33 years later, here I am, about to turn 42 as I write the epilogue. Those lyrics still pump my blood and touch my heart the same way. The only difference now is that I'm no longer that snotty-nosed kid—I'm far from it. That's the power of well-written lyrics: they age as you age, but when you die, they remain immortal for future generations, just like kingdom come.

I've enjoyed vibing to other artists, musicians, and groups as well, and I strongly recommend adding the following to your playlist—they represent Haiti in the most authentic and powerful way.

Songs by Michel Martelly (musically known as Sweet Micky): Ou La La, Tout se Martelly, and Ouvè Baryè.

Throughout his career, Michel Martelly's lyrics were often controversial, as they explicitly addressed themes such as violence against political figures, sexuality, hate speech, freedom of expression, and religious bigotry. He was widely regarded as a "bad boy" or troublemaker due to his. Martelly never shied away from his character; however, he was denounced by many, particularly conservatives and traditionalists, who felt that Sweet Micky was challenging Haiti's norms and defying the status quo.

However, his music was incredibly popular as they come, bringing a different flavor to Konpa music as his name stage hints his music had that sweet taste that his fans craved. His lyrics stuck in everyone's tongue and mind; he entertained the crowd because his lyrics resonate to the masses; you couldn't pay radio stations enough money not to play his music. In songs like "Ou La La," I remember singing along to his catchy and classic chorus:

Chorus

Ou la la, ou ou la la ***(Line 1)***
Pwason te fè dlo konfyans ***(Line 2)***
men se dlo ki bouyi li ***(Line 3)***
Ou la la, ou ou la la ***(Line 4)***

As a seven or eight-year-old kid, I took two steps with my skinny legs in the front yard surrounding coconut and palm trees. Every letter, word, and line moved—and so I grooved. Sweet Micky's greatest attribute was his magnetic personality, which pulled the audience to center stage as they would match his stage energy. His presence on stage was contagious; he had brilliant, catchy lines and hooks or chorus in every song he released to keep everyone on their feet and maintain complete control of the audience.

Songs by Nu-Look: Big Mistake, Cauchemar, Loving You, Legacy, and Is it real?

Some people might disagree with my list—especially my cousin Rovinel from Union County, New Jersey. He's a historian of Konpa music and has listened to, and analyzed, most if not all Haitian songs.

If I had to pick a favorite song out of the four mentioned above, I would have to go with "Is it real?" because the opening line captures the song's theme so beautifully. It is something to die for when the singer connects with the audience from the first opening lines:

Verse I
Mwen gon'w problem Kap ravajèm **(Line 1)**
Ki moun ki kapab edèm? **(Line 2)**

Translated version of Line 1, "I have a problem that is bothering." Line 2 is translated as follows: Who can help me?

Additionally, Line 1 poses a question one will ultimately need to answer. This is an excellent way for a writer to connect with the audience.

To conclude, before I move on to other genres that have been instrumental to my growth, I have never written a song in Haitian Creole. Nevertheless, Konpa has strengthened and shaped my mind lyrically and musically as it has broadened my music arsenal, providing a different perspective on analyzing a single or record. It has kept me open-minded to welcoming or accepting different sounds; I get the best of both worlds. If it were not for vibing and listening to those profound lyrics at an early age, I would not be chasing this crazy dream.

Moreover, I would love to write an entire book on Konpa music, outlining how original and instrumental Konpa is to Haitians, including those who never set foot in Haiti. Still, since this is not the intent of this book, I must defer; perhaps I would base my next book on Konpa if God is willing. I hate to adjourn this genre that means so much to me—well, all good music or things must come to an end. So, before I press "Next," please sing with me as I chant the pre-chorus of *Legacy* at the 0:53 mark.

If I die tomorrow, pa bliye **(Line 1)**
O, pale jenes la toujou kanpe **(Line 2)**
Pou yo defan'n dwa yo **(Line 3)**
Si yon jou'm pa ta la **(Line 4)**

REGGAE is to Jamaicans what Konpa is to Haitians. As a kid, I recall reggae flooding radio stations and dance floors like tropical hurricanes and cyclones. As distinctive as it sounded in my tiny ears, uniquely different from Konpa, the songs punctured my eardrums and heart slowly and beautifully.

However, I could not fully understand every word, line, and lyrics of every song as these singers or artists would sing in English, which was mainly blunted or coated with Patois (a Jamaican dialect/language derived from British English), which I knew little about at the time. Nevertheless, I managed; let's keep it at that.

As I grew up listening to more reggae and perfecting my English in my English class, I found or discovered that reggae is blunted on reality, just like the Fugees' debut LP (or Long Playlist) " Blunted on Reality" scored in 1994, I found reggae to be pure, unapologetic, authentic, and joyful, there I was in my early teenage years, probably twelve or thirteen years old; obsessively listening to those lyrics, taking mental notes along the way, and wondering if there would ever be a place for me to write similar lyrics; the answer was always "not a slim chance." But, the word discourage never crossed my mind, as it is not in my nature and un-Haitian ever to give up, as I was born with a capital R on my chest, and I am resilient.

The more I listened to reggae, the more I familiarized myself with artists such as James Chambers, known professionally as Jimmy Cliff, and the late great Robert Nesta Marley, universally known as Bob Marley. They were so influential musically and spiritually that you could not impede the spreading of their music, never mind their tone of voice, their voice became louder in my head; their music became my voice when I could not speak.

Once again, I fell in love with the lyrics because I was touched profoundly, every line cutting my spine slowly. I believed I could do this; one day, I could write similar lyrics, paint pictures with words, and prove words matter and, when appropriately used and efficiently, may speak louder than actions. Words unite people, cultures, and traditions, especially when harmonizing with soothing sounds. I aspired to be a lyricist.

Subsequently, these two exceptional influencers paved the way for aspiring artists like Alpha Blondy and Buju Banton, who I idolized so profoundly because of their astonishing raw voice and delivery and sharpened lyrics that could cut through the cement of every dance floor and penetrate the dance floor, yet provided lyrics that related to hope and happiness, empowerment sexism; songs like "Destiny," to this day has been one, if not one of my favorite songs all time, brilliant music. How could I forget another masterful song from Buju Banton, "Walk Like A Champion." These lyrics made me doubt myself; I have no shot at accomplishing such lyrical stardom, let alone being a decent lyricist. Buju was young, just another young boy or bwoy (or Bwoy in Patois) from Kingston, Jamaica, the first successful one being Bob Marley, who took the world by storm, penning lyrics that were controversial at times, yet they were so authentic and compelling as these stories revealed the ugly and beautiful side of Jamrock (Jamaica), and globally.

I was blown away by his lyricism, though; I could not sing, still can't sing, I could not play the guitar, still can't play, even if I was given a fortune, but his lyrics traveled everywhere from the Caribbean to the motherland, to Europe then to the fatherland, not sure if there's such a land. Still, I am sure you understand; I am trying to explain that his music was influential and instrumental to my mind because every time I would press play, I listened to poetry in motion.

The revolutionary Bob Marley had me thinking deeply about songs of freedom from a personal level. I was free in my mind. As young as I was, not growing up in his era, I understood one of his most significant messages—his unwavering dedication to the People. Nothing more, nothing less.

More impressively, Bob Marley was not only the message-bearer during his lifetime; through his lyrics, he became the message in the afterlife and beyond.

Also, I remember listening to artists like Alpha Blondy from Ivory Coast, Africa, Lucky Phillips Dube from Ermelo, Africa, Bennie Man, and Sizzla, but Bob Marley was the pioneer; in my young eyes he embodied exceptional and generational talent, which was unmatched not because of his singing abilities and lucent lyrics, but the way each song seamlessly covered a myriad of topics from poverty to inequality, from injustice to hope, then love, which is outlined in song such as "Would You Be Loved."

I felt a sense of peace listening to his songs, even when Haiti was in turmoil, historically speaking, often. The great Bob Marley brought nothing but a peaceful melody; his guitar hits my soul, so much that I would feel no pain, calamity, or gravity to pull me down. It was such a beautiful sound. I would listen and analyze his lyrics; they had no boundaries regarding impact. Bob Marley was fearless musically, putting his life and career on the line in every verse and every lyric line intended to combat injustice. I was amazed and inspired while studying how music from this biracial artist from the heart of Kingston, Jamaica, could have such a global impact. Songs like *I Shot the Sheriff and No Woman,* No Cry from the critically acclaimed album *Burnin'* left a lasting impression. Bob Marley later revealed in a 1997 interview that he chose the line "I shot the sheriff" because saying "I shot the police" would have caused an uproar with the government—a decision he explained brilliantly.

His prowess as a songwriter and lyricist was unmatched. I was sometimes jealous—truthfully. I envied his lyricism because his lyrics spoke to kids like me who wanna be lyricists and dreamers. He was a true musician; he could sing, write, and play the guitar, embodying what it truly means to be a musician.

Furthermore, I was hooked by the way his hooks were written; embedded with honesty, integrity, purity, and quality, he never deviated from his self-image; by reading his lyrics over the years, I could conclude he did not care how society perceived him; or his personality, he solely cared about his self-image. As I visualized myself as a lyricist, I valued those traits profoundly. I wanted my lyricism to mirror his and mimic his lifestyle. That's the audacity of ambition and hope.

As a result, when I started thinking about a stage name early in my wannabe lyricist journey—or maybe just in my fantasy mind—I came up with the alias **"Jah23."** *Jah* because of Bob Marley and Buju Banton, two artists I idolized tremendously, who often referenced Jah as an adherent of Rastafari to mean God. Then came the number **23,** chosen in honor of Michael Jordan—MJ—the undisputed greatest basketball player to ever lace up on the court. Although the alias was short-lived, it reflected where I was as a writer. I believed this dream was a gift from God, so the reference to Jah felt fitting. Coupled with 23—who could beat that? Not to brag, but I felt like I was balling like Spaulding with a stage name that made me think I had game.

Over the years, I have been in Jamaica on numerous occasions, specifically Negril and Montego Bay, beautiful beaches by the way, where the water is sky blue, but I have yet to step foot in the Bob Marley Museum located in Kingston, Jamaica to pay my respect to the great Bob Marley; simply because I don't believe I have written any songs or lyrics that would make him smile down on me. Until then, I feel undeserving and unwelcome to visit the Bob Marley Museum as I would not want to disappoint one of the greatest legends and songwriters ever.

Before I move on to other genres that have fueled this unquenchable dream of mine, allow me to share my favorite reggae songs of all time. These classics are my unprescribed holistic medicine—songs that penetrate the soul and heart, coated with a dose of joy, happiness, and peace. They will never leave me, not for a single day of my life. Here they are:

Songs by Bob Marley: Stir it Up, Iron like Zion, Three Little Birds, and No Woman No Cry

Songs by Buju Banton: Destiny, Single Parent, Love Sponge, and Circumstances

Oh man, I get the chills playing these songs. They are unforgettable; they remind me of the good old days, jamming and vibing to exceptional music.

BACHATA, CALYPSO, DANCEHALL, MERINGUE, SALSA, SOCA, TROUBADOUR, and ZOOK

I am not a historian; I do not claim to be one. However, as a student of music, I would say these genres connected the islands closer to each other, not just musically but also culturally, all across the blue beaches of the Caribbean: Haiti, Saint Lucia, Guyana, Jamaica, St. Thomas, Barbados, and Trinidad & Tobago. Each genre has unique sounds, beats, and joyful and warm lyrics. Overall, West Indians do not discriminate as they take pride in crowding dance floors, parades, carnivals, and Mardi Gras, regardless of which genre happens to be played at a particular time.

So, early on, exposure to these genres further influenced how I viewed songwriting and how people's mood is altered while listening and dancing. These early experiences highlighted a basic fact: there is no music without the people, and there are no people without the music. Hence, any artist, in this case, any lyricist such as myself, has one main goal or task: inducing a mood in an individual or audience as desired. Or give the people what they want.

As I was getting older, my musical taste was being seasoned and sweetened with songs like:

DANCEHALL

Ting-A-Ling by Shabba Ranks, Mr. Lover Man by Shabba Ranks, Who Am I by Bennie Man, Girls Dem Sugar by Beenie Man, and Temperature by Sean Paul, and Settle Down (Destiny) by Mavado

SOCA

Jump by Sponge & Blue Ventures, Superblue by Tribute to Sundar, Tempted to Touch by Rupert Clarke, and Give Me Soca by Byron Lee & The Dragonaires

ZOOK

Sye Bwa by Kassav, Zouk-La Se Sel Medikaman by Kassav, and Se Pa Pou Dat by Alan Cave

being played on the airwaves and at local parties. These songs bring positive energy and happiness that I could only describe as smooth vibes, where everyone moves their feet, hips, and body flawlessly and effortlessly. This made it practically impossible to pay close attention to every verse, every rhyme, and every line.

SOFT ROCK & POP

Furthermore, as more diaspora and tourists visited Haiti, the music scene in Haiti was evolving rapidly. I experienced the impact firsthand as so many of my relatives had immigrated to the United States in the early and late 1970s. Similarly, some relatives had immigrated further up north, northward as Canada, seeking better lives and opportunities in the cold or anywhere.

Consequently, I was introduced to Canadian and American artists dominating soft rock and pop culture. One Canadian artist, in particular, was a best-selling artist named Bryan Adams; if I recall, the year was 1995 or 1996, when one of my older cousins played the following songs: "Rescue Me," "Please Forgive Me," and "Straight From the Heart." Bryan Adams, a fantastic singer and songwriter with a voice uniquely different, made me itch. More importantly, his voice was mesmerizing, moving fans in live concerts worldwide.

Although other songwriters co-wrote some of his songs, his voice supplied those lyrics the oxygen that fans were dying for; fans sang every word melodically as if they had written these lyrics. I found his lyrics simple yet perplexing in how they were structured and composed musically, so I studied and listened to more Bryan Adams songs and some more Bryan Adams as a songwriting blueprint.

Until another mega artist from Canada came along, Celine Dion, singing her heart out in "My Heart Will Go On" as the theme soundtrack of arguably one of the greatest films ever.

"Titanic," although she did not write the song, was written by Will Jennings, who, by the way, is deserving of all the accolades and songwriting credits he has obtained for penning the lyrics, rightly so.

As an aspiring lyricist and writer, I am biased and tend to religiously and steadfastly give songwriters and lyricists credits before everyone else, singers, composers, and producers. However, I must defer this time because Celine Dion did such an astounding job. From the opening line, she softly took everyone's heart away, I mean everyone. One could not resist, as you knew your heart would go on across the ocean or wherever you were as you sang along.

Celine Dion's beautiful and moving voice is the heartbeat of Jenning's every verse and chorus. Without Celine Dion, Jenning's lyrics would have literally and lyrically hit the tip of the iceberg. I genuinely believe that. That's my assessment and my story. I am sticking to it.

Hereafter, I conclude every great songwriter, lest a lyricist, needs a great singer; one cannot coexist without the other. It's like having Elton John writing lyrics without Bernie Taupin (an English-American Lyricist). Better yet, Frank Sinatra needed Paul Anka (credited for the English lyrics, as the Gille-Thibaut and Claude Francois had penned the French lyrics in the original song "Comme D'habitude) as much as Paul Anka needed Frank Sinatra to deliver a marvelous song like "My Way," released way before my time, 1969 to be exact.

Those are some of my early memories of soft rock and pop song lyrics, which are a memorable part of my teenage years as a fan of music and songwriting. I have treasured these beautiful memories in my heart just like my grandmother's souvenirs; they never get old.

Vinyl

How can I forget those music players and recorders? But I don't recall, nor do I remember, the first record I ever saw placed and musically played on the Turntable Platter. However, I remember vividly standing in front of this gigantic wooden record player the size of a refrigerator. The only difference was that it was lying horizontally on the tiled floor in my childhood living room.

Family history has it that my uncle Wilnaire purchased it at a corner store in Newark, New Jersey, in the 80s, then shipped it to Haiti to my late uncle Rodrigue, who brought the record player home. I must have been eight or nine years old, which would have been the early 1990s. I had never seen one before; for a naive kid, it was mind-blowing; as the turntable turned, my head would turn, moving and dancing slowly to classic and unaged records that were ever recorded.

I would stare at the turntable, which would begin to spin when the arm, I mean the "Tonearm," was moved toward the record. The entire process was fantastic and unbelievable; the other lever, which is called a lift, my uncle Rodrigue would push the lift lever forward to lower the arm slowly onto the desired position on the record to begin playing. I was fortunate to be introduced to such a musical piece and a unique one at such an early age, as only a few households, even Haitian kids, had one or ever seen one, for that matter. This early encounter certainly emboldened and lured my liking for music and classic records to levels beyond my years.

Walkman

What can I say? I was a boy then, or I had not become a man yet, but the Walkman had me walking like a man, so much so that I felt like I was moonwalking in Michael Jackson Florsheim's shoes; RIP, Michael Jackson. I don't recall precisely the brand of Walkman I was given or gifted, but it may have been a Sony or a Panasonic. I do remember it was bright yellow, with a hook that would hang on your waist. I would insert the cassette tape and press "Play" to let the heavenly music take me away; my whole body would transform. I would enter this world where calamity, sorrow, and pain were nonexistent. I would close my eyes and press "Rewind." I listened to the same song repeatedly, the same lines over and over; it didn't matter how many times I listened to a specific song; my feelings remained unchanged; I was unbothered by the outside world. I would get this unwavering feeling listening to incredible lyrics ever penned. Looking back, the Walkman was one of the coolest gadgets in the 80s, which was exciting technology in those days. It became one of my loyal companions, accompanying me wherever I would go. Listening to the lyrics attentively as you walked was like running the Boston Marathon; the lyrics kept coming with no finish line.

During that time, I began to anticipate the last word in a line, the last line in a verse, and so forth. For instance, when I hear a song for the first time, I would anticipate or predict the preceding word, line, or even rhymes. My predictions were not always on point like an arrow, but for the most part, I guessed the correct answer six out of ten times. The more I listen, the more I develop this writer's mindset, enabling me to visualize other writers' writing and thought processes. It's not abnormal or uncanny in the world of artistry, where one artist sees through the eyes of the other artist without a prior encounter or conversation. It's like reading someone's lips, in this instance, the writer's words, theoretically speaking.

Compact Disc (CD)

The introduction of CDs in the late 1970s rapidly changed the world of music; it changed how music was produced, stored, played, and marketed. Although I did not possess one from the beginning, it technologically obsoleted the era of cassette tapes.

It would be unfair not to share some of my favorite Long Playlists (LP) or albums and Extended Playlists (EP) that influenced my lyrical curiosity and albums that I used to jam religiously in the mid-90s, prior to my voyage to the United States.

In case you're wondering about the difference between an LP and an EP—Music 101: an EP typically contains four to six tracks, whereas an LP or album includes at least seven tracks.

One of the first CDs, if not the best CD, I have ever gotten as a gift was "Love Always" by R&B duo K-Ci & JoJo, the first LP I ever played. In the summer of 1997, one of my cousins, who resided in Brooklyn, New York, was vacationing in Haiti for a few weeks. She had brought the CD with her and listened to it ceaselessly. I remember approaching and asking her, "What are you listening to," She replied, "All My Life" by K-Ci & JoJo. As she listened to the song, she moved so smoothly and placed her hand on her chest, touching her heart as if the music had poked a hole into her heart. It was beautiful to witness how her body was musically transformed moving by the sound of music. I remember asking her if I could have a dose of what she was listening to as there was something indescribable. She didn't hesitate; she quickly gave me a dose, placing the headphones on top of my head and gently placing the foamed rounded earpieces over my small ears, which were wired and connected to the port jack port located on the left side to ensure the sound remained in my eardrums.

Thereafter, she instructed me to heed the sound and the lyrics. I nodded, suggesting that I understood her instructions. She examined the Maxell black headphones; once she noticed I was impatient, she rewound to the same track, Track 11 "All My Life." It was then the music hit my soul, making me lose control.

It took me to a place I had never been before, a place of pure joy and love. I instantly understood why the music moved my cousin. Even though I had not mastered the English language, my level of comprehension was good enough; thus, the words were easy to comprehend, not to mention the lyrics were simple, yet so exceptionally written, which made it impossible not to list

"All MY LIFE" as one of my favorite R&B records of all my life; I mean "of all time."

My cousin returned to New Jersey a few weeks later, but she had kindly gifted me the LP. Although I was reluctant to take it, she insisted I should have it, so in the subsequent months, I found myself listening to the entire LP daily, vibing and tapping my feet to other tracks: Track 4, "Just For Your Love," Track 6, Don't Rush (Take Love Slowly), and Track 7 my second favorite record on the album "You Bring Me Up" fantastic lyrics with uplifting tempo beat always bring my spirit up, spiritually.

The more I listened to the LP, the more I appreciated these songwriters and their peers, whose hard work and dedication made it possible to deliver one of the greatest releases and albums of the 1990s.

2000

The 90s pinnacled with masterful music; music was rolling just like the rolling stone. But, this book would be incomplete without mentioning how influential music was to my life in the 2000s and beyond. Figuratively speaking, music saved my life; I would not have made it this far if it had not been for song lyrics that kept my mind sharp and sane.

In the early 2000s, as I was transitioning and adapting to my new life in the United States, I faced a multitude of personal challenges: identity, isolation, immigration, family, and social issues.

Consequently, my music preference and playlist widened as a coping mechanism, navigating through new genres and types of sounds that I was not accustomed to: Country, Rock & Roll, Rap, Hip-Hop, Jazz, and hiplife before the world popularized it as Afrobeats, thanks to all my Ghanaian, Ivorian, Liberian, and Nigerian friends and former classmates from Lowell, you know, who you are.

Not to get off topic or go off on a tangent, residing in Lowell, Mass, made the introduction to new genres seamless; because of its exquisite culture and diversity, it was hard. I firmly believe Lowell is the mecca of cultures, even a closed-minded person would be cultured and become open-minded once one gets a taste of the different cuisines, dances, languages and dialects, not to mention Lowell's history is exceptional, as the city was known as the cradle of the American Industrial Revolution because of its textile mills and factories.

While attending Lowell High School (or LHS), I perfected my English as a second language in my ESL (English as Second Language) class. Honestly,

I should have been enrolled in ETL (English as a Third Language), since French was already my second language and had occupied that linguistic slot. But there was no such course as ETL—and now that I think about it, taxpayers would have vetoed such a proposal anyway.

It was at LHS that I met a dear friend, Ebenezer, who remains one of my best friends today—a brother from another mother, from the motherland. We had met through a mutual friend a year earlier, and he quickly introduced me to East Coast Hip-Hop artist Cory McKay, better known by his stage name Cormega, or simply Mega.

Cormega's lyrics were exceptionally crafted. Lyrically, I firmly believe he belongs in the same league as AZ, Nas, and other great emcees I have yet to honor in this book. I guess you could say I'm saving the best—the greats—for last. Although Mega and Nas didn't see eye to eye for years, their feud, chronicled in diss tracks, reached my lyrical radar. Eventually, they reconciled and even featured on each other's songs, but those years of tension were legendary for Hip-Hop culture.

I was inspired by Mega's lyrical abilities because his words were informative and educational. His delivery and flow were something to die for. He instantly became one of my favorite artists, showcasing his greatness in his debut LP, *The Realness,* which included tracks like "The Saga" and "Fallen Soldiers." I must have listened to that album countless times, studying each track to help me cope with my own struggles.

Even though *The Realness* was released in 2001, Ebenezer and I still take trips down memory lane, greeting each other by reciting lines from Mega's songs—a tribute to pure lyricism.

Between 2002 and 2003, I started gravitating toward rap because many of my acquaintances, friends, and classmates were obsessively listening to Hip-Hop. You could say peer pressure played a role, but the music was so powerful I couldn't resist. The more I listened, the more I fell in love.

Rap lyrics illustrate the lives of minorities—the Black, the Brown, the marginalized—and immigrants as well, which I happened to be at the time and will always be.

As a result, I began purchasing rap and Hip-Hop CDs to broaden my music arsenal. There were so many releases—demos, mixtapes, EPs, and LPs to choose from; it didn't matter where you lived; the street alleys, the corner stores, and the retail store shelves were fully stocked with records. I started collecting CDs from artists or groups such as Notorious Big, The Fugees, DMX, Jay-Z, Rakim, Mos Def, Talib Kweli, and Outkast, who had already given Hip-Hop fans and recording labels a sneak peek of what Hip-Hop would become.

Although I arrived on the Rap and Hip-Hop scene late as far as being introduced to it, simply because I was an outsider, an immigrant, Hip-Hop quickly pulled me closer to American culture and the English language as well, so I embraced it. I sought old records that had been released ten to fifteen prior, so I could better understand the genre that had paved the way for newer artists. I was destined to be a savvy Hip-Hop fan; I wanted to be well-informed and relevant, not only be able to critique albums, songs, verses speak on lyrics, but also be able to educate others on the history of Hip-Hop or Rap to those who only listen to music just to be excellent; lacking the lyrical knowledge.

My idea of being excellent from the inception was studying those song lyrics as if preparing for a midterm exam. I could not flunk it. I never wanted to take anything in my life for granted, never took any shortcuts, even if I cut them. So, I cut to the chase like Chase was on the case; I kept buying more albums, not singles. An album provides the artist's fan base with a complete tracking list, providing the full scope of the artist's story, whereas a single only provides a snippet. Moreover, it did not matter how bad or great an album was; I've always felt a need to listen till the end, listening to every track of an album so I could get the full scope of the artist's intent.

The album CDs were superb not just because they were new technology but because the lyrics were provided within the package; only some of the albums would give the lyrics. Whenever they were enclosed, I would study them and memorize the writers' names. Surprisingly, this is how I discovered most singers don't write their songs; they use Ghostwriters or co-writers. For instance, "My Love is Your Love" by the late Whitney Houston was written by Wyclef Jean and Jerry Duplessis; creating a hit record requires a team, let alone a classic album, where you have the best producers, composers, songwriters, singers, and lyricists under the same recording studio.

Lyricists are often, if only sometimes, anonymous compared to the famous singers or artists they write lyrics for.

Do you remember FYE (or For Your Entertainment)? Subsequently FYE became one of my favorite stores to scoop or shop for the newest releases. I thoroughly read and studied the enclosed lyrics for every album I ever bought. In addition, I pay respect to the authors, the songwriters, and the lyricists. So I always turned my attention to the Credits section to pay my respect, and in doing so, memorizing their names, at least I would try my best because so often there are several co-writers involved.

I take great pleasure and pride in admiring the contributors to a particular project. For me, it's an essential part of the experience. They, too, play a role; therefore, they need to be respectfully acknowledged.

To me, tormenting any aspect of artistry is unethical; not reading or acknowledging the Credits section of an album is as unethical as leaving a movie theater without waiting for the credits to roll out on the screen.

Furthermore, for every song I ever listened to, I would not only take the time to read about everyone involved but also key my eyes on the lyricist's or songwriters' discographies. Additionally, I would read and study the lyrics in their entirety, analyzing song structure, pattern, rhyme, and wordplay. Over the years, I must have read other artists' song lyrics for benchmarking purposes. I wanted to know if they were terrible or excellent lyrics. They all provided a little spice to what I was craving and needed lyrically.

They were all fuel, lighting this lyrical fire inside of me, ablaze that I deeply need to keep this passion ablaze. The more I studied those lyrics, the harder I worked on my craft and the more sleepless nights I had thinking about what line or verse I would come up with.

Failure was not an option; thus, I immersed myself in Rap music, especially song lyrics. When I did not have two pennies to rub together, I would compensate by bootlegging the latest releases and downloading and burning my own albums via file-sharing websites such as Limewire or Pirate Bay. Long ago, there was no digital media service offering music (e.g., Spotify, IheartRadio).

Some artists got better lyrically after each LP, so I tried to keep up as much as I could, benchmarking my lyrical skills against lyrical geniuses to make sure I was on the right path. I had learned a long, long time ago that one could come or drive a long way but end up in the wrong location.

Therefore, I periodically paused and asked myself, "How did I fare?" after writing my own lyrics to make sure I was going in the right direction. Whenever I felt my lyrics were not going in the right direction, I would make a U-turn and rewrite them from scratch.

As aforementioned, Cormega was my first favorite rapper, but along the way, I fell in love with these lyrical geniuses of Hip-Hop:

Jay-Z, Eminem, Notorious B.I.G., Lil Wayne, Andre 3000, and Talib Kweli—these artists put the word art in artists with textbook lyricism and compelling stories that have influenced my writing. Over the years, I have become a die-hard fan, watching their lyrical intellect on the sideline, paying close attention to every word, line, bar, and rhyme they would rap on each LP they ever released. They possess a brilliant mind vis-a-vis lyricism in every sense of the word.

Forevermore, I admire them even more for never cheating the art of lyricism. They have proven repeatedly and consistently that they are living proof that rap lyrics have a special place in society, in Hip-Hop, and in American culture.

Their prowess is on top of the Rap spectrum with exceptional wordplay, rhyme, delivery, flow, cadence, and the whole Hip-Hop yard. Their way of playing with words is like playing chess, whereas every other rapper is not even playing checkers but watching checkers being played.

I have listened to all of their LPs including features with other peers. Yet, I am still blown away to this day because I discovered a piece or unhidden message that I had missed. The answers to their lyrics are embedded in every verse, yet it takes time to digest and consume the message they are brilliantly conveying; that is what I call textbook lyricism. These rappers have more compelling stories than a library. One cannot put these artists and rappers in a box; not only that they think outside the box, they are the box, elevating and raising the bar of rap excellence with bars.

Other artists also inspired me, even though they never made my list of all-time favorite rappers. Still, they deserve mention: Lauryn Hill, Nas, AZ, Styles P, DMX, Mos Def, Tupac, Jadakiss, Obie Trice, Rick Ross, 5' 9 Royce, and Joe Budden, who were brilliant on the microphone delivering lyrics and knowledge beyond their years; popping everyone ears with flow, melody, wordplay, rhymes, metaphors, touching on a variety of topics, who inspired not only me but upcoming artists around the world.

Although some of those artists are not actively releasing songs and albums as they once did in the early years of their music careers, their lyrical intellect and versatility are cemented in Hip-Hop culture. Consequently, their impact is transcendent in my writing as a fan and student of songwriting.

Nowadays, I could choose from only so many influential lyricists as the lyrical landscape of true Emcees and lyricists is dried or deserted, but if I had to pick some renaissance rappers that have been watering the dryness. I would say these subsequent new generations of rappers have had my ears; as they are a handful lingering examples of a dying breed:

Che Noir, Nicky Minaj, Kendrick Lamar, J. Cole, Kodak Black, and fellow Massachusetts native Joyner Lucas. Their lyrics contain compelling stories and songs that portray not only images of their surroundings but lyrics that take you to the heart of their upbringing and, more importantly, Hip-Hop culture. They have stayed true to the art of lyricism, obeying the rules of a true lyricist, consistently, may I add, dropping bars, skillful with wordplay, and getting better lyrically after each album as their predecessors.

ALBUM VI
WHO'S CALLING?

"Your calling isn't something that somebody can tell you about. It's what you feel. It's a part of your life force. It's the thing that gives you juice. The thing you are supposed to do. And nobody can tell you what that is. You know it inside yourself." Oprah Winfrey

After over two decades of listening to every genre of music, albums, songs, and records, being influenced by so many prestigious artists, and having so many valuable materials, I was still wondering if becoming a lyricist was nothing but a trance as I had not had an eureka moment and had not ascertained my lyrical path; unsure and unconfident where I belonged as far as being a writer, primarily a lyricist. It was becoming more apparent that I was a lost cause or writer who would never be found in the lost and found. My mind was traveling all over the place like a nomad. Still, I kept telling myself, "JUST KEEP WRITING," "JUST KEEP WRITING," and "JUST KEEP WRITING," it does not matter in what form of literature; eventually, the heavens above or the earth beneath would give me a purpose.

In 2005, I found my divine calling; where everything changed. In the early Spring of 2005, I had just gotten kicked out of my father's house on 15 May Street after a late-night heated argument with my father over a cracked window; I had inadvertently broken while trying to get inside the house five or six months earlier because my house keys would not unlock the entry doors; front or side for some mysterious reasons that solely my father could elaborate on and disclose.

As a result, I moved in and sojourned in my high school friend Ralph's mom's house, which was in a vacant bedroom for the remainder of Spring 2005. After that, I moved into a Townhouse basement in the summer of 2005, owned by Jill. Who is Jill?

The reason I moved into the basement on 112 Methuen Street can be summed up in four words: Jill, the animal lover. She was also a brilliant and passionate former history teacher from Lowell High, who had taught a few of my colleagues—friends I had grown close to over the years. One day, I ran into her outside her townhouse while she was mowing her lawn. As we

chatted, I told her I was looking for an inexpensive apartment to rent or a bedroom before starting the Fall semester at Middlesex Community College. Surprisingly, she unhesitantly said, "I have a finished cellar, vacant. You could move into it while you find the ideal apartment or bedroom." At the time, I didn't have enough money in my savings account. When I asked her how much the rent would be, she replied, "It's not—it's not for rent." Surprised, I asked, "Then why am I moving into your basement?" In her unmistakable South Boston accent, she said, "Your high school friends were troublemakers. You always seemed like a good kid. You can stay in the basement while you get yourself together."

So I gathered my belongings from Ralph's mother's house—which wasn't much to begin with—and settled into the basement.

I was happy but unhappy that I was not financially contributing to her mortgage or paying a significant amount as I should have. But sometimes in life, you have to count your blessings and swallow your pride; I did just that. I unashamedly swallowed that pill of so-called pride with a sip of tears that were coming down my eyes because Jill providing a helping hand was God's plan. One day, I would understand and return the favor; that is exactly what I told myself.

In the first two or three months of living in the basement, every second, hour, and day seemed longer, and the load of so-called life was getting heavier and heavier to carry. I was barely keeping my head above my shoulder. When I tried my hardest to pull myself up and get my life together, I felt this gravity-like force pulling me down closer to rock bottom.

Somehow, I fought and won some of the personal issues or battles I was dealing with or going against, but some problems, emotions, and struggles were too overwhelming; I just could not defeat them.

I remember one day grabbing my pen and notebook, purging all my anger and emotions, cursing my dad out, and cleaning out my closet as if I had stolen a line from Eminem's rhyme or lyrics book. I penned a few rap verses, and I felt relieved. I felt the pain and anger that I endured in that period, escaping through one of the basement's windows. I could not believe I could write such emotional song lyrics; they were authentic, unapologetic, and remarkable.

This became my **"EUREKA"** moment; I guess you could ascertain the argument with my father was a beautiful disaster because had it not been for him, I would have never found my purpose. All praise to the almighty God.

Thereafter, I went on to write rap lyrics to conquer and detonate any issues or battles that life launches in my physical and mental radar. Subsequently, I would not proceed any day of my life without writing a few words, a few lines, and verses. Even through sickness and health, I have stayed devoted to writing lyrics. I love it so much that I feel as if I am married to it, and I hope one day I will have a kid with it.

Consequently, I started working on this project during that time, which would later become known as The Soundtrack Of My Life.

ALBUM VII
THE SOUNDTRACK OF MY LIFE

This album illustrates and chronicles a pivotal and transitional part of my late teenage years and early 20s: growing up in the Caribbean or West Indies and emigrating to Massachusetts.

It is the genesis of sojourning, confronting challenges, searching for answers, adapting, and accepting life and a new culture. I had only been living in Massachusetts for about five to six years, speaking broken English like, getting kicked out of my father's house, and residing down in the cellar. I was constantly dreaming of becoming something in life, dreaming of making my lovely mother proud, dreaming of exceeding the expectations of my late cousins Richard (T-Michel) and Nicko (Rony), dreaming of becoming a Dentist, ultimately majoring in Nutrition, dreaming of proving everyone that ever doubted me, especially a father who I barely knew and got along with, to say the least.

I also found myself dreaming of making a name for myself, dreaming of crossing the road to success, dreaming of the American Dream well, a divided American dream, as the black American dream is quite different from the White American dream. Even though, as a Haitian immigrant, I always felt my dreams should be gravitated towards achieving the Haitian Dream, which is deeper, of course. But I have always asked myself.

What is the Haitian Dream? Quite frankly, I am not sure what it consists of, but as a kid, I would sit on my doorstep daydreaming of having all the material things that most kids should have, glazing at the sky and counting stars, and watching every move of the moon as it illuminated the blue sky, wondering if one day I would become someone important and contribute to society. Perhaps that was my Haitian dream; I didn't have the answers then, and I still don't have the answers now. Because when you come from a place like Haiti or any rough and underdeveloped neighborhood where there are not too many options to peacefully go to sleep and have those sweet dreams and actually work towards achieving those dreams, by default one starts dreaming beyond the borders, beyond those walls, and beyond your actual neighborhood. We become dream chasers, dreaming and chasing dreams of another society or country millions of miles away from home, like the American Dream, to make sure we become successful in life and ensure history does not repeat itself; another black kid never amounts to anything, like a planted seed who got washed away and never grew.

Moreover, this album encompasses a lustrum of song lyrics I had written, then collectively collated and organized into one project and theme. Now that I consider myself a seasoned lyricist, I find those early lyrics to be terrible — not good, not great — but I could not exclude them from this book. They are part of my story, and I would not be doing this book justice if I only highlighted the good.

As with any album, some songs may not make the final cut for a myriad of justifiable reasons: contracts, clearances, and record-label restrictions, to name a few. The same unwritten rules apply to my debut project; some songs were excluded simply due to personal preference.

Call it insanity, but I treated my early days of writing lyrics as if I were a new artist about to release my debut LP, anxiously waiting to see if one of the tracks would become a commercial hit and chart on the Billboard Hot 100 in its first week.

Without further ado, I present to you; the tracklist of "The Soundtrack Of My Life" including images depicting my come up in the lyrical scene, my early work as a wanna be lyricist. I hope you enjoy it!

Tracklist:

01. **Those Years**
02. **Where Are You Boo?**
03. **Divided State Of America**
04. **Naturally Gifted**
05. **Untold Stories**
06. **Marie-Michelle (Mother of All)**
07. **Deeper Than Music**
08. **Think About That**
09. **Death & Pain**
10. **Joy**
11. **509 (Where I'm From)**
12. **A Letter To God (Prayer)**

Track 01♪♪♪Those Years

Intro

Time ain't waiting for no one

Verse I

Coming from a third country
May cause a lot of damage
Somehow I didn't suffer brain-damage
Years later after that voyage
Big up red & blue, we stick like glue
I still remain true to my heritage
No place like home, 509 is my heart
I will never pay homage
After I expose my life like an open book
Save the page that has engraved
Many scars on my face, personality, mind
Then you will understand why
On October 31, 1999 I took a voyage
When the next day is a sequel of yesterday
Church and your soul are the only bandage
Now I'm sitting so comfortably, like cleavage
Babe girl got the full package
Above my game better than average
I barely consult the mileage
'Cause I have the Lord's message
And every bible passage in my storage
So I am stronger than cartilage

Chorus

Even though, those years are gone
Deep down inside I refuse to say goodbye
'Cause of those years
I've learned the true meaning of living
I have become a man
So I'm not leaving those years behind
Will cherish them, I need an encore
Because of those years
I've learned that being happy poor
Is a great gift worth dying for
"Cause of those years I've given my life to God
And I pray every day God is at my door

Track 01♪♪♪Those Years

Verse II

If the word Patience is the topic
No Interpreter is needed
You're speaking my language
Let's get engaged, last name Petit
But so many angels with me, I'm large
Had been broken many times, never shattered
No loss of faith through breakage
Can be sacked near the line of scrimmage
Somehow I still manage, to stay sage
In the bible, God created man in his own image
Knowing that my personality is less
Important than my self-image
Keep me out the cage
Not everything in life is achiral
Like my left hand is a non-superimposable
Mirror image off my right hand
No matter how they are oriented
Only a few will comprehend this message

Chorus (Repeat)

Verse II

Don't you ever let anything demolish
Your self-esteem and confidence
Stay confident, family as your confidant
Don't let this world dictates your life
Be cautious who you choose as a wife
Ladies be prudent who you sleep with
Spring Break don't mean wildlife
HIV is sharper than a knife
Don't let sex brings you down
Keep your head up higher than a giraffe
He who always does what others want
Searching for what the others have
Knowing he can't have
Cars, mansions that he can't afford
Just to fit in and to be loved
Don't believe in the freedom of the will

Track 01♪♪Those Years

Might as well make a will, what's the deal?
I don't care if society don't love me
As long as my loved ones will
I'm cool if my house ain't in Beverly Hills
As long as my children tuition is prepaid
My family can eat their daily meals
And I'm not in debt, I can pay my bills
I'm gonna keep it real, use money wisely
Knowing money is not everything
Money is the only thing, don't be an imbecile
Chorus (Repeat)

Verse III

Certain things money cannot buy
Like Manley being so patient
Focused and humble, of all people
Who am I really? nothing much in reality
But, environmentally not the same scrawny
Who had grown up in the poorest country
I vowed mom I wouldn't act silly
Took an oath to play this game of life fairly
13 years later, I've not acted silly, seriously!
So when I traced my footprints at JFK
Told myself if I don't get assassinated like MLK
Life will be better than okay, Hey!
I knew then that the cover will come off
Didn't know how, but I was determined
Not to let my past be a sequel
Of a covered barrel
So, my expectations have excelled
Farther than Microsoft Excel
Now, I'm writing music that
One day will sell as much as Adele
Now not only I can see the sunshine
I've located the stars in the sky
Time is money, so I abuse the time
To make sure the money don't slide by
Chorus (Repeat)

Track 01♪♪Those Years

Verse IV

A thin line btw the lower and upper-class
Quite frankly, its not prosperity
Uncle Sam gives opportunity
Well, lately with uncertainty
So I've been working my butt off
If hard work really pays off
When all is set and done
Should be surrounded by 18 holes
Playing golf, on my days off
Even if I hit rock bottom
I'll be back where I left off
This is the good life, hate it or love it
You got a dream you have to follow it
I got my first taste of success at Tricia's
Looking at the future, the past, I'm off that
I don't know if its nature or nurture
All I know is life ain't been the same
If you knew how far I came
You'd know why I hate being benched
Or waiting on anyone
I don't drink Gatorade, but boy
I'm in the game, life is too short
That's why I'm playing this game
Everybody wants to win
Nobody wants to swim to get the fame
Why swimming when homicide
Can contribute to fame, that's ashamed
This world is so bewildered, the victim
Survivor is less respected than the shooter
Who's to blame?

Chorus (Repeat)

Track 01♪♪Those Years

Verse V

Things happen for a reason
The horizon changes every season
It's amazing how things change
When you're traveling in a different time zone
You start looking things differently
From what you are used to in Boston
Appreciate what you have son
'Cause life isn't sweet under the sun
Trust me! This is nonfiction
Never was a writer till
My tempered father kicked me out
Never thought I'd forgive pop
For tossing me out (get out)
Till I realized what fam is all about
Family falls apart, never truly departs
Don't even know why I'm telling you this
I must have a purpose, we all have a purpose
What's your purpose? Ask yourself

Chorus (Repeat)

Behind the Lyrics

As beautiful and powerful as lyrics can be, they often come with ambiguity, leading to potential misinterpretation by fans and listeners who may seek further clarification. So, let's take a pause and go backstage, behind the lyrics and the lines, as we explore the mind of a lyricist.

After relocating from the heart of the Caribbean, Haiti, to the East Coast, I spent time reflecting on my past, present, and future, particularly regarding cultural differences. I wrote this song to chronicle my life after having lived in the Northeast for over five to six years. Naturally, I titled the first song in the album "Those Years," which outlines the life I once lived in Haiti—not the Haiti of today, but a Haiti of the past filled with beautiful memories, struggles, and a hopeful future for the youth.

I belonged to a society enriched with some of the most resilient people in the world who have endured so much yet continue to thrive under difficult conditions. As I sat in the cellar with a pen and pad, reflecting on those years, I felt an unprecedented loneliness being away from home. There truly is no place like home; regardless of the circumstances or how Haiti is perceived, my love for Haiti remains unchanged. However, as reality set in like the sunset just outside the cellar at 112 Methuen, I had to confront the future as an immigrant—specifically as a Black immigrant, and more specifically, a Haitian immigrant in America.

My mind was a whirlwind of emotions, and I wanted to share my story as truthfully as possible. Yet, I struggled for hours to compose a verse. Eventually, I managed to write these three lines:

Verse I

Coming from a third country	***(Line 1)***
May cause a lot of damage	***(Line 2)***
Somehow I didn't suffer brain damage	***(Line 3)***

Once I penned these lines, the rest began to flow like water. I allowed my pen to express my thoughts freely; I wanted to lay everything on the table for others to digest my lyrics, reflecting my background and my experiences coming to America from my perspective—not Eddie Murphy's. Next, I wrote the second verse, Verse II, where I touched on the lifestyle of Americans.

Verse III
Depicts my journey of adapting to life in America and my goals as a writer. One of those goals is to sell music as successfully as Adele, as I mention toward the end of the verse. Some may consider this ambition excessive, and I wouldn't disagree. However, what is a dream without ambition, and what is ambition without a dream? This duality inspired my verses. Nineteen years later, I remain as ambitious as ever—still writing, still rhyming, with a strong desire to achieve my goals. Furthermore, Verse IV highlights the significance of hard work and the importance of overcoming failures and setbacks.

Verse V
Serves as a reminder to myself and to others not to take this land of opportunity for granted. There are children and people around the world who die from malnutrition daily, suffering from starvation and lacking access to basic necessities like shelter, electricity, hygiene supplies, and clean water. I conclude this verse by reflecting on my past relationship with my father. Despite the conflict that led him to kick me out of the house, I found the courage to forgive him for what I believe was primarily his fault. Ironically, this incident inspired me to write my first verse. I wish I could share it with you in this book, but unfortunately, I haven't been able to locate the piece of paper I wrote it on. I'm sure the letters are fading away, just like my feud with my father faded over the years.

Track 02♪♪♪Where Are You Boo?

Intro

Where are you, boo? Hopefully, the radio is on
You never know what you've got till it is gone
Perhaps I should've secured it on my own
Where are you, boo? I can't wait to see you
Come back so we can fix things, boo
Like Jay-Z raps, "I can't see em' comin down my eyes
So I gotta make the song cry."

Verse I

If there is a problem let it be known
I had told you that our problems
Shouldn't be recycled at the beauty salon
Word on the streets that you are gone
Can't believe my ear that we're done
You could've hit me on my cell phone
Boo you know it's always on
I'd have lowered my tone
And let you increase your tone
To let you express your feelings
I just I can't leave you alone
Please come back, I'm home all alone
We can work it out, call the house phone
I can explain in my own words, like Ne-Yo
Tell me what's on your mind I ain't Ms. Cleo
Just teach me which way to go
I will be your Clyde and your alibi
If you stay by my side, I'll be on every ride
Loneliness is good for the soul
But somehow I'm losing control
I won't be happy girl if we divide
I want you to be my bride
Without you my life is incomplete
I will even swallow my pride
Because I can't let you slide

Track 02♪♪♪♪♪♪♪♪♪♪♪♪♪♪♪♪♪♪♪♪♪♪♪♪♪♪♪♪♪♪♪♪♪♪♪♪♪♪♪Where Are You Boo?

Pre-Chorus

What am I gonna do without you?
Boo I'm in love with you, let's undo
What I did and didn't do
Boo you already know I'm in love with you
Tell me where you're, I'm coming for you
Can't sleep without you, Where are you?

Chorus

Your homecoming is overdue
Where are you boo? Where are you boo?
Your homecoming is overdue
Where are you boo? Where are you boo?
Your homecoming is overdue

Verse II

Why did you leave me? I am so cold
I'm worthless 'cause I'm so old like gold
I want to play my role, so let the scenes unfold
I nicknamed you 'Precious'
'Cause you're as beautiful as a diamond
I childishly treated you like a real diamond
Should have known little things meant
More to you than diamonds
That explains why you like almonds
Then I stopped doing certain things
Like rubbing your hair
Massaging your lower back
Running my finger on your belly button
I took you for granted, now I'm writing this
How good is Christmas
Without your name on my Christmas List?
You're what I ever wanted, All ever needed
No question, I foolishly took you for granted
Now I can see that diamonds aint forever

Pre-Chorus & Chorus (Repeat)

Track 02♪♪♪♪♪♪♪♪♪♪♪♪♪♪♪♪♪♪♪♪♪♪♪♪♪♪♪♪♪♪♪♪♪♪♪♪♪♪♪Where Are You Boo?

Verse III
What I did wasn't clever
I know you won't believe that
Come back so I can show you that
I said in 'Thought of a Philosopher" that
My patience will never denature
Boo, I got no patience within me
Come home , then you shall see
I'm about to hop in my whip
Because I can't wait no more
About to put the pedal to the metal
To Baltimore or Singapore
Best believe I'm coming for sure
I am demanding an encore
Please don't say Au revoir
Life without you is a drained reservoir
Pre-Chorus & Chorus (Repeat)

Track 02♪♪Where Are You Boo?

Verse IV

Remember how we used to hang out
So romantically in the backyard
Top or bottom then didn't matter
We did the whole nine yard, slow or hard
And afterwards we'd watch the sunset
While I pierce a hickey on your neck
Give you something Maybelline can't undo
When your girlfriends say what the heck?
And what happened to your neck?
You can reply that's how my boo and I do
Otherwise give them a rain-check
I wasn't perfect, but treated you with respect
We didn't have to travel all the way to Tibet
But always on the go, to go down low
Till you reached the highest peak, Mt. Everest
Please come back to me, your sex game
Is a perfect sunset, mine will leave you wet
Press play! So Rihanna can bring us an umbrella
Impatiently waitin, put yourself in my shoes
Where are you Cinderella? Please holler
I'll be waiting in the cellar, or in my Impala

Pre-Chorus & Chorus (Repeat)

Track 02♪♪Where Are You Boo?

Verse V

We haven't even tied the knot
But, sweetie if you willingly return
To your impatient boo, I don't see why not
I am not, believe or not
Writing this to get recognition
just saying this cause I love you a lot
In case you were wondering
Yeah, I have been wandering
Went to your mom's spot
I even went to that parking lot
Where we used to sway
That vehicle off the ground
I'm saddened that you ain't around
Nowhere to be found
I still remember how your voice sounds
Like my Bose surround sound
How crazy is that? You missed the day
I wore that cap and gown
What could top this verse?
All I ever dreamed of was
How I could make you proud
I am clueless what love is
Oh boy! Love is too profound
I don't want to be drowned
Come rescue me, how does that sound?

Pre-Chorus & Chorus (Repeat)

Outro

They say you never know how much you love someone until they are gone. I don't need you to disappear from my life to realize how much I love you.

Behind the Lyrics

I'm trying to remember exactly how this song came about. I do recall sitting down in the cellar, contemplating what it would be like if my girlfriend or partner just vanished without saying goodbye. How would I react? Would I care enough to chase after her? Initially, I thought I would write a song about it, expressing my feelings and emotions. More importantly, I would seek answers; I would want to understand the reasons behind her sudden disappearance. And so, let the story unfold.

Verse I

This verse sets the stage for the story, highlighting the events that occur before her departure. Initially, I was uncertain about the ideal location for this narrative. As I developed the song in my mind, I realized that a beauty salon would be a perfect setting. Many women use salons not just for personal care, but also as a therapeutic sanctuary where they can vent about personal issues, particularly relationships. While this may not be universally true, there is some validity to my premise. Wouldn't you agree? At the beauty salon, they don't just wash hair; some women go there to "wash their dirty laundry" as well. No topic is off-limits—whether it's about sex, relationships, or anything else you can think of.

The Pre-Chorus and Chorus

These sections clearly express my feelings: I couldn't find her and didn't know where she was. I want to remind her that I still love her deeply. If she could come back and give me another chance in her heart, I would do everything to make it right for her. I use the chorus to emphasize the main message of the song by repeating "Where are you, boo?" four times.

Verse II

The text highlights the impact her departure has had on my soul, as our souls were once deeply intertwined. I admire her for being a simple girl, rather than someone who is materialistic and loves diamonds. She finds joy in the simplest things in life, as noted in Line 6: "That explains why you like almonds." Additionally, I provide specific examples of the things I used to do for her consistently, which I have inexplicably and unjustifiably stopped doing. In Line 1, there is a statement that ends with "I am so cold." This not only reflects the cold winter climate of the basement but also expresses the emotional chill I feel in her absence.

Verse IV
This verse illustrates the good times and the memories I once shared with her, as referenced in Line 1, Line 2, and Line 3:

Remember how we used to hang out ***(Line 1)***
So romantically in the backyard ***(Line 2)***
Top or bottom then didn't matter ***(Line 3)***
We did the whole nine-yard, slow or hard ***(Line 4)***

Line 4 is my favorite line features clever wordplay, beginning with "backyard" and extending to "the whole nine yards," which adds depth to the song. I considered adding a more suggestive twist by saying "the whole 69 yards," but I felt that would have been too obvious.

Verse V
Until now, I hadn't provided her with a convincing reason to come back. Simply saying that I miss her and asking, "Where are you, boo?" probably isn't enough. In this verse, I'm expressing my heartfelt feelings and making a promise about my dream of marrying her soon.

Track 03♪♪♪♪♪♪♪♪♪♪♪♪♪♪♪♪♪♪♪♪♪♪♪♪♪♪♪♪♪♪♪♪♪Divided State of America

Intro

In 2005, then-President George W. Bush occupied the White House as Hurricane Katrina came ashore and devastated the Gulf Coast of America. The category 3 storm killed over 1,500 people in Louisiana, left almost 1 million Louisianans without electricity, hundreds of thousands of people were rendered homeless, tens of thousands were left stranded, and tens of billions of dollars in damage occurred." Are we really united? Is America united? Are you united?

Verse I

Some say life is like a rope
Others arguably say nope
According to the Bureau of Justice
1 in 3 black can expect to be in a cell
For something such as selling dope
No opportunity to even see that rope
While sitting in a cell they cope
By reliving what they wrote
My life is what you see
Every now and then its a slope
But somehow I manage to cope
People change and grow, but
America doesn't do neither, take note
It doesn't stand united, so divided
We all have our little secrets
We keep burying away
America has its problems, yet
The chief keeps deporting our troops away
Helping others during their darkest day
Thus the rest of the world believe
America is so helpful, so problem less
We as a nation get carried away
As a result, Katrina occurred
The government didn't know what to say
Then the president has the audacity to say
We are fully prepared, you better pray

Track 03♪♪♪♪♪♪♪♪♪♪♪♪♪♪♪♪♪♪♪♪♪♪♪♪♪♪♪♪♪♪♪♪♪♪♪♪♪Divided State of America

Chorus

One nation under God
The so-called United States of America
One nation under God
With so much segregation among us today
This is a new era
Say hello to, Divided States of America

Track 03♪♪♪♪♪♪♪♪♪♪♪♪♪♪♪♪♪♪♪♪♪♪♪♪♪♪♪♪♪♪♪♪♪♪♪♪Divided State of America

Verse II

Every time someone is holding a bomb
That's about to blow,we always on the go
The truth is one cant please everybody
Internationally known for saving others
Nationally known to be a disgrace to others
Mainly to my sisters and brothers
Katrina didn't take 24 hrs to become a catg 5
Someone should've given the order
To stop the water, they just didn't bother
Damages still linger three years later
Should I go further?
Now I'm scanning my environment
Wondering what the blacks have
To face in this nation
It hit me, we have limited options
Against discrimination
Sports our best occupation, in my opinion
The time is now, we have to stop relying on
The NFL, the National Basketball Association
Look around you, discrimination's everywhere
Listen up son, go get an education

Chorus (Repeat)

Track 03♪♪♪Divided State of America

Verse III

Truthfully, education changes perception
17 years ago I was off the radar
7 years later, I'm under the microscope
All eyes on us, We ain't even a star
But, because of what and who we are
We are at war, so you are at war
Racism burns hotter than the sun
But, we can't be Ushered, Let it Burn
They want you to tear your skin off
So you can be called Mr. Jackson
Just 'cause we're outnumbered
We must fight as if were King's son
Can't let this sh*t gets the best of us
Cause it's distressing every ghetto
Every project, which is all of us
That's the reason after Katrina
So many of us got lost
Look at New Orleans, then flip a $ bill
In God We Trust, now it's time for us
To understand only God can save us
Red Cross and FEMA get lost

Chorus (Repeat)

Track 03♪♪♪♪♪♪♪♪♪♪♪♪♪♪♪♪♪♪♪♪♪♪♪♪♪♪♪♪♪♪♪♪♪♪♪♪Divided State of America

Verse IV

I was seconds away from criticizing
Bush like Kanye West
But, my critics were interrupted
What if God had given Katrina a MapQuest
Racism would've found a way
To destroy our people, save them father
Even though they killed so many people
Now some might say
I ain't supposed to be concerned
I should keep silent, like the lambs
'Cause I ain't from New Orleans
But black is black, right?
Even thru the brightest light
A nigga doesn't turn white
Not even for one night with Ms. White
That's against our nature
Which is equivalent to nine figures
With racism, there is no pleasure
For the culture, it's time to fight back
Before our children get sacked
In fact, we can't keep fallin' back
Like a bad quarterback
Because we were enslaved once
We don't want the same thing twice
With no education, lives will be
in jeopardy, if not in double jeopardy
Cause they won't know their 5th

Chorus (Repeat)

Behind the Lyrics

This song is dedicated first and foremost to all the families who lost loved ones during Hurricane Katrina. Additionally, I want to dedicate this song to the city of New Orleans and the surrounding areas. My message to you is to always rely on one another: your fellow New Orleanians, your neighbors, and most importantly, your children, sisters, and brothers. Historically, the government has prioritized wars over the welfare of Black individuals and minorities, so it is essential to lean on each other during tough times.

As I got myself acclimated to the U.S. and getting more comfortable and feeling less confused about my new life in America, I started to see a divided America, an America incapable of prioritizing and fulfilling its duty; keeping a nation united and safe, incapable of saving those who had fought and given their soul to this land. Then, hurricane Katrina happened, validating my early theory or philosophy. Hurricane Katrina not only proved me right, but it also proved that just because one, by one I am implying a black person is born in America does not necessarily make you an American, because people were forced to live in uninhabitable conditions, forced to live un-American, forced to sleep on rooftops, forced to loot for baby food.

As pictures and photos were shared by the news media, and with social media becoming an integral part of these platforms, I was overwhelmed by anger, sadness, disappointment, and mostly confusion. I found it hard to believe that in the greatest nation in the world, people could be left stranded and empty-handed to die. If someone had told me this could happen, I would have replied, "IMPOSSIBLE."

Well, it did happen only in America. The pain was excruciating, knowing America possesses supplies and resources to supply its citizens and the world. As an immigrant from Haiti who had seen a share or myriad of cyclones and hurricanes during my adolescent years, it was inexplicable, so much so that I had a hard time getting the picture of my black people on the roof out of my mind.

Verse I

The first verse highlights some of the issues America faced from the beginning of the 2000s, specifically from 2000 to 2005. I mentioned the ongoing struggle with drug-related crime, noting that the war on drugs continues, particularly affecting Black and Latino communities. Additionally, I expressed support for bringing the troops home, as families had been waiting impatiently for their loved ones to return after being deployed to fight in wars. I believe that we cannot fight every war or win every battle. As an immigrant, I also observed that social, cultural, and workplace inequalities in America were growing, creating even deeper divisions within the country. The bridges that could unite us had been damaged long before Hurricane Katrina, and the devastation from that event only highlighted an already eroded trust in a government and system that has consistently neglected the needs of Black and Latino communities.

Verse II
As tragic as the actual hurricane was, the aftermath proved to be even more devastating. The Federal Emergency Management Agency (FEMA) was virtually nonexistent, seemingly swept away in the Gulf of Mexico. They failed to fulfill one of their key responsibilities: management. I wanted to convey a clear message to them, which is expressed in the last line of Verse II.

I also discussed the importance of education. It's crucial to recognize that one does not necessarily need a four-year college degree to be educated. However, it is essential to understand and acknowledge the gaps in your knowledge, and to know how, what, when, and why to seek out the necessary information.

There is a reference to sports in this verse meant to remind Black and brown athletes of the importance of education in combating racism, discrimination, and inequality within the confines of White America. Since we have limited options to tackle these issues, any platform, such as sports, should be used as a tool to confront racism and discrimination. We must leverage these opportunities to break barriers and open doors for our fellow sisters and brothers to make a meaningful impact. We should strive, at all costs, to cross that line—the so-called baseball color line—just as Jack Roosevelt Robinson did. Otherwise, we will never be prepared for the next "racism-icane."

Verse III
I wanted to determine whether the root cause of the hurricane could be traced back to then-President George W. Bush. Ultimately, it became clear that Bush was not responsible for the hurricane itself, as it is a natural occurrence. However, how we prepare for and respond to such a natural disaster falls under the responsibility of the agencies appointed by the government officials and policymakers we elect. Therefore, while Bush was not directly to blame for the hurricane, he could be considered culpable for the lack of effective leadership, the inadequate evacuation process, and the

overall emergency management during the crisis—unless it could be proven that race did not play a role in these failures.

As I reflected on these issues, I felt overwhelmed with emotions. In an attempt to find clarity, I decided to close my thoughts on a positive note, inviting those affected by the hurricane—particularly in the context of racial inequality—to join together and stand against the broken systems that have let them down and may continue to do so in the future.

Track 04♪♪♪♪♪♪♪♪♪♪♪♪♪♪♪♪♪♪♪♪♪♪♪♪♪♪♪♪Naturally Gifted (God Given Gift)

Intro

For this extraordinary gift, I am deeply grateful to God, whose divine hand has blessed me with this amazing talent. To my beautiful mother, **Marie Michelle**, I could not have written those verses and lyrics without your inspiration.Thanks for teaching me the importance of writing. I love you for that, Momma. Finally, I'd like to thank my late cousin T-Michel for tutoring me when I couldn't write a perfect essay for my French class. You guided me. RIP, Homey! It's time to unwrap this gift. Shall we?

Verse I

I just took the gift out, check me out
Perhaps, my lyrics would create a blackout
But, if one listens attentively
My verses will take your pain out
'Cause they're similar to a BIC Wite-out
I ain't ghost writing, I'm chilling out
If you love this song, knock yourself out
Well, if you don't, its time to cash out
Nah, I'm just teasing, this is pure poetry
Patience is handing out, don't cash out
Please listen, listen till you passed out
Naturally gifted, I don't copy and paste
Quite frankly, I don't plagiarize
I just sit back in the cellar and analyze
If you think otherwise
I'll make sure you recognize
Sometimes, I can't believe
I'm writing this with apparent ease
I should be nominated for a Nobel Prize

Chorus

I'm naturally gifted
Take this as a gift, to be lifted
A God given gift, you can't be seated
My gift is limited
I'm naturally gifted
Take this as a gift, to be lifted
A God given gift, you can't be seated
My gift is limited (God given gift)

Track 04♪♪♪♪♪♪♪♪♪♪♪♪♪♪♪♪♪♪♪♪♪♪♪♪♪♪Naturally Gifted (God Given Gift)

Verse II

I'm not writing this for the paper, but Manley
I'm mean, manly, it's for my identity
Till my name becomes a byword for poetry
This God given gift is like ESPN classic
Sorry if you can't see me, your cable is basic
Every line is a matrix
I took in advanced mathematic
My hooks are permeable unlike Glad plastic
Words will touch anyone, it's asymmetric
A ghostwriter, yet my words are vocally sick
Crick enough for you to feel my lyrics
Through your muscle
From 509 to 978 I'm that lyricist
After this, my street credibility
Would be like Cormega or Jadakiss
I bet you, I won't get all the credits
Cause my lyrics are not in your Playlist
I'm writing this for free, take it as a gift
If you don't like it, Peace!
I'll catch you in the West Indies

Chorus (Repeat)

Track 04♪♪♪♪♪♪♪♪♪♪♪♪♪♪♪♪♪♪♪♪♪♪♪♪♪♪♪♪♪Naturally Gifted (God Given Gift)

Verse III

If the previous verses made no sense
I suggest you check your contact lens
Then you'd see my verse has no sequence
Regardless of your acceptance criteria
I'm gonna be patient till I get to the top
'Cause I got perseverance
But, when I get on top
My doubters gonna need a reference
Since you doubted Patience
I'll need my celebrity distance
I'm not rapping, I'm ghostwriting
I ain't a rapper, but I might be an emcee
Considering w/o any beat, I'm writing for free
Once again, A God given gift, can't you see?
I'm killing this verse lyrically
Called me by my Government name
Mr. Patience not Manley, but, isn't he?
Nah, Mr. Patience is the new me
The one who is gifted naturally
My pen bled for four days literally
Last time I had a writer's block
I vow my pen to keep the flow going
Like Styles P from D-Block
Finding this God given gift, ain't no shock
That I got this song locked
I got the key lyrically this verse can be unlocked
This is what I called a writer's antilock

Chorus (Repeat)

Outro

Never be afraid to try new things in life
As destiny is powerful and unpredictable.

Behind the Lyrics

If the Soundtrack of My Life were my debut album, "Naturally Gifted (God-Given Gift)" would be my first single. This song not only highlights my abilities as a lyricist and writer but also solidifies my passion for songwriting and rhyming. Writing has never felt like a job to me; it has never felt like a nine-to-five. Songwriting has always felt like something I was destined to do.

This song represents my journey and shows that I was on the right path. It was written in 2005 or 2006, about five to six years after I graduated from ESL class to a regular English class. I understood that I still had a long way to go, but I was making significant progress, both literarily and, most impressively, lyrically, if I may say so myself.

Moreover, this song played an important role in my mental state. Like any dream, there are moments filled with self-doubt and periods of hopelessness. If you let go of the rope for even a split second, it can be detrimental, turning dreams into nightmares, so dreamers need to be cautious.

I will delve into specific verses since each verse serves one clear purpose: to showcase my ability to create rhymes and wordplay while being thoughtful and insightful, without being boring. Who would have thought that this timid kid would one day find the art of songwriting enjoyable and exciting? Honestly, I had no idea that words would lead me down this path. Although I have not yet reached my final destination, this song carries an "I MADE IT" aura. I apologize for getting ahead of myself, but one cannot deny how I truly feel; lyrically, this song has a unique essence. If you, too, are naturally gifted, don't let a single day pass without sharing your talents with others, as they are limited. As highlighted in the last line of the chorus, if you don't use it, you will lose it.

Track 05♪♪Untold Stories

Intro

Nothing lasts forever, right? Look around you; racism, obesity, warfare, and miseducation still exist.

Verse I

I know poetically I'm pretty sick or ill
Know, I aint sh*t, I'm no big deal
Life ain't the same since my cousins got killed
I have flaws, I'm not better than you
Everyone has their shortcomings
So I don't show off, I just chill
Some need to self-administer a chill pill
I'm only living 'cause of God's will
My mom survived the quake I'm thrilled
Almost lost the only woman who
knows my DNA, for real
You think you know me well, but
Which side did you get to know, for real?
'Cause naturally there are two sides
The good and the surreal
When your back is against the wall
Some insanity may come out
Like Uma Thurman in Kill Bill

Chorus

Some stories have been told
Yet so many stories are untold
Let your voice be heard
While I let these untold stories unfold
I need your help 'cause these untold stories
Have been on hold too long, too long
Racism, miseducation, obesity, warfare are so wrong
It's time to say so long to these untold stories
I pray that God blesses my verses
And my pen don't run out of ink, as I think
Until then, this is nothing but a song
Let your voice be heard and sing along, sing along

Track 05♪♪Untold Stories

Verse II

Growing up I didn't think it was possible
for a Nigga to be a real doctor
'Cause all I ever knew was Dr. Huxtable
And Smith's uncle, what's his name? Dr. Phil
Shout out to those in school, you know the drill
If you ain't Kobe-ready with a smooth skill
Or can't top The Miseducation of Lauryn Hill
You are nothing but a fire drill
Young black kids stay in school
Can be a doctor or the next president
I vow your dreams will be fulfilled
Whenever going to class seems hard
Just envision Gabby the "flying squirrel"
Flipping on uneven bars, strong as steel
On another note, blacks voted for Obama
Thinking racism is forever sealed
Not too long ago, going to Wells Fargo
A white biker called me Negro, for real?
I took it as a reminder that America
Is still surrounded by white walls
So they called it the White house, still
Obama has placed a band-Aid on racism
But after his 2nd term, the band-aid will
be removed just like a banana peel

Chorus (Repeat)

Track 05♪♪Untold Stories

Verse III

Look closely, lesions of racism have yet to heal
Believe it or not its a chronic incurable disease
Don't need a CAT scan or MRI
To diagnose all blacks with lesions of racism
A large tumor of racism will be revealed
It is immortal, ask Jena six how they feel
Who will eradicate racism?
Perhaps your unborn neonate will
I guess, we will have to wait and see
Until then, I don't know who the hell will
Now I don't have to explain to you why I feel
So apprehensive running, jogging, or walking
In my own neighborhood after 7:09 PM
'Cause of how my hoodie cover my skin
R.I.P Trayvon Martin
The verdict got the nation on its heels
In the end only his parents need Advil
If you feel their pain, stand up for a purpose
Don't just march to march
March to change the justice system
March to change "Stand- Your- Ground" law

Chorus (Repeat)

Track 05♪♪♪Untold Stories

Verse III

Osama is dead, congrats to Mark O. the SEAL
Our troops are in the Middle-East, still?
I don't follow politics, but its politics as usual still
Our soldiers are not home. What's the deal?
I know the answers are concealed in Capitol Hill
The money we spend fighting, approximately trill
Recession is worsening, families working 3 jobs
Still can't pay bills, why do you think some steal?
Moms got no choice but working on high heels
Just to provide meals
Some are sickened by exposing' their body
Have no strength to appear on Oprah or Dr. Phil
And the damn govt is spending money daftly
No wonder America has lost its appeal
The govt. bailout putting the money on the hands
Of those living happily in Beverly Hills
And their kids' tuition prepaid at Tar Heels
While seniors can't even afford an OTC refill
Some died cause those illnesses weren't healed
The govt. is not trustworthy, for real
If you are looking for someone to trust
I suggest you flip a dollar bill, a dollar bill

Chorus (Repeat)

Outro

Women lie, men lie, and numbers don't; they are real. According to the NCHS, more than 35% of men and women were obese in 2009-2010, unreal.Don't be surprised because America has been on a burger diet without a treadmill. I firmly believe it's time to address these issues, I have faith; ask Faith Hill.I hate to disclose these untold stories, but when you don't stand still, you will fall for anything. If you know how I feel, let's join forces to fight.

Behind the Lyrics

As the introduction suggests, this song addresses racism, obesity, warfare, and education—specifically, miseducation. However, the first verse presents a different perspective.

Verse I

This verse is misleading, as it doesn't address the aforementioned issues. As a lyricist or writer, my opening line— in this case, the verse—often serves as my warm-up or rehearsal before diving into the song's main theme.

Although I sometimes found it difficult to silence those stories, my lyrical instincts would not allow me to remain muted on the issues America has been facing for years. I could not shy away from topics that have remained unresolved for so long. In all honesty, some of these challenges may never go away, but as a nation and responsible citizens, we cannot ignore them while pretending they will miraculously be resolved. Instead, we must continue to fight these issues with all our power, platforms, and resources so that our children, and their children, do not inherit the problems of our past.

Verse II

This section distinguishes between reality and fantasy as I began to adapt to life in Lowell. I became a sports fanatic; in addition to watching soccer, known globally as football, I also turned my attention to basketball, football, hockey, and baseball, even though I had only played soccer growing up. Nevertheless, the other sports captivated me, and as a resident of Massachusetts, it is both impractical and unethical not to support a team in a city filled with champions.

Furthermore, I started watching a lot of sitcoms featuring talented and remarkable actors and actresses on television. Initially, I was thrilled to see people like myself excelling in major sports, which are predominantly represented by Black athletes. I thought, "That's awesome!" However, I also grappled with a concern: this dynamic can become a form of oppression, as many young people today may not aspire to be anything beyond entertainers, specifically professional athletes or movie stars.

This creates a deeper issue, miseducation; the uneducated, even the educated kids, start believing, idolizing, and mirroring their life and lifestyle to those of the entertainers, being televised glamorously on TV. Therefore, as a society, we became brainwashed, so brainwashed blacks, including minorities, get discouraged, abandoning a 2-year or 4-year college degree to pursue professional sports, which further deepens these issues that we have been struggling to resolve.

Don't get me wrong, some black kids were heaven-sent and born with a God-given gift to play and compete with the best athletes and artists in the world, but not every kid was born to be a generational talent like the late Kobe, Pele, Lauryn Hill, H.E.R, Prince and the list goes on and on. The disparity was evident that blacks were inferior, even in their dreams, as their parents and grandparents did not empower them to dream beyond the walls of their bedroom. Some parents may have empowered their kids to focus on education, Some may have, but I would proclaim the vast majority did not; even those who were empowering their children to be anything they could be in life had to cross the frontier, like the Barracks of the world to reinforce the importance of education. Lastly, there is a reference to the " band-aid" that was intended figuratively that the fight against discrimination and racism would be halted suddenly, but it is a continuous process.

Verse III

First and foremost, I want to salute those who have risked their lives for our safety and well-being, especially the soldiers who have prioritized our lives over their own and their families. They have spent years fighting wars that are often not worth fighting for.

If I recall correctly, the reference to Mark Owen, a Navy SEAL, came to mind after I watched an episode of 60 Minutes, one of the greatest and most iconic television shows, where he was featured and interviewed. The conclusion of the segment highlights the impact that wars have on the United States and, more importantly, on families across the nation. One of my most poignant lines is, "No wonder America has lost its appeal." As an immigrant who is now a naturalized U.S. citizen, I realized while writing this back in 2008 that political views play a significant role in how one perceives and evaluates the United States.

To conclude, how can one forget the 2008 Emergency Economic Stabilization Act, which was a national disaster that rescued and funded the wealthy while the middle class and working class struggled under the weight of debt?

Track 06♪♪♪♪♪♪♪♪♪♪♪♪♪♪♪♪♪♪♪♪♪♪♪♪♪♪♪♪♪Marie-Michelle (Mother of All)

Intro

This one's for you, momma. I'm sorry for all the drama I have caused you. I'm writing to thank you from the bottom of my heart for your courageous, passionate, and undying love.

Courageous- For raising three silly boys on your own.

Passionate- For having and expressing tremendous love for 52 weeks, 356 days, every year. Even in a leap year, you always have that One Love left to embrace your three sons. I applaud you

Verse I

Momma, I don't even know where to start
Hopefully, you can hear me out
Feel your son's words wherever you at
Reminiscing, when I used to sit on your lap
So comfortably, I'd catch a power nap
A proud child, you deserve a standing ovation
Where your three sons can clap
Never heard you complaining abt muscle pain
Your courage, strength is insane
This song is dedicated to you
Marie Michelle, I'm talking to you
Sometimes, I wish I had kissed you more
And showed you that I love you more
Spent more time when I saw you in 2004
Knowing I'd be Gone Till November
Sadly, I kissed you bye and left like Wyclef
I wish we could control destiny
Hope you understand your son's journey
Sorry I have never said that before
I ain't gonna stop saying it, cause I mean it
Michelle, I promise I'll get you that mansion
You won't be forgotten, even if I was in a coffin

Chorus

Marie-Michelle, Marie-Michelle mother of all
With no father around, you stood tall
You are the mother of all
Just for your love I'll give you everything
Matter of fact, you can have it all

Track 06♪♪♪♪♪♪♪♪♪♪♪♪♪♪♪♪♪♪♪♪♪♪♪♪♪♪♪♪♪♪♪♪♪Marie-Michelle (Mother of All)

Verse II

Who knew huh? I'd be writing this for you
You knew, 'cause mama ain't raise no fool
Momma, if I could start from scratch
I would have never left you
It's painful, these days when I have to cook
My own flavorless food
That's when I deeply miss you
I know I'm getting too deep
But in reality growing up
I had no father to look up to
So I studied and followed your footprints
That's how I grew
This made me stronger, tougher
Life wasn't sweet, but together w/o a father
We made it sweeter than fructose corn syrup
That's how I know I love you
I'd plead the 5th 'cause you're my heart
I'd take a bullet for you, take the chair for you
If you needed a heart, I'm braver than John Q
You ain't no artist, but, considering how you
Brought us up , that's a piece of fine art
You should be treasured at the Museum of Arts
God created a Petit man, but you birthed Man-ley
Love you till the end, our love will never bend

Chorus (Repeat)

Track 06♪♪♪♪♪♪♪♪♪♪♪♪♪♪♪♪♪♪♪♪♪♪♪♪♪♪♪♪♪Marie-Michelle (Mother of All)

Verse III

They say like father, like son
But growing up father wasn't home
Before I turned one, he was gone
To pursuit the American dream
But, you still made it a sweet home
I never screamed, cried no tears
You'd raised me for 17 harsh years
Never saw any falling tears
I admire you for all, the mother of all
This song is just a sneak peek, that ain't all
'Cause after my this verse
Best believe, I'll buy a phone card to call
Now, I'm grown to say like mother, like Son
I'm blessed to be you son
Judged me, if I'm wrong after this song
There's no way you gonna go to hell
'Cause raising 3 boys, you'd lived thru hell
I swear your soul is like Patti Labelle
I'm sick like Ne-Yo when you ain't well
That's how bad your son cares, good night!

Chorus (Repeat)

Behind the Lyrics

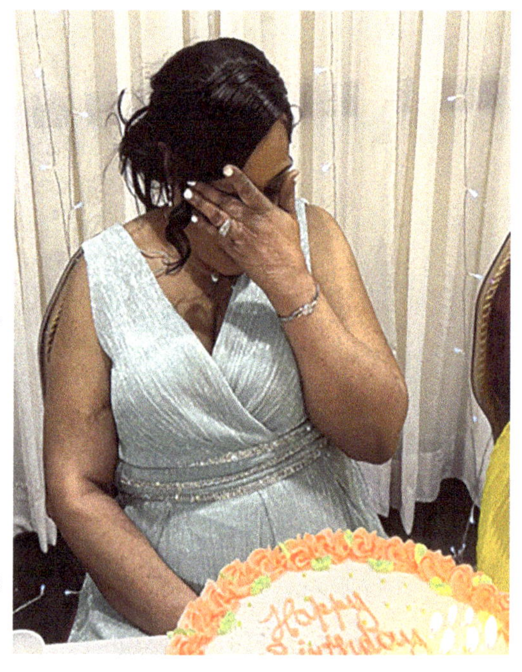

I acknowledge that we live in a society where many men are raised by women, as I was raised by a woman—my single mom, to be specific. It's common to say that behind every man, there is likely a single mother. This song is deeply personal and dedicated to my wonderful mother, Marie-Michelle. There are also many reasons I want to dedicate this song to her that I struggled to articulate for years. It wasn't that I didn't want to express my feelings to her; rather, I didn't know how, nor did I have a role model to help me understand those vulnerable emotions during my younger years. I wasn't taught to show my softer side, especially not to the one woman who knows me best, as I outline in Verse I of "Untold Stories."

However, as my isolation from my mother grew—she was living in Lakou Kokoye and I was living in Lowell—I felt a surge of emotions that compelled me to write this song. The emotions were so overwhelming that tears flowed freely, with no need for gravity to assist. I realized this was my moment to give my mom her flowers while she is still alive to appreciate them, even though we are miles apart.

Verse I

This section highlights my early childhood with my mother. Honestly, I can't recall my exact age during this time, but I remember that Marie-Michelle never took a day off and never neglected us—by "us," I mean my siblings and me. To this day, her dedication to her job and responsibilities has not wavered. I witnessed a single mother whose sacrifices and hard work were unmatched and unparalleled. She cared for, loved, and devoted herself to raising three boys, all while enduring pain and struggle that we were shielded from. She created for us the life she had dreamed of—a life filled not only with the challenges of parenting but also with the uncontrollable difficulties arising from the unstable environment of Haiti. Yet, she remained steadfast and persevered.

After I permanently moved to the United States, it was painful to wake up in the following weeks and months without seeing my mother around. I missed the aroma of her homemade omelets or fried eggs wafting from the kitchen into the hallway. I longed for the sight of my school uniforms and clothes pre-ironed and ready for the next day. Most sadly, I just missed her. To complicate things further, I would travel to Haiti annually to visit her, but as I look back, I realize that I did not cherish those moments as much as I should have. I should have spent more quality time with her, as exemplified in the lines below:

Verse I
Sometimes, I wish I had kissed you more **(Line 1)**
And showed you that I love you more **(Line 2)**
Spent more time when I saw you in 2004 **(Line 3)**

Verse II & Verse III
They provide concrete examples of the relationship my mother and I share to this day. While I love my father, my mother, Marie-Michelle, truly makes my heart beat. I took the opportunity to describe her in ways I never had before I migrated, highlighting her strengths, courage, and dedication. Ultimately, these traits have been instilled in me, though I'm unsure if she realized it. On April 13, 2024, during my speech at her surprise party, I had the chance to thank her for being both my mom and my dad, showcasing her courageous strength. As I trembled with emotions during the speech, I somehow missed the moment when she tilted her head down, hiding her teary eyes. Everyone else in attendance saw this, but I did not. Thankfully, one of the guests captured this moment for me, allowing me to cherish it for years to come. She is truly the Mother of All.

Track 07♪♪♪Deeper than Music

Intro

This is deeper than music. I say, this is deeper than music.

Verse I

After years of simply writing
To purge myself from pain
The way I was brought up
Made it harder to express myself
That's why I need a notepad and pen
So, on a stressful day , that's when
I press play, to get a peace of mind
While I'm sipping on some Henn
After I had nursed a cold Heineken
To ensure the pain is lessened
Sometimes I imbibe more than ten
If the alcohol don't weaken the pain
I say, Jesus, I know you can
Came from the bottom, that's the reason
Sometimes I want to get so high up
And be somewhere in the moon
Where there is no gravity, no calamity
To pull me back down
Croix-des-Missions my hometown
I have been racing for many years
Still can't see the finish line
I did a U-turn, head back to church
Then God gave me a sign
Life ain't a race, so I'm taking my time
Even if I don't time it right all the time
I'll get it right 2 times, like a broken clock
Some are speeding, doing 120 on a 65
But would they reach their destination
That remains to be seen
Life is a movie with so many scenes
The choices will shape our life forever
Further, those choices that did not kill us
Will only make us stronger, years later

Track 07♪♪Deeper than Music

Chorus

This is better than music
I said this is better than music
This is deeper than music
Deeper than music
Whether you're feeling sick or weak
Best believe, this music will do the trick
No need to call a Dr. just one teaspoon
Sky's the limit, things will get better soon

Verse II

Let the truth be told
We're a generation of men raised by women
I was raised by a single mother
Had to learn on how to be a man
Hope you understand, ladies and gentlemen
It's ironic 'cause my name is Manley
Still don't have what it takes
Someone once said, every man
Trying either to makeup for his father's mistake
Or live up to his father's expectations
Not trying to live up to his expectations
But, thank him for inspiring me
'Cause never was a ghostwriter till
My tempered father kicked my butt out
Never thought I'd forgive pop
Till I learned the meaning of forgiveness
Look at me now ten years later
It was business before pleasure
I came up, against all odds, that's odd
What a wonderful treasure
This is the soundtrack of my life
Listen to it on your Ipod, read it on your Ipad
This is my everything, my life, my struggle
I am God's son thus, I feel invincible

Chorus (Repeat)

Track 07♪♪Deeper than Music

Verse III

Success is in the eye of the beholder
I first tasted success, I was like I made it
Didn't know what else to do anymore
Was happier than a toddler at a candy store
But after the quake I exited the store
Saw my loved ones by the rubble
My jaw almost hit the floor
Seeing them sleeping on the floor
I got a dozen cemented blocks
Made my bed on the floor
Whoever lives with worry of riches
Is actually very poor
Rest in Peace to Mother Theresa
The quake had shattered their shelter
Yet moving like nothing even matter
Seeing one around me is poor
Don't know how one can be successful
If his fam can't afford a prescribed pill
When they're ill, it makes no sense for real

Chorus (Repeat)

Behind the Lyrics

Why did I write "Deeper Than Music"? I remember it as a day when I was deeply reflecting on life, particularly the lives of those who have less. My focus shifted away from creating music to engaging in some self-reflection, which has always been a healing process for me. It allows me to calm my racing heart and prevent burnout. Taking a day for reflection is essential; it helps me check myself before I wreck myself, clears my mind of debris and unwanted distractions, and refuels my spirit with positive energy. It's important to dedicate time to pause and reflect.

The song represents a moment of contemplation, as outlined in Verses I through III, illustrating that the impact of songwriting on my life goes deeper than music—whether I'm writing lyrics or simply listening to them. From the start, I felt that poetry was always stirring within me whenever I wrote down my ideas in my composition notebook. The art of songwriting has always captivated me, and I often wonder what the greatest lyricists would think of my work. This particular song serves as a reminder that music can break down barriers and walls with profound and uplifting lyrics—lyrics that resonate with the masses through my personal perspectives and experiences.

Verse I

This is an exciting introduction as I reflect on the history behind my writing: "After years of simply writing to purge myself of pain." Isn't that intriguing? Most importantly, I was embracing the present moment, contemplating who I had become as a man. I also began to envision what life might have in store for me, recognizing that tomorrow is never guaranteed. I observed a world where everyone is pursuing similar goals but at different paces and times.

Ultimately, I spoke about the significance of choices; both good and bad play a crucial role in shaping our lives and futures. I remind everyone—including the listeners—to be patient. Life is not a race, and those who rush may not reach their destination. It's not about who finishes first; rather, it's about being the last one standing on the podium.

Verse II

It has been well documented that I was raised by my single mom, Marie-Michelle. Therefore, it should not be surprising that there have been times in my life when I reevaluated my identity as a man; this reflects the first part of verse II, which deals with an identity crisis.

Every family experiences turbulence, some more than others. However, the fact remains that family is important, a theme well portrayed in the 1989 sitcom "Family Matters." It took me decades to fully understand the concept of family. While I was in the process of forgiving my father, who had kicked me out, it became evident that parents are critical to a child's upbringing. I felt victimized by my father's absence, but I knew I had to take the high road and move forward with a healing heart; after all, he is my father.

I remember a saying from my childhood—though I can't recall the French version, the English version goes like this: "After the rain, here comes the beautiful weather." In my case, after my own conflict with my father and during the forgiveness process, I discovered songwriting. So when one of my songs eventually becomes a hit, don't be surprised if he is credited in the song credits section, as he inadvertently contributed to my songwriting career. Isn't that something?

Verse III

This verse stands out to me, especially as I reflect on my trip to Haiti a few months after the earthquake. At that time, I felt accomplished—I had just completed my bachelor's degree in Nutritional Science from UMass Lowell, was working full-time at a clinical laboratory in Woburn, MA, and living in a semi-luxury apartment. I believed I was successful in every sense of the word. However, witnessing the earthquake survivors, including my loved ones, changed everything. They used concrete blocks from the rubble as makeshift box springs for their mattresses. There was no shame in their actions; they piled the concrete blocks with a calmness that shattered my heart. In that moment, my sense of success and all my accolades felt insignificant. Since that experience, my understanding of success has been forever altered. It no longer aligns with dictionary definitions; it's much more nuanced and personal. The key takeaway from this verse, Verse III, is to define your own success on your own terms. That's the story behind this verse, and it's yours to take or leave.

Track 08♪♪♪Think About That

Intro

Think About That. Guess who's back? It's been a minute since I wrote a song. I guess when everything goes wrong, your mind is gone mentally. I recently lost my grandma, Louisiana. So I had to vanish for a sec; her life goes on. Now that I'm back expect some insightful poetry. Because I got wiser and stronger lyrically, mentally, and physically. I'm back at it again; check it! Real talk

Verse I

They say every time someone is gone
A baby boy is born
So while I'm writing this song
I thought abt that warrior who gave
His life for Patience to be born
If my philosophy is not torn, like cooked-corn
When a baby dies, his warrior must be reborn
Think about that, my poetry is a fact
No matter where you at
May be a place you never wanted to be at
But, if you see things like I see things
You would say it's a good start
'Cause destiny is something that
One can never figure out
Therefore fall back, relax
Your turn will come, after the storm
Hold on tight, never give up
Go for your dreams, no matter what
With faith one day you'll be in the sky
Flying higher than a kite

Chorus

Have you thought about that?
Before you turn the lights off
You got to light out, if not
The blackout will knock you out
Think about that
You can't know everything inside out
Before your next act, you gotta think twice
If it's worth the sacrifice, think about that

Track 08♪♪♪Think About That

Verse II

Think about that, and then analyze this
Joy wouldn't feel good, if it wasn't for pain
I would go insane if I didn't have a pen
I guess you can say no pain, no gain
Because after I wrote "Death & Pain"
Joy has emerged, and absorbed the rain
What a sunny day, damn
Can't believe I escaped the rain, this is insane
Now if you take the time to fight pain
When joy comes you won't cry again
'Cause same things make you laugh
Makes you cry, if you ask me why?
I guess, happiness ain't always painless
Nor is it priceless
Therefore, the MasterCard commercial cost
More than two shoes from Pay less
After watching the Pursuit of happiness
I see why some have tears of sadness
This game of life is so hard not to act reckless
Thanks Mr. West, I hope I die careless

Chorus (Repeat)

Track 08♪♪Think About That

Verse III

I'm from a place surrounded by poverty
Believe me, 2 days seem like a century
If not an infinity
So being broke is a b*tch
Your life can't be hauled
'cause the leash in which
We're in is limited like a dog leash
I have no relish
You can move all you want to
But you won't vanish
Your energy won't replenish
Being broke is not a joke
That's why I won't judge one selling coke
Nor would I judge you from judging he
Who sells dope, nope!
The more the melanin the darker the skin
The darker you're, the less loot in savings
Only my black folks are starving

Chorus (Repeat)

Track 08♪♪♪Think About That

Verse IV

A good friend tries to do the impossible
To return a favor
A fake one won't even remember
The favor's flavor, who's your savior?
God is my confidant and savior
Those who tell you they're your friends
Always the first one to bounce in the end
Some might choose to stay for a sec or two
But, when sh*t hits the fan, they gotta go man
So I'm paranoid when it comes to friendship
Had divorced some, as if I was in a relationship
That's when I say "it's not you it's me"
Sometimes I wanna open up to more friends
But the word trust, can't be given
Got to be earned, something I've learned
On the low, I have gone AWOL for a few
Just to live a reclusive life
Even purged those I knew in high school
I mean, we cool, but their BS, that's old school
Friends change, family to enemy
That's not how sh*t supposed to be
People show me love 'cause I got little dough
But, jealousy will arise when I blow
Hope they know, for show, better yet for sure
After all is set and done, I'll flutter out this city
To north shore, now it all makes sense to me
life is fear, jealousy and envy, feel me?

Chorus (Repeat)

Behind the Lyrics

Think About That is a song about nothing—just kidding! In April 2007, I flew to Haiti to attend my grandmother's funeral, who had passed away a few weeks earlier. While I was on the plane from Logan Airport in Boston to Mais Gaite, Port-Au-Prince, I felt my grandmother's spirit traveling alongside me in the window seat. I was reflecting on the circle of life—life, then death, followed by rebirth. This contemplation inspired the lines I drafted for Verse I.

They say every time someone is gone ***(Line 1)***
A baby boy is born ***(Line 2)***
So while I'm writing this song ***(Line 3)***
I thought about that warrior who gave ***(Line 4)***
His life for Patience to be born ***(Line 5)***

I seized the opportunity to share an uplifting message with those grieving the loss of someone they cherish. Death often leads us down a path filled with feelings of hopelessness, fear, confusion, and sadness. It compels us to view life through a different lens, highlighting just how fragile it can be. This reflection on the stages of mourning inspired the title "Think About ..."

Verse II

This verse is likely the most insightful in the song, in my opinion. It reminds us that experiencing pain and hardship will ultimately make the sunny days feel more meaningful. Once we have gone through those dark times, we will never take joy and happiness for granted again.

Verse III

This verse addresses poverty in Black communities, not only in America but globally. It is painful to witness, and even more so when poverty continues to ravage the Black race with no end in sight. While one might argue that poverty exists everywhere, it is important to recognize that in many cases, its root causes stem from systemic power dynamics originating from other countries. This results in a cycle that affects not just one generation but the next as well.

The impact poverty has in those communities of melanin is enormous, resulting from unlawful behaviors such as violence, drug dealers, robbery, and prostitutes, just to name a few. In the end, it makes one wonder, do you condone this type of behavior? Or do you have to let the abnormal become normal as your rationale? If you consider or think that being broke is not a joke, would you judge someone who chooses to sell Coke? I let you be the judge.

Verse IV

As I reflected on my inner circles, I realized that I had developed close relationships over the years. For the first time, I began to assess each friendship. Are those people really my friends? Who do I truly consider a friend? Honestly, I struggled to differentiate between my true friends and those who weren't at that time. It took me years to come to this understanding, and I truly hit rock bottom before I could clearly distinguish between fake friends and genuine ones. I believe friendship has different levels, and it should be recognized as such. Friendship is essential for many reasons. From a social perspective, I have learned the importance of opening the door to see which types of friends are knocking, but one must be cautious about who they invite inside.

Track 09♪♪Death & Pain

Intro

Death strikes like 60 caplets of aspirin. Whether there is sunshine or rain I still feel cohesive pain. Ever since my 2 cousins got killed, man, I feel as if death is perpetually circulating in my cell membrane. I've been trying to extract my cousins' death out of my brain, but I don't think I can.'cause death and pain can't be banned. It's like trying to stop the rain

Knowing well mother nature will always win, feel what I was feeling at the time, feel my pain

Verse I

Oh God! Can I express this calamity?
I learn tomorrow's uncertainty
All I can do is living for the moment
I barely live for tomorrow
Cause this life is spiritually borrowed
After life death will follow
You win some, you lose some
When my cousins got killed, man
I deeply lost some
My cousin Rony was the first one
I used to look up to my dog
A man's best friend, not just someone
I would trade all my achievements
Just to recuperate this one
God bring me back my mentor, Benson
Nowadays, nothing even matters, son
Like Ne-Yo I suddenly feel sick
My health and strength may fail
Cause death and pain hit me so quick
Damn I feel so weak

Chorus

Some cope with pain
By injecting something into their veins
To eliminate the pain
I just think abt the second life in heaven
To stop my pain, till then
One has to cope with death and pain

Track 09♪♪♪♪♪♪♪♪♪♪♪♪♪♪♪♪♪♪♪♪♪♪♪♪♪♪♪♪♪♪♪♪♪♪♪♪♪♪♪Death & Pain

Verse II

My dreams are broken, pain won't go away
Trying to be strong with my inner strength
But I see death coming half a mile away
I decided to accelerate, but my cousins'
Death is still on my way
Now I'm sitting in the cellar reminiscing
About my dog and feeling so down
I hope he's smiling down
Thinkin how we used to kick it downtown
I treasured those memories from 96
And revive them 24/6
Looking at your pic across my window
All I can see is your shadow
I'm dreaming, so I decided to follow
But, death misled me to my first sorrow
And then my stomach got hollow
Cousin I want you to feel this flow
Before my pen lay low
Chorus (Repeat)

Verse III

And to my cousin T-Michel, I said peace
I know you ain't here, Rest in Peace
But, gonna make you relive thru these hooks
Remember we used to hit those chem books
Like teacher and student, just by our looks
Truthfully, I miss you, I want you to know it
If I start crying after this line I can't help it
It's hard to proceed 'cause I'm trembling
Can't comprehend why you ain't breathing
Homie, I wish you were at least hospitalizing
So I can see you in the physical form
Can't' believe you're sleeping in a coffin
But, I know you're in heaven
Our relationship was a covalent bond

Track 09♪♪♪Death & Pain

We both know this a little basic chemistry
Which is part of our memory
Only God can measure what you meant to me
Never think I forgot, we shared the same heart
Not even death can tear us apart
Chorus (Repeat)

Behind the Lyrics

Verse I

Chorus

Verse II

Verse III

This section above is intentionally left blank because my heart is too heavy to express how much these two individuals meant to me as a child seeking a father figure to look up to.

As much as I would like to delve into the inspiration behind the lyrics of "Death & Pain," I unfortunately lack the strength to proceed with this section. The loss of my cousins still weighs heavily on me; it continues to hurt even now, especially when I read the verses I penned over twenty years ago. Is it fair to say that time does not heal every wound or scar? I thought revisiting and writing about this might be easier, but the truth is, I am still grieving the loss of Rony and T-Michel. As a result, let the song "Death & Pain" speak for itself. I apologize for not being able to analyze and break down each verse as I have done elsewhere in this book.

Outro

This song is dedicated to my cousin and mentor, Nicko, who was murdered in Haiti, and to my cousin, tutor, and protector, T-Michel, who died in Cuba. Rest in peace!

Track 10♪♪Joy

Intro

Oh yeah, it feels good, doesn't it? What more do I need?
Perhaps something new, new challenges, new goals. Starting a family will bring new challenges.What do you think? Haha!

Verse I

Listen well, joy is here, all I ever wanted is here
May never return over there 'cause Joy is here
Honestly, I do not know what else to do
Somebody tell me what needs to be done
Somebody tells me what I have not done
Kelly Clarkson please tell them
"All I Ever Wanted" I have already gotten
Lately everything's going according to plan
Gonna keep doing what I've been doing
Stick to the script, from working overnight
And sleeping and snoring during class
Can't even count how many classes I skipped
Still earned 120 credits in my transcript
Car and apartment under my name
Which smells better than the basement
From the basement to leasing an apartment
I aint supposed to be here
If someone had told me I'd be here
I would have said it wasn't apparent
Everything is possible in life
As long as you have a mind
Never say you cannot
Don't take anything for granted
Could have been a zoe sleeping in a tent
Got places to go, no one to see
So after this song I'm gone
Cause I'm happy with what I've done
Ain't the type to get excited, but, man!

Track 10♪♪Joy

I love the way this one feels, I got chills
Excited just cause I put a big smile
On someone face, had it been my face
Happiness would have had a bitter taste
You should have seen momma's face
I've learned the path to happiness
Is better to give than to receive
That's correct! I'll be the quarterback
You play wide receiver

Track 10.♪♪Joy

Chorus
During my odyssey I'd slipped
Didn't fall when I was near
I still don't know why I didn't fall
But I do know with God there is no fear
Now I can proudly say joy is finally here
Don't know how long this excitement will last
Could be a second or years
But, I'm certain that I'll seize the moment
Until joy forsakes me and disappears
Bad ass job, I can't help it
This feeling is so enjoyable, Joy

Track 10♪♪Joy

Verse II

Enjoying this one in a lifetime moment
Me, myself and I
Somewhere nice by the ocean
While I survey the blue sky, why not?
I did it my way, not too long ago
I was in the basement by myself
Scooping four litter boxes, by myself
Not too long ago
I was placed in academic probation
Thought that college was overrated
Almost dropped out, then I asked myself
How am I gonna pay my financial aid?
From that moment on
I spent more time in the library
Than a school nerd and the Librarian
Not too long ago I was pulling all nighters
To obtain a passing grade
It's only fair now that I upgrade
Love you, all my supporters
And thanks to all the doubters
Should I say my motivators?
Some will not comprehend what
It takes to be me, but its okay
Others will not fully understand
At times what I say
'Cause ESL, so to compensate
I've mastered the art of writing essay
Any type of success brings envy, touché
If you weren't part of my success
Please leave me alone as I pray

Chorus (Repeat)

Track 10♪♪♪Joy

Verse III

Some can't believe, how much I've grown
But, those who've stayed with me
Through thick and thin
Knew it was a matter of sec, I'm gonna win
I hope all the doubters are ready
When they find out what I'm gonna do next
I did it my way, bad ass job with two jobs
Could pay for two bjs
Sill have left over for anything at BJs
But, I ain't gonna do that
I've been there and done that, I am off that
Don't know what life would be
Without the obstacles, the pain, and tears
God has miraculously put my life in order
I'd been waiting for this moment
Say goodbye to all life's disorders
Now they're history as the future is clear
Need a fresh start, please bring water
Nah, this ain't my baby shower
Bring the gospel choir, thank you Lord
Nothing is a problem until God says it is
It's my time now, you know what it is

Chorus (Repeat)

Behind the Lyrics

This song represents my victory lap and graduation party, celebrating my achievement of graduating from college, which has always been one of my goals. After studying tirelessly and working incredibly hard for five long years—first at Middlesex Community College and then transferring to UMass Lowell—I finally heard my name, Manley Petit, echo through the speakers at the commencement ceremony. This moment marked the completion of one of the most important goals in my life and, more significantly, in my career, as education holds great significance for both me and my family.

Following graduation, I began my professional career and started to enjoy the fruits of my labor. I was able to own a better and more reliable car, lease a semi-luxury apartment, and financially support both myself and my mother.

That moment was a pivotal step in my journey to success, allowing me to start tasting the American dream—or the Haitian dream, whichever comes first. In my case, I was unsure which one it truly was.

Verse I

How can one express joy? In the first verse, I convey the joy of achieving something that neither my mother nor my father was able to accomplish: graduating from college. I do not intend to brag or criticize my parents for not achieving such academic success, as their opportunities were different from mine. However, Boy-oh-boy,the feeling of joy I experienced is truly wonderful. I worked two or three jobs to stay afloat and keep my dream alive. Working overnight shifts, which are among the toughest schedules one can endure, made it particularly challenging. I even skipped classes, as mentioned in lines 10 through 12: "sleeping and snoring during class—I can't even count how many I skipped."

Verse II

This is a reminder for everyone to embrace happiness and joy as much as possible, as they often have a fleeting nature. Additionally, I want to express my gratitude to all my supporters and motivators, including those who doubted me but contributed in some way to my success.

As I prepare to leave behind 2009 and 2010 and look toward the future, which appears brighter than when I first arrived in the U.S., I reflect on my next steps and goals. The reality of the moment feels like the sunset on Sunset Boulevard, prompting me to consider my future plans.

Verses III and IV

I wrote these verses to acknowledge the power of the Lord. This achievement would not have been possible without Almighty God. He made it all happen. My first ten years in America were spent trying to catch up, watching other immigrants who had fully acclimated sit in the front row of success while I felt stuck in the back.

As immigrants, our stories share similarities but arc also uniquc to cach individual. There are different levels of success and excellence, especially for those of us coming from underdeveloped countries like mine. Time is not on our side, so we must hustle every day, using education as the driving force to climb the mountain known as corporate America. It is not easy; the journey is filled with complexities. Not only do we face discrimination from whites and those who have privilege, but sometimes we also encounter hostility from fellow Black individuals who may feel superior due to their immigration status. They might worry that their jobs are at risk. However, once you surpass them academically, you can have important conversations with them, reminding them that we are also battling racism. They need to recognize that being born in the United States does not solely define someone as an American.

It's also important to remind them of who they are and encourage them not to let opportunities in America pass them by. These thoughts came to mind as I was writing this song and discovering my voice.

Track 11♪♪♪509

Intro

Once again, this is your messenger, Patience The Ghostwriter.
I'm about to take you to 509, where I am from, Haiti. Haiti welcomes you!
Are you ready? Let's go!

Verse I

Welcome to 509! Sak Pase? or Sak Ganla?
Where I'm from its like TNT
We know drama
Poverty, violence, and struggle
Aren't excluded in our drama
Everybody is a survivor
Which is a product of our environment
The street life can't be taught
If that is what you thought
To survive what we're going through
Whoever tries to mimic our lifestyle
Will end up in a coma, if you succeed
You must be the bravest warrior

Chorus

At the end of this song
You'll understand where
I'm coming from, 509
Where I'm from ain't fun
Not anyone can come
It seems like there's
Always a thunderstorm
Where everyone is scared to come

Track 11♪♪509

Verse II

Where I'm from money can
Easily issue you a diploma
As long as you can distinguish
A period from a comma, man
Money is more important than a person
That's the reason Nicko Benson
Got smashed son
Now we live for the moment
There's violence in our environment
Due to poor government
Can't stop inhaling the cemetery's scent
With so much violence
We look forward to attending an interment
And wonder who's next to go in a coffin
Hopefully from the coffin to heaven
If he never committed a sin
Unfortunately we all have sinned
One keeps on praying
Cause a gunshot is promised
On anyone chest, regardless
If you got a bulletproof vest
Stop the violence! So I can stop saying
Peace and rest, I mean, rest in peace

Chorus (Repeat)

Track 11♪♪509

Verse III
My heart is still coated with 509 residues
Enough to teach you the don'ts and dos
For instance always pay your dues
'Cause if you don't, you might as well
Say hello to the Haitian voodoo
Which doesn't know who is who
You better payback or watch your back
'Cause injustice is justice, no peace
So 509 is similar to the Middle East
Only God knows when the violence
Gonna cease with ease
Kidnappers going after your niece
Food is fundamental to all life on earth
Kidnappers won't hesitate to take one's breath
Kidnapping your two 2-yr old daughter
Starvation is sadly turning to murder
Hunger will pull the trigger
Chorus (Repeat)

Verse IV
509 is a corrupted zoo
Corruption is a part of every issue
Kidnappers demanding large ransom
To deliberate your boo
Some might request a few loot
If they got love for you
If you have no clue
Where to get 'em the loot
Your days would be numbered
And I feel so sorry for you
If they ever release you, you can't sue
We don't got lawyers that go through cases
Can't press charges
So 'em robbers can easily recapture you
And tie you up with their shoe laces
Chorus (Repeat)

Track 11♪♪509

Verse V

Where I'm from so many have nothing
So we're constantly struggling
To turn life into something
Some got addicted to school
Hoping, one day things gonna be cool
But in reality, they end up selling tools
Such as stools to afford 'em books
Lives be slipping halfway to school
Some try standing tall
But not enough loot in their savings
So they practice fasting
All you can do is witnessing
Young poor Haitians starving and dying
I expect this song to give 509 some hope
Mainly, to those students who choose
Not to kidnap or sell dope
But keep climbing life's rope
As they cope while being broke

Chorus (Repeat)

Behind the Lyrics

As someone who was born and lived in Haiti until the age of 17, I consider Haiti my home, despite its challenges with poverty and instability. Throughout my early years in the U.S., I made a conscious effort to protect and represent Haiti at every opportunity. I often downplayed and defended the country's ongoing issues—violence, corruption, poverty, you name it. Defending Haiti felt like defending a family member—a father, mother, or brother. The unwritten rule is to love them unconditionally, flaws and all. I have shared those same sentiments regarding Haiti.

However, as time passed and I lived outside the country for nearly a decade, I began to swallow some of that pride. I came to accept that Haiti is, indeed, what it appears to be as portrayed on television.

I know many Haitians struggle with the perception that our country is the poorest and grapples with significant issues. Some believe that the media only showcases the negative aspects of Haiti, and to some extent, that may be true. However, the positives of Haiti can often feel minimal compared to the larger, prevailing struggles faced by most of its citizens. The harsh realities I once overlooked in my youth became clear as I assessed the country as a whole, forcing me to acknowledge the uncomfortable truths, even though it was embarrassing.

As I matured and learned to compare different situations, it became evident to me that Haiti is in dire straits, plain and simple. It's difficult to address multiple issues effectively when the challenges are so vast. While there could be improvements in some areas, the core issues remain.

This song addresses the persistent problems highlighted by news outlets—poverty, violence, and corruption—while also offering a sense of hope, pride, and beauty. When I was writing this song between 2005 and 2006, I found beauty within the struggle and poverty. Looking back seventeen years later, I am amazed by how far I've come lyrically. These verses still resonate with me as I analyze and explain the theme and concept behind "509."

Verse I

I was reflecting on my upbringing and how my mother and family protected me and my brothers from poverty, violence, and hardship. Despite enduring these challenges, themselves, they never displayed the scars of such difficult experiences. Because of this, they became my superheroes, creating a

nurturing environment largely free from violence and poverty. In retrospect, I realize that I was not as poor as the name of Haiti notoriously hints. My family, living overseas in the U.S. and Canada, traditionally supported us back home, providing enough sustenance and necessities for life. We also received help from relatives in Haiti who had stable jobs as teachers and business owners.

Furthermore, I never considered myself poor because, as a child, I was content and happy with what I had, rather than focusing on what I lacked or what my family couldn't provide.

I learned early on that comparing what I had to what others possessed could easily lead me to feel poor. Some days, I could sense my Spidey Sense tingling that my mother was struggling to make ends meet, especially when the Western Union agent didn't arrive at our house as expected with my father's or a relative's monthly allowance. However, my mother's hustle, strength, and resilience always ensured that we managed to get by.

Our support was not just financial; we were provided with material things that kids in our neighborhood could only dream of. Even if we received these items when they were released on the market, sometimes a decade later, after they had gone out of style or become scarce, we eventually owned them. Not many kids in my neighborhood could relate to that experience.

Everybody is a survivor **(Line 6)**
Which is a product of our environment **(Line 7)**

I wanted to highlight the impact my environment had on my family and upbringing. The setting I grew up in could make or break a person; there was no in-between. While I never witnessed anyone being shot at in Port-au-Prince, I did see dead bodies lying in the streets on my way to school on a few occasions. I continued with my day, never interfered, and allowed it to remain just another part of life, as it was for most pedestrians. Reflecting on those experiences, I realize they shaped how I cope with both death and life. They compelled me to keep living despite the struggles, pain, and violence surrounding me. I considered myself a "survivor" long before Destiny's Child sang, "I'm a survivor, I'm gonna make it." I am living proof that, despite the horrific conditions in Haiti during my childhood, those experiences ultimately contributed to shaping me into a good person. That's the image I wanted to convey with this message. Looking back, I recognize that I could have expressed the lyrics differently.

Verse II and Verse III

These lines highlight the influence of money and its effects on a historically corrupt nation. The financial consequences are harmful across all sectors, including education, agriculture, infrastructure, and the justice system. In Haiti, the pursuit of financial gain permeates every level of society, including the government, which is one of the fundamental causes of the ongoing issues that need to be addressed and resolved.

Verse V

This verse is one of hope and encouragement, aimed at inspiring the nation, especially the youth, who represent the future of a brighter and more promising Haiti. It serves as a message to the diaspora communities, urging them to continue supporting their parents' or grandparents' homeland and not to turn their backs on Haiti. Additionally, it reassures tourists and visitors that one day, Haiti will regain its alluring and welcoming charm.

Track 12♪♪♪A Letter to God

Intro

Some men see things as they are and ask why. I dream of things that never were and say, "Why not?" I just want to thank you, Lord; thank you!

Prayer I

Dear Lord, first and foremost
Thank you for just being there
When I need you the most
I love the fact that you always stay
By my sight, never forsake your post
You've followed me everywhere
From Lakou Kokoye to the East Coast
Let's celebrate with a toast
Loving this writing gift you gave me
That's the reason I penned these verses
As a form of letter, instead of a prayer
Loving the enduring patience, you gave me
Please, don't let me lose my patience

Chorus

In my mind, I'm always a fighter
But thanks to you, God, I'm a believer
Thank you so much, you are a true savior
There were times I'd been broken
But, you never let me shattered
Do not know what life would be
Without you, so as my Father
Please accept this letter

Track 12♪♪♪A Letter to God

Prayer II

Loving the fact that you're never late
Cause nothing starts till you arrive
Don't make decisions till I talk to you first
Because you know what's best
I have no alternative, but to put you first
And in second position is my family
I don't get upset, nor do I complain
When things don't go as planned
Because everything I have planned
Can only be attained, if it's your plan
Things I thought were just fantasies
But with you I can, proudly say,
YES WE CAN, unlike John McCain
God, you've strengthened my courage
In order to break the unbreakable
Undo the impossible, do the possible
This is not a confession letter,
But thank you for forgiving me
Understand, I'd tried to be perfect
But in the end I am only human
And you are God, thus I must sin
Although to live is to suffer, God
I wish death was easy on us
Cause between me and you, God
Life is hard
I hope I live till my last day
Please don't take me off guard
Chorus (Repeat)

Track 12♪♪A Letter to God

Prayer III

God, sometimes when I talk to you
You don't say anything back
I hope you ain't turning your back on me
Please watch my back
Let me know what I have to do
So you can take me back
God, I feel so alive and right
When I write, even when I'm not alright
But knowing that you're here with me
When I can't see through the darkness
Makes everything so right and bright
Let there be light, so white

Chorus (Repeat)

Prayer IV

God, you've given each one of us a gift
Thanks for the patience, the writing gift
Never take them for granted, I'm blessed
Grateful for any car with four wheels
Because it beats two heels
I am satisfied with a decent income
As long as I can pay my bills
There is no such thing as success
If you know how failure feels
Failure is a better teacher than success
In that case God, hitting the bottom
Is a pop quiz, not a test
I don't want anything else

Chorus (Repeat)

Outro

I realize that none of it matters—not the diploma, the car, or the money. What I truly need is my health, and I'll let nature take its course. Once again, thank you, God, for helping me with this album. It would be incredible if "The Soundtrack Of My Life" goes platinum.

Behind the Lyrics

This song is more than just a letter to God; it is a heartfelt prayer of thanks to the Almighty. Until now, I had not taken the time to genuinely express my gratitude for the creative gift that has been so instrumental in my mental, spiritual, and physical well-being. I also hadn't paused to thank God for everything I have experienced, overcome, and learned throughout my life. I believe this song effectively conveys my spiritual connection with God.

Through this song, I can speak to God openly, seeking forgiveness, asking for help, acknowledging my blessings, and requesting guidance to illuminate the dark paths that lie ahead.

While every verse is self-explanatory, I won't go into a detailed breakdown of each one. One significant change I made in this song is replacing the word "Verse" with "Prayer." I would have kept "Verse" had I intended to submit it for recording purposes.

Verse I

Dear Lord, first and foremost **(Line 1)**
Thank you for just being there **(Line 2)**
When I need you the most **(Line 3)**

I truly believe that everything happens for a reason, regardless of the season, your background, or where you come from. God always has a purpose, one that is too profound for humans to fully understand. My journey was not an accident; I was born in Haiti and then migrated to Lowell. It was all part of God's plan. Moreover, my patience is a blessing from God; I am more patient than a doctor. Although I didn't fully grasp this as a youth, I began to recognize it when others acknowledged it in me. For these reasons, I want to express my gratitude to the Lord: "Thank you for just being there."

Chorus

But thanks to you, God, I'm a believer **(Line 2)**
Thank you so much, you are a true savior **(Line 3)**

The main message of this chorus is not simply to believe, but to truly be a believer. Merely believing does not make one a believer. I became a believer the moment I placed my faith in God. There have been times in my life when I felt broken and lost, but somehow, I managed to find the scattered pieces of myself and miraculously put them back together. For this, I credit God, my faithful savior, as referenced in Line 3.

Verse II

I don't get upset, nor do I complain	***(Line 7)***
When things don't go as planned	***(Line 8)***
Because everything I have planned	***(Line 9)***
Can only be attained, if it's your plan	***(Line 10)***

The following lines are my favorites because they contain perfect rhymes (i.e., complain, planned, attained, plan) from Lines 7 through 10. Additionally, these lines serve as a reminder or aide-memoire that while human beings can create or propose any plans they wish, ultimately, it is God who determines the outcome—whether it leads to failure or success. This concept is reflected in Proverbs 19:21: "Man proposes, but God disposes."

Verse III

How did these verses come about? They originated from a conversation I had with the Lord above. It is human nature to question our existence, and it's understandable. Life and death are difficult concepts to define. Therefore, I often plead with God for answers. However, when God does not respond quickly, I sometimes feel as though He is turning His back on me.

Verse IV

This verse emphasizes the importance of being modest and humble rather than stubborn. It encourages living life with a spirit of humility and being content with what you have, recognizing that your possessions are a luxury. Your true needs depend on God, who will provide for your desires. Therefore, be grateful for every gift given by God and trust Him to care for your needs in the future, as He is the King (2 Kings 4).

After completing my first album, "The Soundtrack Of My Life," I found myself uncertain about what to do next. I asked myself, "Now what? What is my next move?" I had already shared most of my song lyrics with friends and family for their feedback, particularly with Ebenezer and anyone I was dating at the time. I received positive responses; some would say, "Manley, you should sell these! You should connect with so-and-so. You're really good. Did you actually write these lyrics?"

I often responded to feedback with the same unthoughtful line: "Those lyrics are alright, but they could be better." I never felt that I had reached the summit or pinnacle where the great songwriters stand. While I welcomed their feedback, I realized my lyrics hadn't been truly tested, nor had I passed the test of great songwriting. My lyrics lacked validation and challenge, especially from A&R (Artist and Repertoire) professionals. I needed to figure out what to do with my lyrics, let alone how to promote or market them, as I had never considered the business side of music.

Musically, I knew that I needed help when it came to walking into a recording studio—whether at Universal, Atlantic Records, Interscope, or Def Jam Headquarters—to submit unsolicited materials for my album. I found myself feeling bored and uninspired, lacking ideas for the songs. As I continued pondering, it struck me: I didn't have an album cover. Every album deserves artwork. So, in the meantime, I decided to design my own album cover, which I think turned out pretty well.

Now that I had created the artwork, I found myself shaking my head and asking the same questions: "Now what?" and "What's next?" My friends and inner circle were also curious about my next steps. Financially, some would ask, "Are you making money?" I'd respond with a firm "No," reminding them that this process is not simple.

During this time, I kept writing like a full-time employee, taking advantage of every school break and every downtime at my security job to focus on song lyrics.

Coincidentally, my creative writing skills skyrocketed and improved significantly. I transitioned from having a writing tutor to tutoring ESL students in a community service program for newly emigrated Vietnamese and Cambodian adults on Middlesex Street. I found myself proofreading papers for others, including native speakers. I was writing at full capacity; composing essays, research papers, poetry, rhymes, wordplay, and verses became much easier. Yet, I often questioned how good I really was. That was the million-dollar question to which I had no answer. So, I kept writing—spending money on Papermate pens, expanding my vocabulary by reading more words in the dictionary, and striving to find meaning in my writing and in this crazy dream of mine that I had embraced wholeheartedly.

What comes next? Being influenced and inspired to write lyrics is important, but what is the ultimate goal? How valuable is a dream—or even a goal? If one does not aim for the stars, how can they expect to score. I knew I needed to succeed, but how could I make that happen. Was there someone out there searching for a budding lyricist like me. These questions lingered in my mind. After conducting thorough research online, I discovered the A&R (Artists and Repertoire) division. A&R representatives are responsible for finding promising new artists for record labels or music publishers, and the word "promising" gave me a glimmer of hope, even though I wasn't certain I was a worthy candidate as a new writer.

I reached out to the A&R division and managed to schedule a 15-minute consultation for a small fee of $25, which was quite reasonable. Since this was my first meeting with an A&R representative, I made sure my cellphone was fully charged, the volume was turned up, and I was on time and well-prepared. Although I had not been provided with a direct phone number, I anticipated that I would automatically accept the call. I was ready to swipe "accept" even if the caller ID showed "scam likely." Within minutes, my cell phone rang loudly, reminiscent of church bells on a Sunday morning, awakening the late sleepers around me.

If my memory serves me correctly, the conference call was scheduled for 5:30 PM EST (Eastern Standard Time), but my phone rang at 5:29 PM. Perfect timing, I thought, but I was incredibly nervous, so it felt less than perfect. I answered the phone politely and calmly, and I heard a soft voice on the other end: "This is so-and-so. May I speak to Manley P……?" Before the A&R representative even had a chance to pronounce my last name, I quickly responded, "Yes, this is he," while searching for my side notes.

The A&R continued, "How may I help you?" I took a deep breath. I formally introduced myself and provided some background on my writing experience. I mentioned that I have been writing song lyrics across many genres, including rap, hip-hop, R&B, pop, and gospel. Suddenly, I was interrupted. "It's great that you write, but what specific type of music do you focus on?"

I replied again, "From rap and hip-hop to R&B, pop, gospel, and even jazz." I could sense that he wasn't pleased. He elaborated, "You can't be all over the place; you need to choose a specific genre and pick a lane. Then we can schedule another session down the road." As I ran out of time and didn't have a chance to ask any questions about his feedback, I simply said, "Thank you, and have a nice day."

From that one consultation and meeting, I realized that the music industry is like a highway. You need to pick a lane to navigate your way, and later, you might switch lanes. Otherwise, the industry may dictate your path for you.

Even though I didn't pay much for the consultation, I found myself wishing for a refund because part of me felt it wasn't worth it. However, another part of me believed that life is like a classroom, and there's always a lesson to be learned. As a result, I started to review all the song lyrics I had written so far, assessing which genre I excelled in, which I was mediocre at, and which I struggled with. I took the constructive feedback from the A&R seriously; in the end, I had to choose a lane.

I couldn't definitively determine which genre suited me best. I kept telling myself that I would eventually figure it out and choose a lane, so to speak. Until then, my lyrics would wander through various genres, primarily Rap and Hip-Hop.

I continued writing, but this time I slowed down and took a more reflective approach. I went back to the drawing board, buying old records, singles, and classic albums that had topped the charts, such as Reasonable Doubt by Jay-Z, The Score by the Fugees, The Album by the Firm, It's Dark and Hell is Hot by the late D.M.X. Ready to Die and Life After Death by the Notorious B.I.G., It Was Written by Nas, The Miseducation of Lauryn, by Miss Hill, and The 18th Letter by Rakim. I was determined to explore the early and mid-90s music thoroughly, leaving no record unplayed. My goal was to learn about wordplay, rhymes, delivery, flow, and punchlines, and I began to listen more attentively to their lyrics and songs.

As 2015 was waving goodbyes, I hadn't committed to a specific musical style or genre; I found myself writing without any particular direction in mind. I often browsed the internet, searching for platforms to promote or pitch my song lyrics, hoping to connect with artists seeking songwriters and lyricists. At that point, I was simply desperate to collaborate with any musician. Unfortunately, 2015 ended on a bleak and bad musical note with no hope.

If I remember correctly, in the fall of 2016, on a late autumn evening, I continued my search for artists online. I came across a local musician, a young white male in his early twenties, from the Merrimack Valley area of Massachusetts.

I initially contacted him via email, and after exchanging a few text messages and phone calls, we set up a face-to-face meeting. Despite not having met in person before, he sounded enthusiastic and eager to hear my story, making me hopeful that I could pitch my song lyrics to him.

After a long day at my nine-to-five job, I drove home to rest briefly. Then, I packed my laptop and headed to a nearby 99 Restaurant to meet the young artist. Although the restaurant was within walking distance, I arrived a few minutes late—my friends would jokingly refer to this as "Haitian Time."

Unbothered by my tardiness, I quickly surveyed the venue to see if I could spot the young fellow. We located each other without embarking on a historic manhunt. Fortunately, the restaurant was not packed like sardines, which made it easier to find him.

We introduced ourselves formally and started with general questions like, "Where are you from?" and "Do you live in the area?" As we transitioned to the main topic of our meeting, the waitress approached our table, which was near the entrance. Every time a customer entered or exited, I felt the evening chill softly brushing against my eyelashes.

Suddenly, the waitress interrupted us, asking, "Hi, something to drink?" I remembered that we both ordered a beer, though I couldn't recall which kind. I guessed mine was probably a regular Corona with lime. The young man followed suit, kindly saying to the waitress, "I would have a beah also," but his request was breaded with a thick Boston accent.

Since I wasn't hungry, I told the waitress we wouldn't be eating, which wasn't entirely true as I hadn't eaten since leaving work, despite stopping home briefly. I wanted to focus on discussing music without the disturbance of the waitress's constant check-ins, asking, "Are we ready?" or "Are you guys ready to place the order?" Thankfully, the young artist wasn't hungry either, so my strategy worked

I explained to him that I couldn't sing and had never been a singer. Instead, I write lyrics—that's what I do. Am I good at it? Well, that remains to be seen. I told him I was looking for someone to pitch my songs to and write for, which is why I had contacted him. Ultimately, I wanted my name in the credits, recognized as one of the writers—for that, I needed acknowledgment.

I reaffirmed my dedication and passion for writing lyrics. To illustrate this, I positioned my Surface on the dining table at an angle where he could see the screen. I opened a subfolder titled "The Soundtrack Of My Life," which contained around twenty complete song lyrics. I didn't want to waste time, so I quickly clicked on the first song, allowing him enough time to read through every verse and chorus. I then clicked on another song, providing a quick overview of the concept. He kept reading and skimming through the lyrics as I moved on to the third song, and so on.

Then suddenly, there was a pause, and I noticed his pupils widen. He asked, "You wrote all of this? All these songs?" I replied confidently, "Yes!" with a huge smile on my face. Without needing him to elaborate, I felt a spark of hope in my mind, hopeful that something good would come from this meeting, even as the restaurant grew louder than when I first arrived. I took another sip of my warm beer, which had been cooling off on the table for close to an hour.

He cleared his throat to gather his thoughts and then unexpectedly shifted the conversation: "Where did you say you were from again?" I proudly replied, "Born and raised in Port-Au-Prince, Haiti."

I wanted to specify that I was from a small town named Lakou Kokoye, but I didn't want to lose his attention or deviate from the purpose of the meeting—pitching my song lyrics instead of delving into geography. I wasn't sure if he knew where Haiti was located.

Unsurprisingly, I was not shocked that my Haitian accent still lingered. He seemed impressed, though I was puzzled about whether it was my accent or my lyrics that wowed him. The conversation took another U-turn to the earlier question: "You wrote all of these? English is not your first language, correct?" I nodded and confirmed with some confusion, "Yeah!"

I added that I had been writing for years and had improved over time. As he analyzed and reviewed each song with a magnifying glass, I was hoping this could be a breakthrough moment, hoping he would find a tiny particle of excellence and brilliance in my lyrical DNA (a tiny particle of brilliance in my DNA under the microscope as he analyzed my writing with a magnifying glass).

"Wait for it! ... Wait for it! ... Wait for it!"

He then said, "These are pretty cool lyrics, but... but... but…" The rest of his words seemed to get stuck between his teeth.

"But, but," somehow, he was able to floss out his words: "I do not see myself singing any of these song lyrics. Don't get me wrong; you have penned some great lyrics, but I cannot relate to them"

He continued, "I want to sing about topics that reflect my lifestyle: dating chicks, partying, breakups, and so on."

I silently thought, "I GET IT." I glanced at the time on the taskbar and realized that twenty to thirty minutes had passed, and I noticed that the waitress had been very respectful and cooperative, not interrupting us frequently.

Thereupon, he instructed me to open YouTube so he could play a few songs he had released and uploaded on his channel months earlier. I watched and listened attentively to the lyrics, then resumed our conversation.

Then he mentioned that wanted to be the next Justin Timberlake. I replied, look!, I still think we can make this work. Give me a month or two, and I will have some songs catered to your liking or taste." The conversation ended with a bittersweet taste, even the beer could not wash down, but that's life; you have to keep your head up and persevere.

As we exited the restaurant, I thanked him for meeting with me, and I promised to stay in touch. Honestly, I was not satisfied but satisfied, but felt content knowing I could use his feedback as inspiration to challenge myself to create songs that align with his lifestyle and vision.

I realized that I couldn't just write for or about myself; pouring my life into my lyrics didn't resonate with a wider audience. I needed to connect with a large audience, comparable to those at major events like the Coachella Valley Music and Arts Festival or Summerfest.

Was the young artist, right? Yes, yes, and yes, the young artist was completely right. I lacked materials suitable for rising stars or emerging singers; instead,

I had songs that reflected my personal experiences. This prompted me to re-evaluate my approach when pitching to others.

As I brainstormed, I began drafting a few songs aimed at being relatable to him. Despite reaching out multiple times to update him, he was unresponsive. I continued to write and managed to complete three songs. I emailed him one of the songs, and although he promised to get back to me, he never did.

After several unsuccessful calls and emails, I decided to move on. I didn't lose my patience, but I felt my time was being undervalued. Sometimes, things simply don't work out in life, even if you work hard and stay dedicated, like a gym rat training six days a week, twice a day. Although I didn't get to collaborate with him and our relationship was short-lived, I'm grateful for the experience because it was educational.

I have learned that there is often a root cause for why things don't go as planned, a reason that may be beyond our understanding. Therefore, we mustn't lose ourselves and our soul while trying to regain control.

Additionally, I was reminded to broaden my horizons as a lyricist, allowing my lyrics to explore diverse topics, people, and themes outside my personal experiences.

I also learned that sometimes a compliment can come off as an insult. For instance, the remark, "English is not your first language, right?" was intended as a compliment at the time, but in hindsight and retrospectively, I realize it was actually an insult.

ALBUM VIII
THE NEW ENDING OF MY LIFE

This album represents my frustrations, reflections, and maturation as a man. It outlines a clear vision of who I was and where I stood in life. The title of the album originated from a thought-provoking conversation I had with a wise man. He once told me that while you can never change the beginning—because the past is the past—you can always shape the ending and rewrite your narrative.As I narrate this chapter of my life, I had to let go of the past and focus on the present, as the future remains uncertain and unwritten. Now, here I am in my late 20s, approaching 30, allowing these tracks to unfold like a poem in my mind. This album is my present to you, and I hope you enjoy it as much as my first one. Enjoy!

Tracklist:

01. Beautiful
02. Out of Time
03. HSH (Heart, Smile & Happiness)
04. The Good With The Bad
05. Maybe Its A Sign
06. Missing
07. Put Up A Fight
08. Red Light
09. Running by My Side
10. The Old Days

Track 01♪♪Beautiful

Verse I

I've been staring at you from afar
I can see you chatting', dancin by the bar
You look so beautiful in that dress
Are you a bottom model? I mean a top model
A beauty quite like you
Has impaired my ability to speak

Chorus

Your beauty is a handful
Way too much to handle
Someone quite beautiful as you're
Wherever you are
I'll always love you from afar
Just like a beautiful shooting star

Verse II

I've been standing on my two feet
Wish you were by yourself,
His behavior aint match your beautiful face
Let's face it, It shows on your facebook
Can't wait for him to step aside
So I can tell you how beautiful you look
Chorus (Repeat)

Verse III

I'm trying to keep it together
But every time I look at you
You look more beautiful than the last time
It's crazy, I could see you driving me crazy
In the back seat of my blue Ferrari
Sorry babe I'm slipping into reverie
Chorus (Repeat)

Bridge

You are so close, yet so far away
Before I even get closer
You vanish like a shooting star
Chorus (Repeat)

Track 02♪♪♪Out of Time

Intro

Hon, How do I look?

Verse I

Babe, give me a minute or two
I'd say you're the prettiest
with those dimples and sunshine smile
That wouldn't do you justice
Probably got me locked up for awhile
I'd say you're the cutest in skinny jeans
'Cause you attract me like lint on denim
Then again you already know that

Pre-Chorus

Babe, I hate when you ask me
"How do you look?"
'Cause when I try to describe you

Chorus

I always run out of time, out of time
Even when I look at you
A million times
Even when I use my right mind
To find one word
Still run out of time, out of time

Verse II

Babe, don't move your broad shoulders
I think I got it, Oops! sorry
Spoke too soon, it's getting harder
'Cause when you blink your piercing eyes
You look more beautiful than the last time
No wonder why, I'm reading Webster
Searching for the perfect word
Putting all-nighters, just like in school

Pre-Chorus

Babe, I hate when you ask me
"How do you look?"
'Cause when I try to describe you

Track 02♪♪Out of Time

Chorus

I always run out of time, out of time
Even when I look at you
A million times
Even when I use my right mind
To find one word
Still run out of time, out of time

Bridge

I don't wanna lie and say the wrong word
Next time, you should get undressed
So can I tell you the naked truth, ‘cause

Chorus

I always run out of time, out of time
Even when I look at you
A million times
Even when I use my right mind
To find one word
Still run out of time, out of time

Outro

Babe give me more time
So I don’t run out of time

Track 03♪♪♪♪♪♪♪♪♪♪♪♪♪♪♪♪♪♪♪♪♪♪♪♪♪♪♪♪HSH (Heart, Smile & Happiness)

Intro

How a baby has rejuvenated my life, from a dad to a son

Verse I

I feel reborn since the day you were born
I can feel it, I can feel it in my heart
You are not only son, you're my 2rd heart
Knowing even if my heart doesn't start
Or suddenly skips a beat, you will pump blood
Through me, life will repeat
Amazing moments I have ever had
Was listening to your loud heartbeat
From that moment on
I knew from the bottom of my heart
And nothing will never take us apart,
If anyone ever attempts to split us "apart"
Don't you worry, don't you worry,
I will always be there like a treasured art
You won't have to wonder where's daddy at
Like I used to ask mom for so many years
Who and where was my father?
She'd answer, but I'd go to bed with tears

Chorus

You are not only my son
You are my second heart, my heart
Deep down you aint only my heart
You are my smile, my smile
Deep down you aint only smile
You are my happiness, my happiness
You're my HSH (Happiness, Smile, Heart)

Track 03♪♪♪♪♪♪♪♪♪♪♪♪♪♪♪♪♪♪♪♪♪♪♪♪♪♪♪♪♪HSH (Heart, Smile & Happiness)

Verse II

You're not only my heart, you're my smile
When I'm desperately searching
Searching for something
To cheer me up, so often a smile
Just thinking of you or veering
To my monitor screen
Seeing your face, gives me reasons to smile
Those moments I'll cherish for a while
No matter how far you're, thousand miles
I'm coming home to capture your smile
Just so I can smile
I want you to know that your smile
Has become my smile

Chorus (Repeat)

Verse III

You are not only my smile
Cause your presence is happiness
Just watching you sleep, watching you eat
Witnessing your baby steps
I will be with you every step, of the way
I once believed in, "The pursuit of Happiness"
Something that everyone has to pursue
You have brought eternal happiness
Which follows me like a shadow
Forever be happy, more than I could ever show
We share so many traits, I can barely do the math
Hope one day you do the math
I can proudly say just like father like son
In the end, MJ, I hope you draft your own path
Be better than your father, the better half

Chorus (Repeat)

Outro

Dedicated to my HSH, my son MJ

Track 04♪♪The Good with the Bad

Verse I

Remember, I grew up poor
Now chauffeur opens door
Buy you red bottoms
To show you when it rains, it pours
Marble floor you never seen before
Girls trip in cars with suicide doors
No need to gaze for shootin' stars
Cause that's how beautiful you are

Pre-Chorus

But a kiss goodbye
Before I hit the road
Always seems to start a war

Chorus

Take the good with the bad
Love is bittersweet sweetheart
Take the good with the bad
Love is like oxygen sweetheart
Take the good with the bad
Love is sweet so is time
Take the good with the bad
Otherwise we won't survive
Take the good with the bad
Fame is a purse and a curse
Take the good with the bad

Verse II

I should have done more
To dry those waterin' eyes
Sorry my apology took awhile
I've been on top for so long
Fans singing lines of every song
Got lost in the midst of it all
Didn't know fame has a downfall
Till our love started changin' like fall

Pre-Chorus

But a kiss goodbye
Before I hit the road
Always seems to start a war

Track 04♪♪♪The Good with the Bad

Chorus

Take the good with the bad
Love is bittersweet sweetheart
Take the good with the bad
Love is like oxygen sweetheart
Take the good with the bad
Love is hard to define
Take the good with the bad
As I keep this lifestyle alive
Otherwise we need a 9-to-5
Take the good with the bad
A jag comes with a price tag
Take the good with the bad

Bridge

It's true, we argue all the time
Name a couple walkin' a fine line
Loving in the spotlight, without a fight
Where a misstep gets scrutinized
Don't let lights, camera, actions
Make you blind, so, would you?

Chorus

Take the good with the bad
Love is bittersweet sweetheart
Take the good with the bad
Love is like oxygen sweetheart
Take the good with the bad
Love is sweet so is time
Take the good with the bad
Otherwise we won't survive
Take the good with the bad
Fame is a purse and a curse
Take the good with the bad

Outro

Take the good with the bad
As I keep this lifestyle alive
Otherwise we need a 9-to-5

Behind the Lyrics

The title of this song is self-explanatory as I reflected on the life of an artist—someone who is a star or part of the rich and famous—living in the spotlight. It brings to mind the lights, cameras, and action, along with the red carpets that glorify and illuminate a person's persona and private life to an extreme degree, often in a way that feels inhuman and overly perfect. I also contemplated how "fame" can have both direct and indirect impacts on an artist's personal life, particularly affecting their significant other.

For example, an artist must go on tour, leaving their lover or family behind for weeks or even months at a time—similar to what Wyclef Jean described in his hit single "Gone till November." I understand this reality; it comes with the territory of being an artist. They signed up for all of it: the cars, the mansions, the paparazzi, the interviews, the concerts, and the red carpets—even those with "red bottoms" or "bloody bottoms." However, do their loved ones, including their children, sign up for the loneliness and the long hours spent apart while their partner travels like a nomad? Probably not.

As a society, we often perceive celebrities and famous artists as if they can do no wrong. We view their fame as a gift, ignoring the darker, more complicated side of it—the curse that can come with such a life. Thus, this song serves as a reminder to "take the good with the bad," as the same thing that brings laughter can also bring tears. If you don't believe me, listen to every line of this song, "The Good with the Bad."

Verse I

I went through numerous drafts of Verse I before settling on these lines after months of editing and refining. In the first two lines, I aimed to illustrate the evolution of an artist from an economic standpoint, highlighting the journey from poverty to wealth. I included the line, "Now the chauffeur opens the door," to provide context about the artist's current lifestyle.

Remember, I grew up poor	***(Line 1)***
Now chauffeur opens door	***(Line 2)***
Buy you red bottoms	***(Line 3)***
To show you when it rains, it pours	***(Line 4)***
Marble floor you never seen before	***(Line 5)***
Girls trip in cars with suicide doors	***(Line 6)***

Additionally, Lines 3 through 6 celebrate the extravagant lifestyle that he provides for his significant other, thanks to his wealth and fame. For example, he buys her designer red-bottom shoes and cars, allowing her to enjoy trips with her friends. She is living her dreams as he invests all his riches into their relationship. Line 4 is particularly striking to me, as it symbolizes the abundance of gifts she has received due to his rise to stardom.

Line 6, "Girls trip in cars with suicide doors," surprised me. At first, I found myself repeatedly humming the words "Girls trip," but I struggled to connect them to the previous lines. However, once I considered the word "doors," which rhymes with "poors" from Line 4, the line began to take shape. I was finally able to complete it and understand its significance:

Girls trip in cars with suicide doors **(Line 6)**

As a lyricist, I often find myself navigating the intricacies of language much like a contestant on the Wheel of Fortune; spinning the wheel of locution. The key difference is that there are no other contestants, no prizes, and no money involved.

Pre-Chorus

I wanted to rain on his parade. Despite his wealth and fame, she despises that he is never home. He kisses her and then hits the road, as penned below:

But a kiss goodbye **(Line 1)**
Before I hit the road **(Line 2)**

This is how she perceives the relationship. One of her main fears, perhaps her most prominent fear, is infidelity. While I didn't explicitly detail this in the song, the concept of infidelity did cross my mind while writing the pre-chorus. More importantly, the pre-chorus is very expressive; it reveals what she truly values as a woman. It also highlights her primary love language, which I only learned about during couples' therapy—she values quality time and physical touch more than receiving gifts.

Chorus

The central idea behind the song's chorus is that "beggars can't be choosers." The line "Take the Good" refers to the luxurious gifts she is being offered—gifts that many can only dream of. However, the downside is that she must come to terms with loneliness, which tears her heart apart each time he leaves. Additionally, I included his responses to her concerns in the subsequent lines:

Otherwise we won't survive **(Line 9)**
Take the good with the bad **(Line 10)**
Fame is a purse and a curse **(Line 11)**

"Fame is both a gift and a curse." I believe this is one of the best lines ever. The "purse" symbolizes wealth and material success. He's willing to give up his fame and extravagant lifestyle, but he warns her that it would come with a price or cost, leading to a mundane nine-to-five job and an ordinary life instead of a lavish one. Would she choose that path? I decided to leave this question unanswered.

Verse II

He empathizes with her, shows compassion, and begins to understand the impact of his absence in these opening lines, Line 1 and Line 2:

I should have done more **(Line 1)**
To dry those waterin' eyes **(Line 2)**

Yet, he continues to sing the same old song, "Take the Good with the Bad."

Bridge

This bridge takes a reflective route. I aimed to normalize or generalize the situation by acknowledging the undeniable truths about real relationships. Every relationship experiences its highs and lows, especially when lived in the spotlight where everything is magnified, as highlighted in lines 3 and 4.

Loving in the spotlight, without a fight **(Line 3)**
Where a misstep gets scrutinized **(Line 4)**

Furthermore, in Line 5, every relationship experience through peaks and valleys, where lights, camera, and actions can blind couples, as penned in:

Don't let lights, camera, actions **(Line 5)**
Make you blind, so, would you? **(Line 6)**

Hence, couples must work to keep their relationship strong. They should take the good with the bad. Otherwise, fame and wealth—the lights, camera, action—can ruin everything, even with fans singing every line of every song.

Track 05♪♪Maybe Its A Sign

Verse I

You've said you love me
Maybe two times
something along those lines
But I don't feel anything
Your love must be traveling
'Cause it hasn't reached my spine
Not even my heart

Pre-chorus

Just so you know
You still haven't crossed the line
Near my heart

Chorus

Maybe it's a sign, maybe it's a sign
you don't really love me
'Cause your love is a bunch of words
I'm sorry to say, I'm loss of words
Maybe it's a sign, maybe it's a sign
You don't love me anymore

Verse II

Don't know what your love is made of
'Cause you keep telling me
Instead of showing me
Start doing things that make me
Wanna say babe you didn't have to
If you wanna win my heart

Pre-chorus

Just so you know
You still haven't crossed the line
Near my heart

Chorus

Maybe it's a sign, maybe it's a sign
you don't really love me
'Cause your love is a bunch of words
I'm sorry to say, I'm loss of words
Maybe it's a sign, maybe it's a sign
You don't love me anymore

Track 05♪♪Maybe Its A Sign

Bridge

It's easy to put into words
"we're deeply in love"
I'm yet to feel loved
Remember actions speak
Louder than words

Chorus

Maybe its a sign, maybe it's a sign
You don't really love me
'Cause your love is a bunch of words
I'm sorry to say, I'm loss of words
Maybe it's a sign, maybe it's a sign
You don't love me anymore

Track 06♪♪Missing

Verse I

Baby, please pick up, it's me again
Remember how I told you back then
I didn't need you, ooh
So I left without saying goodbye
When I got your text asking why
My reply, " it's not you, it's me "
A typical excuse for a guy
It works every time

Pre-chorus

But this time
Being on my own
Something just don't feel right (nah)

Chorus

'Cause baby, since you been gone
Part of me is missing, missing
Ooh baby, without your loving
Part of me is missing, missing
I need you baby, ooh yeah baby
Ooh baby, without your kissing
Part of me is missing, missing
Cause you're the part missing
Missing, yeah baby

Verse II

Baby so much pain, I need aspirin
Baby seeing your makeup stain
On the pillowcase drives me insane
I'd flip it over, away from my face
But your smell is embedded in my head
Its a reminder, We Belong Together
Comeback to put our differences to bed
Same way we used to go to bed

Pre-chorus

But this time
Being on my own
Something just don't feel right (nah)

Track 06.♪♪♪Missing

Chorus

'Cause baby, since you been gone
Part of me is missing, missing
Ooh baby, without your loving
Part of me is missing, missing
I need you baby, ooh yeah baby
Ooh baby, without your kissing
Part of me is missing, missing
Cause you're the part missing
Missing, ooh baby

Bridge

AMBER Alert, even after sunset
Will keep looking for you, ooh
Till the day I die, hoping one day
I'll find you in the lost and found

Chorus

'Cause baby, since you been gone
Part of me is missing, missing
Ooh baby, without your loving
Part of me is missing, missing
I need you baby, ooh yeah baby
Ooh baby, without your kissing
Part of me is missing, missing
Cause you're the part missing
Missing, yeah baby

Outro

Please baby, oh baby
Sorry baby, I'm missing your loving
Your kissing, ooh baby

Behind the Lyrics

Let's get straight to the point like an arrow: This song tells the story of a guy who experiences a change of heart after breaking up with his girlfriend. After some time apart, he realizes just how much he misses her and wants to rekindle their relationship. He tries to track her down, but her location remains a mystery. One night, he even leaves a voicemail similar to an Amber Alert, mistakenly thinking she might be missing.

Verse I

Line 1, In the opening line, I aimed to establish a theme so the audience understands the song in context. I know some of my lyrics can be complex, and some might find me perplexing, but this one is as "real as it gets,"in other formal words, as genuine as it gets. I wanted to highlight that it's not the first time he has called his ex-girlfriend, which is why the line ends with "again."

Baby, please pick up, its me again **(Line 1)**
Remember how I told you back then **(Line 2)**

The end rhyming scheme used throughout Verse I is what ultimately dictates the overall structure. Lines 2 through 6 serve as the backbone of this tale or narrative, as he reminisces on how he broke up and abruptly left without saying goodbye, as mentioned in Line 4.

So I left without saying goodbye **(Line 4)**
When I got your text asking why **(Line 5)**
My reply, " its not you, it's me" **(Line 6)**
a typical excuse for a guy **(Line 7)**
It works every time **(Line 8)**

In Line 6, this breakup speech may come across as thoughtless, and many women might consider it "taking the easy way out." However, he did indeed send the message. Lines 7 and 8 were included not to tarnish his reputation or portray him as a victim; rather, he wanted to take responsibility for his past mistakes, as any genuine and honest man should. As the story unfolds, he shares his mental state and feelings of isolation stemming from not being with her in the Pre-chorus below:

Pre-chorus

But this time **(Line 1)**
Being on my own **(Line 2)**
Something just don't feel right (nah) **(Line 3)**

This is probably the simplest pre-chorus I have ever written. The lines are concise and get straight to the point. As any lyricist can attest, our goal is to tell stories within a limited space, such as verses, and to condense longer narratives so that our audience doesn't feel overwhelmed. After all, that would defeat the purpose of music. As lyricists, we do not have much of a window, or even legroom, to make mistakes, as if we were flying Spirits (I am just tripping) as we are provided a small window to take our audience on a journey. Lastly,

Chorus
'Cause baby, since you been gone **(Line 1)**
part of me is missing, missing **(Line 2)**
Ooh baby, without your loving **(Line 3)**
part of me is missing, missing **(Line 4)**
I need you baby, ooh yeah baby **(Line 5)**
Ooh baby, without your kissing **(Line 6)**
part of me is missing, missing **(Line 7)**
Cause you're the part missing **(Line 8)**
Missing, yeah baby **(Line 9)**

I didn't count how many times I repeated the word "missing," but I was surprised to find that the song's title, "Missing," is repeated just as often. However, in retrospect, I'm glad I did. When you're missing someone, it's something you need to voice repeatedly.

Verse II
I must admit that Verse II is more powerful than Verse I, as the imagery is clearly illustrated with no ambiguity whatsoever. What do you think?

So much baby, I need aspirin **(Line 1)**
Baby seeing your makeup stain **(Line 2)**

Line 1, as I annotated earlier, his mental state begins to deteriorate. The more he misses her, the more pain he experiences, as stated explicitly: "So much pain, baby, I need aspirin." However, the following lines convey feelings of loneliness, regret, and a sentimental vibe throughout the song:

On the pillowcase drives me insane **(Line 3)**
I'd flip it over, away from my face **(Line 4)**
But your smell is embedded, in my head **(Line 5)**
Its a reminder, We Belong Together **(Line 6)**

Between Lines 2 and 8, as I was writing this verse, I imagined a male artist or singer recording these lyrics while lying in bed. He once shared this experience with his ex or former partner, which is funny how it all unfolded. The word "reminder" suddenly came to mind, and then the phrase "we belong forever." However, I changed "forever" to "be together" as a nod to Mariah Carey's "We Belong Together." Just kidding—sort of! All kidding and jokes aside- That song is a classic and beautifully performed. I can envision myself writing similar lyrics, and this reference serves as an homage to the writers and lyricists who contributed to such a masterful hit. As I have done on numerous occasions, I feel it's important to give credit where it's due. I appreciate great lyricism, and I strive to paint vivid pictures with words, so I don't consider myself a complete philistine in this regard.

Comeback to put our differences to bed **(Line 7)**
The same way we used to go to bed **(Line 8)**

Lastly, in Lines 7 and 8, as he reaches the end of the voicemail, he kindly asks for reconciliation, saying, "put our differences to bed." Initially, it read, "put our differences to rest." I decided to change it to create a stronger rhyming scheme for the song's conclusion. Do you think I should have kept the original phrase? Overall, this verse really brings the music to life.

Bridge
AMBER Alert, even after sunset **(Line 1)**
Will keep looking for you, ooh **(Line 2)**
Till the day I die, hoping one day **(Line 3)**
I'll find you in the lost and found **(Line 4)**

I want to be honest: the original version of the bridge did not include Line 1, which reads, "AMBER Alert, even after sunset." However, while writing this book, I decided to revise the bridge by adding "AMBER Alert" because there was a recent case of a missing girl that really affected me. The word "missing" resonated with me, especially in relation to the theme of the song.

After sunset, I noticed a recurring theme in movies where authorities and rescue teams often halt searches for missing persons due to reduced visibility or challenging conditions at night. I felt that this was a valuable addition to the song, inviting the audience and listeners to participate in the search for a missing person—in this case, for his ex-girlfriend.

Subtly and indirectly, I wanted to raise awareness about the serious issue of abduction, especially of young girls. It is crucial for each of us to do our best to assist in the search for and safe recovery of abducted children, treating their cases as if they were our own child or loved one.

Track 07♪♪♪Put Up A Fight

Intro

Why?

Verse I

Why am I still living, hoping?
When everyday
I feel like you're fading, away
Don't even remember my name
Never mind your own name
Seems just like yesterday
You were calling me, sweetie
Now you don't even know me

Pre-Chorus

Even though, the road to reach your heart
Getting longer everyday
Till my last breath on earth
Till your last day

Chorus

Darling, we gonna put up a fight
We gonna put up a fight
Gonna put up a fight
'Till this pain goes away
'Till we win this fight
Darling, we gonna put up a fight
We gonna put up a fight
Gonna put up a fight
Everything gonna be alright
'Cause you gonna put up a fight

Verse II

Not long ago, you were showing me
Which way to go
It pains me seeing you in the hallway
Going the wrong way
Sickness or not, we'll find a way
To get right back on track
Remind you, how much I love you
With hugs and kisses everyday

Track 07♪♪♪Put Up A Fight

Pre-Chorus

Even though, the road to reach your heart
Getting longer everyday
Till my last breath on earth
Till your last day

Chorus

Darling, we gonna put up a fight
We gonna put up a fight
Gonna put up a fight
'Till this pain goes away
'Till we win this fight
Darling, We gonna put up a fight
We gonna put up a fight
Gonna put up a fight
Everything gonna be alright
'Cause you gonna put up a fight

Bridge

Won't lose hope, nope
Keep fighting till the end, no dead end
Remember you put the F in Fighter
That's why we fight Forever

Chorus

Darling, we gonna put up a fight
We gonna put up a fight
Gonna put up a fight
Till this pain goes away
Till we win this fight
Darling, we gonna put up a fight
We gonna put up a fight
Gonna put up a fight
Everything gonna be alright
'Cause you gonna put up a fight

Outro

Gonna put up a fight

Behind the Lyrics

I get chills whenever I read these lyrics. I wrote this song after watching the movie "Still Alice," which stars Julianne Moore. The film, released in 2014, is a powerful portrayal of a woman diagnosed with early-onset familial Alzheimer's disease. While I don't know anyone personally who is battling this incurable disease, the experience of watching the movie profoundly touched me. Although the film was quite sad, it inspired me to write this song. It was a painful process, but as a writer, I wanted to create something that could help alleviate their suffering. My hope is that this song can serve as a form of medicine, offering hope, strength, and courage not only to those who are ill but also to their caregivers. Caregivers must remain sharp both physically and mentally to look after their loved ones. After all, if caregivers are not strong and become ill themselves, they cannot effectively support those who depend on them. I hope this song strengthens those who are weakened, as every day presents new challenges and mountains to climb. I believe that each of us knows someone who is fighting for their life. While I may not have a cure for this disease, I sincerely hope my song provides a dose of comfort and healing that they have been seeking. May God bless those suffering with hope, strength, and courage.

Verse I

Why am I still living, hoping? ***(Line 1)***
When everyday ***(Line 2)***
I feel like you're fading, away ***(Line 3)***

This verse begins with the question, "Why?" It's a question that many family members who serve as caregivers ask when their loved ones are battling a disease. As a caregiver, you may not experience physical pain, but mentally and emotionally, the weight of their illness can feel overwhelming. At times, it becomes a burden too heavy to bear, and you may even find yourself exhibiting similar symptoms and signs of distress. In those moments, you say to yourself these three lines:

Don't even remember my name ***(Line 4)***
Never mind your own name ***(Line 5)***

Lines 4 and 5 highlight the impact of the disease, particularly emphasizing the heartbreaking symptom of memory loss. Individuals affected begin to forget important information, such as the names of relatives or details from recent conversations, and they struggle to remember everyday objects. While some diseases can be foreseen through regular screenings and genetic testing, others are unpredictable. Therefore, the caregiver, including the ill, has no time to prepare for it, even if they are wearing the perfect watch. These two lines offer specific examples of rhyming endings.

Pre-Chorus

Till my last breath on earth **(*Line 3*)**
Till your last day **(*Line 4*)**

Initially, I was adamant about not including a pre-chorus in the song. However, after reviewing Verse I, I realized that the ending of Verse I—particularly Line 8, "Now you don't even know me"—lacked an adequate element of anticipation. If I jumped or dove directly into the chorus, I risked losing the audience's interest. I recognized that something essential was missing; I needed an element to heighten the anticipation of the song. To address this, I elaborated on the significant aspects of being a caregiver, such as devotion and commitment. As any caregiver understands, you must be dedicated to taking care of someone else "Till your last day," as exemplified in **Line 4** below, let alone yourself. Now you know the origin of the pre-chorus.

Chorus

The purpose of this chorus is to illustrate that battling a disease is not a solitary act of valor; it requires the support of others. That's why I opted for the first-person plural pronoun "We" instead of using "You" or "I'm" to express the fight. Clever, right? Additionally, I wanted to include some encouraging and uplifting words, so I decided to end the verse with Line 9: "Everything's gonna be alright."

Verse II

As I mentioned earlier, one of the symptoms of Alzheimer's is memory loss. In this verse, the caregiver reflects on the past, trying to remind the individual of cherished memories, the good old days; while also accepting the present situation. Ultimately, the caregiver expresses confidence in the future, despite the illness, as conveyed in these lines:

Sickness or not, we'll find a way **(*Line 5*)**
To get right back on track **(*Line 6*)**
Remind you, how much I love you **(*Line 7*)**
With hugs and kisses everyday **(*Line 8*)**

Bridge

I kept the bridge short so that the audience would not have to wait too long to reach the chorus. It is essential to note that I would only have built the bridge with the word, hope. Hope is something to hold onto as you "put up a fight" worth dying for. So, if you know someone battling any disease, don't give up; keep fighting.

Track 08♪♪♪Red Light

Verse I

I've noticed you been
Trying so hard to please me
Doing things for me
To make sure everything smells brand new
Even buying cars just because
I wish I could do the same for you
Oh babe you got nothing to prove

Chorus

Stop it! Red light!
You don't have to spoil me
You don't even have to shower me
With lux (luxury)
For me to love you
Stop it! Red light!
You don't have to
Cause you've already won my heart,
Won my heart

Post-Chorus

You know it's true
I really love you

Verse II

It feels good how you've been treating me
Its taking time to get used to
Given nice things who'd refuse?
But I feel like I gotta tell you
You got nothin to lose, I'd never forsake you
I just don't want you to burn out
Then get up and leave me

Track 08♪♪♪Red Light

Chorus
Stop it! Red light!
You don't have to spoil me
You don't even have to shower me
with lux (luxury)
For me to love you
Stop it! Red light!
You don't have to
Cause you've already won my heart,
Won my heart

Post-Chorus
You know it's true
I really love you

Bridge
I'd never repay you
Just play your part
And I'll keep loving you
Green light, you can go if you want to

Chorus
Stop it! Red light!
You don't have to spoil me
You don't even have to shower me
With lux (luxury)
For me to love you
Stop it! Red light!
You don't have to
Cause you've already won my heart,
Won my heart

Post-Chorus
You know it's true
I really love you

Outro
Stop it! Red light!

Track 9 ♪♪♪ Running by My Side

Verse I

It's been years
Since you told me not to call anymore
I promised I'd leave you alone
But last night I tripped and fell on the floor
Where we used to lay down
I felt broken this time around
No one else to call and rely on

Pre-chorus

Babe I am sorry for broken our promise
But a part of me aint sorry

Chorus

Cause when I hear your voice
On the other side
It doesn't feel like you're out of my life
It feels like you're home hiding inside
Once I say babe I am home
You'll be running by my side
Running, running by my side

Verse II

Hey it's me, please don't hang up
I know I am not supposed to call
You right, I've crossed that line
Is that your other half in the background?
Last time I called, you were in the playground
Cause I heard the merry go' round
That's when I knew, you've moved on

Pre-chorus

Babe I am sorry for broken our promise
But a part of me aint sorry

Track 9 ♪♪ Running by My Side

Chorus

Cause when I hear your voice
On the other side
It doesn't feel like you're out of my life
It feels like you're home hiding inside
Once I say babe I am home
You'll be running by my side
Running, running by my side

Bridge

Since you left me home all alone
I haven't brought anyone home
Cause I still believe we're lovers

Pre-chorus

Babe I am sorry for broken our promise
But a part of me aint sorry

Chorus

Cause when I hear your voice
On the other side
It doesn't feel like you're out of my life
It feels like you're home hiding inside
Once I say babe I am home
You'll be running by my side
Running, running by my side

Track 10 ♪♪ The Old Days

Verse I

As I look to the days ahead
reminiscing about those nights in bed
When we used to talk for hours
So much, your voice still echoes in my head
"babe don't fall asleep, one more hour"
Since your breakthrough, I barely see you
These days, you let the phone ring
Too busy doing your own things
Only want a quick Hollywood fling

Pre-chorus

Babe what happened to us?
Where did we go wrong?
I just wish

Chorus

We could go back to the old days
to the old days
When the chemistry was there
You were my oxygen
and I was your nitrogen
Together we were fresher than air
Let's go back to the old days
to the old days
So we can breathe the same air

Verse I

I wish we could go back
When we were always drunk in love
Remember? a CD off the rack
And a bottle from the liquor store?
Then we'd be sipping on coconut rum
And dancing to our favorite songs
We were like two kids having fun
Nothing to prove to the media
Cause we had each other to lean on

Track 10 ♪♪♪ The Old Days

Pre-chorus

Babe what happened to us?
Where did we go wrong?
I just wish

Chorus

We could go back to the old days
to the old days
When the chemistry was there
You were my oxygen
and I was your nitrogen
Together we were fresher than air
Let's go back to the old days
to the old days
So we can breathe the same air

Bridge

I don't like the new you
Not even for a second boo
Maybe it was bad timing on our part
I guess all good things must come to an end

Pre-chorus

Babe what happened to us?
Where did we go wrong?
I just wish

Chorus

We could go back to the old days
to the old days
When the chemistry was there
You were my oxygen
and I was your nitrogen
Together we were fresher than air
Let's go back to the old days
to the old days
So we can breathe the same air

After completing my second album, The New Ending Of My Life, I found myself contemplating, "What is next for Patience the Ghostwriter?" At that moment, I did not have an instantaneous answer.

Despite my relentless writing, I could glimpse at the writing on the wall: Patience The Ghostwriter, might need to give it all up and wake from this unattainable dream. The idea of taking a break from it all didn't seem so far-fetched.

I chose to focus on the positives and explore alternatives—any way I could continue this wild journey. As a result, I directed my attention toward promoting my music. While writing song lyrics for this album, my primary goal was to create lyrics for a male artist I had previously mentioned. I began promoting my work by reaching out to artists, record labels, and recording studios both locally and statewide, as well as participating in song lyric contests.

Promoting

Promoting music in this industry is far from easy. It's not as simple as parking your car, walking into a record label, and submitting your materials. These days, it simply doesn't work that way. You typically need an A&R representative, and even then, achieving contact can be extremely challenging. Most A&R representatives are nearly inaccessible; you often have to know someone who knows someone to get in touch. Furthermore, most insiders will tell you upfront that they do not accept solicited materials.

After extensive research online, I discovered a directory of music publishers that included major and indie publishers, complete with their addresses, emails, phone numbers, the genres they cater to, and, most importantly, their policies regarding unsolicited and solicited materials. The reality is that ninety percent of these publishers do not accept unsolicited submissions.

Being a maverick and inherently a cavalier by nature, I decided to disregard the norms and written law of music publishing. I began promoting my song lyrics by submitting unsolicited materials to as many publishers as possible, fully aware that most, if not all, would likely reject them. I approached this with a carefree attitude, acting as if I were oblivious to their rules as I am forever a cavalier and a maverick.

I enthusiastically bombarded their email inboxes with song lyrics, including a Word document containing a brief biography that I had prepared weeks earlier.

Meanwhile, I encountered numerous recording labels and music publishers that did not provide valid email addresses or websites; they only shared business addresses, some of which were P.O. boxes. So, I printed all the lyrics from "The New Ending of My Life" album, organized them, and placed them in yellow, sealed 9 x 12 "Kraft Clasp Envelopes. Then, I drove to the local post office on Main Street in North Andover and mailed them out..

If I recall correctly, there were about seven to ten envelopes. I requested that they be shipped via "priority mail" and ensured I received tracking numbers for each package. I didn't ask the USPS clerk about the validity of those addresses, assuming they would flag any invalid ones if there were any. I presume.

As I headed home and waited for the never-changing red light to turn green, I thought, "This is crazy; what am I doing?" This moment marked my first feeling of uncertainty—not literally or lyrically, but figuratively. I remembered a message from someone's T-shirt I had seen a few days prior that read, "It's only crazy until you do it." I reassured myself that someone would indeed receive and review those envelopes.

Furthermore, I called some record labels and recording studios, as their contact information was listed on the three-page directory before I submitted my materials. Most of the phone numbers went straight to voicemail or were unanswered, and I kept a tally of those calls. A few were answered, but they yielded vague responses like, "You could submit to this email," or "We do not accept unsolicited materials, sorry." In other instances, I heard, "You don't have a full song, just lyrics." I would softly reply, "Yes, just lyrics." The response was often a simple, "Sorry, we cannot help you."

In conclusion, I never received any definitive responses. I continuously reminded myself, "At least I tried," and with that, I moved on.

As I moved on and aimed to write more songs for the young artist at the 99 restaurants. I found myself tripping, not falling on a few minor life's speed bumps and setbacks:

Thumb Drive

As humans, we evolve, and so does technology. Before 2016, I periodically transferred my lyrics onto a 250 megabytes (MB) thumb drive or USB flash drive. For the longest time, I had been transcribing lines, verses, and songs from napkins and sticky notes and store receipts in my composition notebook to ensure I would not forget them. More importantly, this allowed me to avoid carrying tons of paper.

Whenever ideas, lines, words, or concepts surged into my head as a writer or lyricist, I felt the need to jot them down immediately. Then, whenever I found time—which was rare—I would sit in front of a computer or laptop and transcribe the lyrics from my notebook into a Word document. I would save and transfer the lyrics into the designated folder on my thumb drive as well as my personal drive. This process, which I had implemented years ago, worked effectively: it was a way to back up or save all my lyrics in case I lost the notebook

Everything was functioning well until one evening when I couldn't find the thumb drive no matter how hard I looked. I searched everywhere, flipped the house upside down like a mattress, hoping and praying I would find it at a nearby lost and found.

After weeks of manhunting, it became apparent that my luck had run out. Even if I drove to Hand Drive, I would not locate the thumb drive (a little wordplay for your amusement). Therefore, I decided to halt the search with a thumb down!

The last time I remembered having the thumb drive was the night before, when I was wearing denim jeans on my way to a nightclub in Nashua, New Hampshire. I took it out of my pocket so that the bouncer wouldn't have a fit over the metal device and deny me access. Long story short, the new songs I had drafted were all saved on the thumb drive, not in my notebook, as I had started transitioning from using a notebook to solely Word documents.

A week later, I was chatting with a colleague at my nine-to-five job and explained what happened with the thumb drive. He knew about my hobby of writing song lyrics as if it was a second job. After listening patiently to my frustration, he exclaimed, "Man, a thumb drive?!" That is old-school, method man." You need to save your files, in this case, my lyrics, in the cloud," I said with a disappointed smirk," to which I replied, "Cloud." He looked at me as if I had two heads.

I paused and reiterated my question, genuinely confused: "Cloud? What is a cloud?" This time, he looked at me as if my head was in the clouds.

Realizing I wasn't joking, he explained, "Google has something called Google Drive." As we were chatting near his four-by-four cubicle, he pulled his office chair closer and instructed me to:

- Create a Google account with a username and password.
- Open Google Drive instead of a thumb drive—he joked about it again.
- Create a folder within Google Drive to save or upload your files and lyrics.

After his crash course in IT 101, I felt outdated, even though my colleague was only two or three years older than me. From that day forward, I began using Word documents instead of writing my lyrics in a notebook.

But as old habits die hard, I still occasionally rely on my trusty notebook for a helping hand because the notebook is different, in a bizarre way. While the cloud is incredible, I could never completely abandon my pen and composition notebook, which have been traveling with me on this crazy dream the first day the ink touched the first page.

Alas, without the thumb drive, I was able to jog my memory somewhat and rewrite some of the songs from scratch. Alternatively, for those I could remember vaguely, I managed to remember important details like themes, titles, and certain lines to some extent.

Email in My Inbox

When I thought I was a few exits away from hope or establishing some musical momentum and when I presumed good news would soon be coming my way or on the horizon, more setbacks stabbed me in the back when I started receiving feedback, feedback after feedback, from a Writer Relations Coordinator affiliated with a recording studio in Nashville, Tennessee.

Feedback I

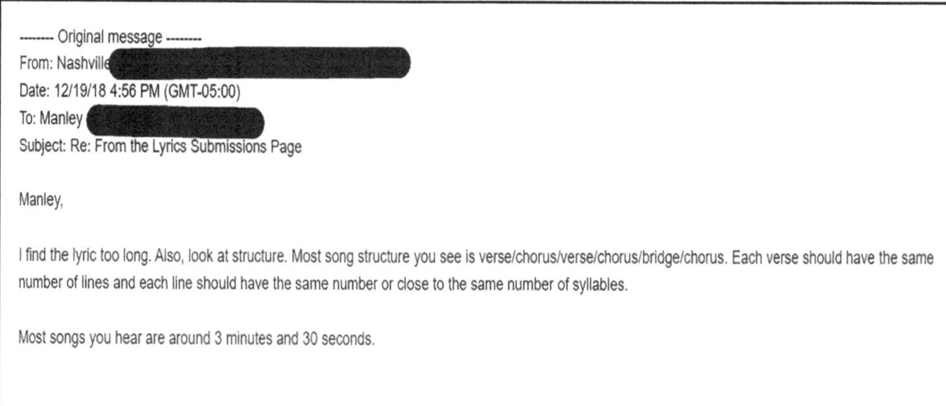

-------- Original message --------
From: Nashvill[redacted]
Date: 12/19/18 4:56 PM (GMT-05:00)
To: Manley [redacted]
Subject: Re: From the Lyrics Submissions Page

Manley,

I find the lyric too long. Also, look at structure. Most song structure you see is verse/chorus/verse/chorus/bridge/chorus. Each verse should have the same number of lines and each line should have the same number or close to the same number of syllables.

Most songs you hear are around 3 minutes and 30 seconds.

Feedback II

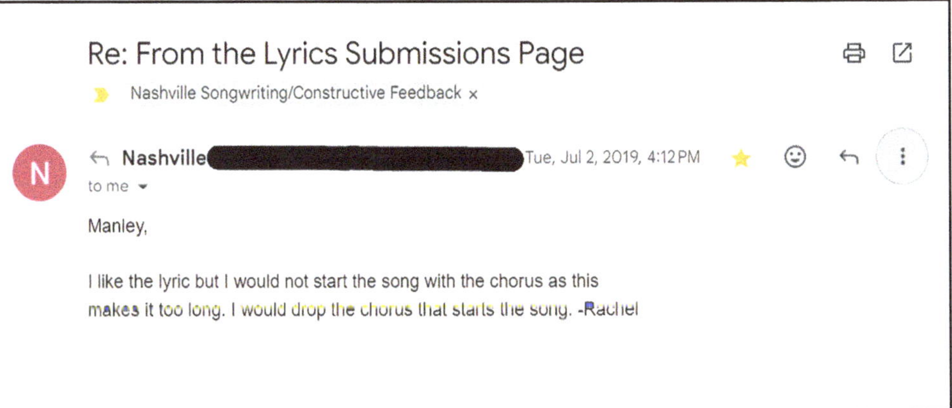

Re: From the Lyrics Submissions Page

Nashville Songwriting/Constructive Feedback ×

Nashville [redacted] Tue, Jul 2, 2019, 4:12 PM

to me

Manley,

I like the lyric but I would not start the song with the chorus as this makes it too long. I would drop the chorus that starts the song. -Rachel

Feedback III

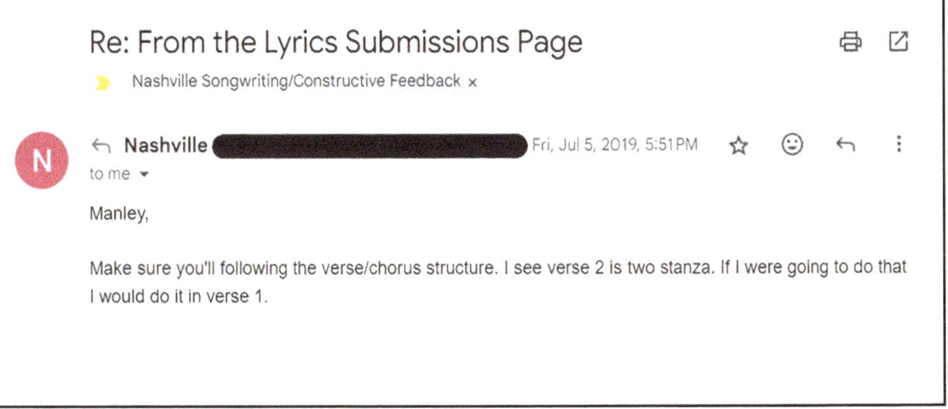

Re: From the Lyrics Submissions Page

Nashville Songwriting/Constructive Feedback ×

Nashville [redacted] Fri, Jul 5, 2019, 5:51 PM

to me

Manley,

Make sure you'll following the verse/chorus structure. I see verse 2 is two stanza. If I were going to do that I would do it in verse 1.

Feedback IV

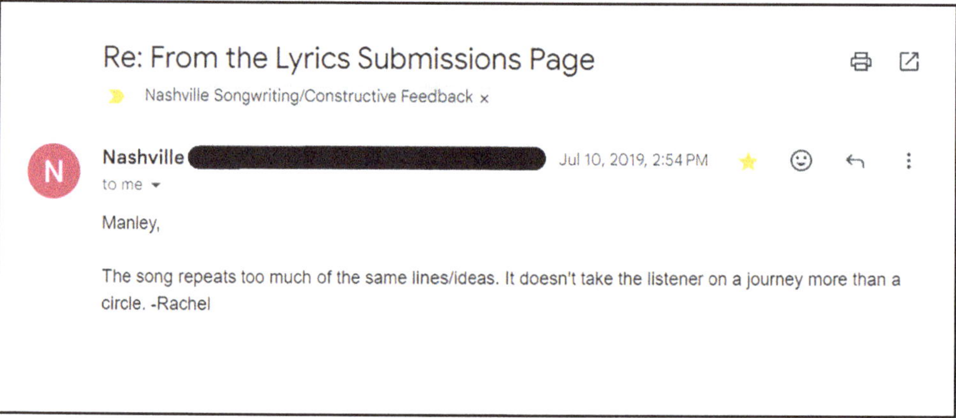

Re: From the Lyrics Submissions Page

Nashville Songwriting/Constructive Feedback ×

Nashville [redacted] Jul 10, 2019, 2:54 PM

to me

Manley,

The song repeats too much of the same lines/ideas. It doesn't take the listener on a journey more than a circle. -Rachel

Feedback V

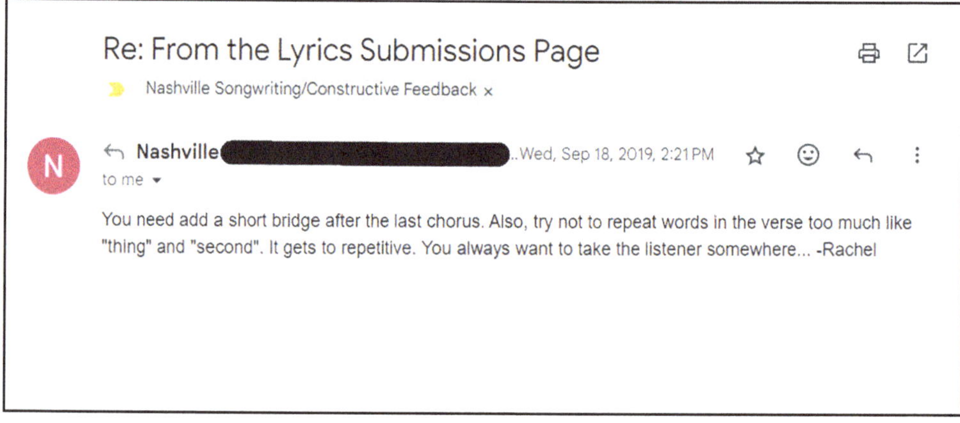

Re: From the Lyrics Submissions Page

Nashville Songwriting/Constructive Feedback ×

Nashville [redacted] ..Wed, Sep 18, 2019, 2:21 PM

to me

You need add a short bridge after the last chorus. Also, try not to repeat words in the verse too much like "thing" and "second". It gets to repetitive. You always want to take the listener somewhere... -Rachel

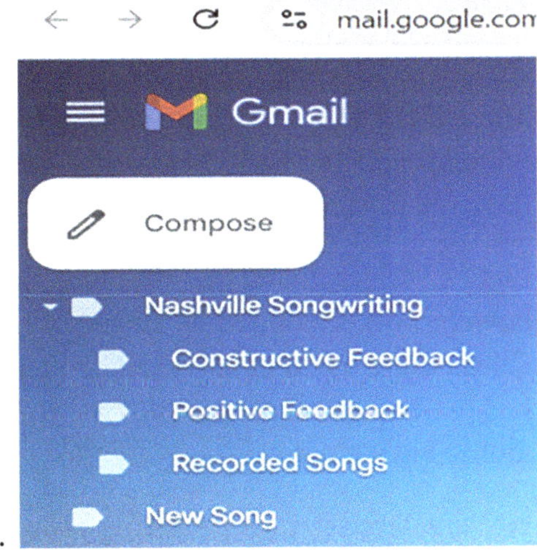

At first, I thought the reviewer's comments were harsh. I also felt like a failure, devoid of hope and direction. This was the first time I had ever submitted my lyrics for review to a Writer Relations Coordinator, so the feedback hit me hard. It took me a few days to process the criticism and realize that the recording company and the assigned reviewer were simply doing their jobs by evaluating my lyrics and providing feedback—whether it was positive or constructive. That said, I felt that Rachel could have shown me a bit of southern love or Nashville hospitality, especially since she is based in Music City, the mecca of the music industry.

In the midst of adversity, I found myself reflecting on how easily a dream could evaporate in thin air based solely on someone's perspective or critique.

Amid adversity, I faced the mirror, took a good look at myself, assessed my situation, and considered her feedback. The reflection in the mirror can either uplift you or bring you down, as it reveals your true colors—your authentic self, in other words your self-image.

A few years earlier, I had learned that there is no such thing as negative feedback; there is only constructive feedback and positive feedback. At that moment, however, my mind struggled to differentiate between the two. The truth is, the recording company's feedback hurt. It was painful to realize that, all along, I believed I was doing a decent job with my lyrics and was on the right path to achieving my dream.

I was suddenly reminded that I needed to work on my lyrics. I began to wonder if this dream of mine was truly attainable. I contemplated giving up, but instead of deleting the constructive feedback I had received, I created a folder in my email labeled **"Constructive Feedback"** to use as motivation.

I did not want Rachel's constructive feedback to derail my destiny or define who I was and could potentially be as a lyricist. Her feedback served as a reminder that in this game of life, you will experience both losses and wins.

Hence, I always count the losses just as I count my wins, but I never counted myself out of the game; not even for a moment. I was not raised that way.

Therefore, I was willing to start from zero, taking baby steps, even if it meant pretending that I had never written a day in my life, as if it were my first day in Pre-K (or Pre-Kindergarten).

Did I consider giving up? Absolutely! I thought about quitting many times; however, I was inspired by stories of individuals who looked like me and defeated the odds. One particular story that inspired me was that of my favorite basketball player, Michael Jordan, or MJ, whom I enormously idolized as a child.

He, too, faced hardships during his high school years. As a sophomore, he was not selected to play for the Varsity team. As he later said on his website, "I think not making the Varsity team drove me to work at my game and also taught me that if you set goals and work hard to achieve them, the hard work can pay off." I genuinely believe his perseverance was one of the by-products of his greatness; he defines and standardizes the essence of greatness.

Like MJ, I told myself it was time to get to work. I worked harder than ever, wrote more lyrics, spent sleepless nights crafting verses, choruses, and bridges and devoted more time to studying lyrical structures across various genres: Country, Jazz, Blues, Gospel, R&B, Rap, Pop, and Soul, to name a few of my favorite genres.

As I read and studied lyrics from those genres, it became painfully evident that I SUCKED! with capital letters. I did not belong in the same league as those prolific lyricists: Eminem, Jay-Z, Lil Wayne, John Legend, Buju Banton, Mega, Bob Marley, Sam Cooke, Michael Kiwanuka, Andre 3000, Talib Kweli, Nicki Minaj, and Alicia Keys— these songwriters paint compelling and timeless stories that are cemented on the concrete of every street corner of America and around the world.

I abstained from submitting new song lyrics to this particular recording studio until I had a lyrical and musical plan. My strategy was not to revise the songs I had previously submitted; instead, I aimed to submit entirely new lyrics that met all the requirements for a hit record.

During this time, I focused on song structure, ensuring that I created compelling stories with strong vibe or flow, effective rhyme schemes, and impactful delivery. These elements were inspired by stories about potential artists I envisioned writing for, rather than my personal life. I imagined writing for top-charting artists like Rihanna, Alicia Keys, Leon Bridges, Ogi, Norah Jones, The Weeknd, Bruno Mars, Son Little, and others. This was my Moment to fully commit and write with passion—until my fingers hurt.

ALBUM IX
SEIZE THE MOMENT

This is a moment of clarity. For the first time, I feel my dedication and hard work finally paying off — almost as if they're settling old debts. For a while, I felt ashamed of my earlier lyrics. Looking back, I realized that my first two albums, *The Soundtrack Of My Life* and *The New Ending of My Life,* were… well, not very good.

Then one night, during a football game, a particular wide receiver changed everything. Somehow, that moment revived my dream — like CPR bringing it back to life. I think of it now as the instant I decided to seize the opportunity instead of letting it slip away.

After months of stepping back, I returned to writing with a new fire. I worked tirelessly in the early mornings, usually between 5 and 7 AM, while the world slept, alarms snoozed, and birds whispered their first songs of the day. In that quiet space, I wrote — and finished — twelve new songs.

Tracklist:

01. Addicted
02. Be Careful What You Wish For
03. Despite Everything, Best Believe
04. Fame (A gift and A Curse)
05. Famous
06. Forgive Me
07. I Don't Forgive & Forget
08. I am Done
09. In Thin Air
10. Never Too Late
11. Seasonal Love (Part I)
12. Seasonal Love (Part II)

Track 01♪♪♪Addicted

Verse I

I wasn't born sick, I'm just an addict
I'm just an alcoholic
I have been fighting
I have been fighting this disease
I have let a lot of people down
Even those who used to look up to me
Save me, save me, yes, I am addicted

Chorus

Help me, help me
I'm addicted, I'm addicted
Yes, I am an addict

Verse II

Don't give up on me
As I fight adversity
Make me part of your family
Don't push me away, I'm telling you
I have been rejected by numerous people
I have tried to stay clean mentally

Chorus

But, my mental illness is real
Help me, help me
I'm addicted, I'm addicted
Yes, I am addicted

Bridge

When I'm away by myself
I have another life, life
This disease cuts deeper than a knife
Don't leave me by myself
Stay with me, please don't shut the door
Don't want to hit rock bottom again
I could end up on the floor, keep eyes on me

Chorus

Help me, help me
I'm addicted, I'm addicted
Yes, I am an addict

Behind the Lyrics

On September 30, 2018, the New England Patriots played against the Miami Dolphins. Tom Brady threw for 274 yards and three touchdowns, leading the Patriots to a dominant 38-7 victory, which handed Miami its first loss of the season. This song's lyrics are not about Brady or the Patriots; they focus on Josh Gordon, a wide receiver who had been traded from the Cleveland Browns to the Patriots just a few weeks earlier. As a Patriots fan, I've kept myself informed about new players throughout the off-season and regular season. That's the Patriot way, and I wouldn't want it any other way.

Honestly, prior to that day, I didn't know much about Josh Gordon's personal life or his challenges both on and off the field. All I knew was that on September 30, 2018, he made his debut for the Patriots, catching two passes for 32 yards in the team's 38-7 win over Miami.

That evening, while watching one of the Patriots' postgame shows, I overheard a commentator discussing Josh's personal struggles, — his battles with addiction, both to drugs and to alcohol. The commentator applauded his remarkable talent but noted that his issues seemed to overshadow his skills, which ultimately led to him being traded to the Patriots. As I sat in the living room, glued to the TV, I couldn't even get up for a water break. I shuffled through the pillows on my couch to find my cell phone. Once I located it, I opened my Chrome browser and performed a Google search with the keywords "Josh Gordon receiver." My search returned several articles and videos, and I remember clicking on one of the videos to learn more.

After reviewing information online and watching YouTube videos, I became convinced that he possessed a natural talent but was also battling demons he had faced since he was a young teenager. His story profoundly touched me, especially his long journey to recovery and the NFL. I felt compassion rather than judgment, recognizing that everyone is fighting battles we know little about, whether openly or in silence, and whether unashamedly or shamefully.

I respected the fact that he openly shared his journey. Therefore, I could not be a Karen; adopt a critical perspective on his struggles through a lens of criticism, understanding that we are all trying to swim in the ocean, the so-called life, to avoid drowning.

As the evening came to a close, I scratched my head, a habit I have whenever I start to feel sleepy. I tried to ignore the signs that it was time for bed;

instead, I found myself lost in thought. I went upstairs to prepare for sleep, but as I approached the den next to my bedroom, I suddenly stopped. I pulled over my office chair, turned on my laptop, and opened a new Word document. Without intending to write a song, I began typing these two lines:

Verse I
I wasn't born sick, I'm just an addict **(Line 1)**
I'm just an alcoholic **(Line 2)**

The rest was history, lest the rest be rehabilitating and therapeutic. I continued sitting there for another 20 to 30 minutes, and in one sitting, I completed the preceding lines.

I have been fighting this disease **(Line 3)**
I have let a lot of people down **(Line 4)**
Even those who used to look up to me **(Line 5)**
Save me, save me, yes I am addicted **(Line 6)**

Next, I moved on to the chorus. At that moment, I visualized a talented NFL player who was battling addiction and willing to share this part of his personal life. He wasn't sharing his story for fame or attention; his talent had already been widely recognized. I saw the good in Josh's story—a kid crying out for help. I intentionally used the word "help" to reinforce his central message. Although I don't know him personally, I felt I could make a difference through my lyrics.

Chorus
Help me, help me **(Line 1)**
I'm addicted, I'm addicted **(Line 2)**
Yes, I am an addict **(Line 3)**

The chorus was short and sad. In Line 3, I wanted to conclude with a line that conveyed accountability and responsibility. As I wrote "Yes," I felt it was important to capture that sentiment. While watching various interviews on YouTube, I noticed a calm, genuine young man sharing his story to the best of his ability. At no point did he say "No" to struggling. I wanted to emphasize this in the chorus.

After that, writing Verse II came effortlessly for me, both in terms of lyrics and overall ideas. I didn't struggle at all to find the right words or concepts; it felt like I had discovered the needle in the haystack along with the rest of the song, including the bridge.

Verse II
Don't give up on me **(Line 1)**
As I fight adversity **(Line 2)**
Make me part of your family **(Line 3)**
Don't push me away, I'm telling you **(Line 4)**

Line 3, in this line, I used "family" instead of "team." I could have kept the original word, but I second-guessed myself and chose "family" instead. Did the Patriots take a chance on Josh? Yes, yes, and yes! The Patriots took a risk on Josh, just as they had with other players who had past off-the-field issues. That's the Patriots' way. Unfortunately, Josh did not remain a member of the Patriots family for long. On December 18, 2018, the Patriots announced that he was "stepping away from the football field for a bit to focus on his mental health." Hours later, the NFL announced that the Patriots wide receiver had been suspended indefinitely for violating the NFL's substance abuse policy.

Bridge
When I'm away by myself **(Line 1)**
I have another life, life **(Line 2)**
This disease cuts deeper than a knife **(Line 3)**
Don't leave me by myself **(Line 4)**

This message is about raising awareness and hope for those who are fighting this battle. To all the fighters out there, remember that every day you are alive is a victory, so don't give up. If you know anyone facing this struggle, join forces with them to offer the resources and support they may need. This song is dedicated to all the fighters and survivors. Keep on fighting!

Track 02♪♪♪♪♪♪♪♪♪♪♪♪♪♪♪♪♪♪♪♪♪♪♪♪♪♪♪♪♪♪♪♪♪♪♪♪Be Careful What You Wish For

Verse I

We breathe the same air
Yet, you hold my expectations
So high in the air, in the air
Can't even afford a bad day
'Cause in your eyes
I'm walking on water

Chorus

Be careful what you wish for
Cause fame is like a gift and a curse
Like a gift and a curse
Be careful what you wish for
Before you open the door

Verse II

I wish you could see the sacrifice
Leaving my family behind
Making every stop for you
'Cause the show must go on
While you're singing along
My firstborn is prob being born

Verse III

Be careful what you wish for
Cause fame is like a gift and a curse
Like a git and a curse
Be careful what you wish for
Before you open the door

Bridge

I 'd trade places in a heartbeat
So you'd feel my heart racing
With no finish line
I wish you'd stop judging me
'Cause it hurts me
More than you know

Track 02♪♪♪♪♪♪♪♪♪♪♪♪♪♪♪♪♪♪♪♪♪♪♪♪♪♪♪♪♪Be Careful What You Wish For

Chorus

Be careful what you wish for
Cause fame is like a gift and a curse
Like a gift and a curse
Be careful what you wish for
Before you open the door

Track 03♪♪♪♪♪♪♪♪♪♪♪♪♪♪♪♪♪♪♪♪♪♪♪♪♪♪♪♪Despite Everything, Best Believe

Verse I

I was four, when we reached the border
I was sleeping when we got detained
Was told to act ill when they started flashing
Was told to close my eyes
When the tear gas was thrown

Chorus

Despite the journey, I'm reaching
Despite the struggle, I'm fighting
Despite the humiliation, I'm standing
Despite everything, best believe
Despite everything, best believe
I am here, I am here

Verse II

Head barely above water
I was told to swim faster, faster
Oh I was swimming, swimming
Dead bodies floating on water
Was praying I could walk on water
Oh I was praying, praying
I could hear them barking and screaming
Get them, get them

Chorus

Despite the journey, I'm reaching
Despite the struggle, I'm fighting
Despite the humiliation, I'm standing
Despite everything, best believe
Despite everything, best believe
I am here, I am here

Track 03♪♪♪♪♪♪♪♪♪♪♪♪♪♪♪♪♪♪♪♪♪♪♪♪♪♪♪♪♪♪Despite Everything, Best Believe

Verse III

I was told to go back on the boat
I was left in the river
Like the river they kept running
I could see them crying and trembling
When I was being taken away
I was told that I smelled
I could see them trying to run away
Like the waves more kept coming

Chorus

Despite the journey, I'm reaching
Despite the struggle, I'm fighting
Despite the humiliation, I'm standing
Despite everything, best believe
Despite everything, best believe
I am here, I am here

Track 04♪♪♪Fame

Verse I

Before the fame
Before you ever knew me
Only dimes under my name
I was poor, but happy poor
Now with fame
I'm unhappy with all this wealth

Chorus

Be careful what you wish for
Cause fame is like a gift and a curse
Like a gift and a curse
I say fame is like a gift and a curse
Be careful what you wish for
Before you open the door

Verse II

Before no one cares
Now pictures being taken
I wish some could be untaken
Videos being posted behind the scene
I guess with fame
Nothing will never be the same

Chorus

Be careful what you wish for
Cause fame is like a gift and a curse
Like a gift and a curse
I say fame is like a gift and a curse
Be careful what you wish for
Before you open the door

Bridge

I hope you get the picture
That I'm struggling
With fame

Track 04♪♪Fame

Chorus

Be careful what you wish for
Cause fame is like a gift and a curse
Like a gift and a curse
I say fame is like a gift and a curse
Be careful what you wish for
Before you open the door

Track 05♪♪♪Famous

Verse I

Where were you in the midst of it all?
When I was stuck on the side of the roads
When I was lost in the hills
Tryin' to make it to Hollywood
Where were you?
When I was chasing this dream
Where were you?

Chorus

You should've listened to me
Believed me (me), loved me (loved me)
Before the fame
Now you can't have me, what a shame
I'm finally famous, famous

Verse II

Now I'm famous
Settin' the world on fire
You feel the flame of my fame
You remember my name
Can you hear the crowd? Can you?
Dreams do come true (come true)

Chorus

You should've listened to me
Believed me (me), loved me (loved me)
Before the fame
Now you can't have me, what a shame
I'm finally famous, famous

Verse III

You couldn't stand me (Remember?)
You told me I never stood a chance
Now I'm standin' on the biggest stage
You wanna stand by me
Telling me you're so happy for me
Now you wanna be a fan
I'm sorry you aint a stan

Track 05♪♪Famous

Chorus

You should've listened to me
Believed me (me), loved me (loved me)
Before the fame
Now you can't have me, what a shame
I'm finally famous, famous

Track 06♪♪Forgive Me

Verse I

I should have known better
Not to hurt the girl I truly love
Sorry I've let you down
I don't even have the courage
To face you and tell you my wrongs
So I wrote all my wrongs in this song

Chorus

Oh girl, please forgive me
I know I don't deserve you
So I 'm begging you
Please forgive me

Verse II

Since you've been gone
I feel like I've been knocked down
You were right, when it rains it pours down
I'm prayin' the rain washes away
All the pain that I have caused
'Cause I don't wanna lose you

Chorus

Oh girl, please forgive me
I know I don't deserve you
So I 'm begging you
Please forgive me

Verse III

Your friends hated me from day one
Keep telling you I ain't the one
The truth is I hate myself
For not proving them wrong
Instead I chose to mess around
I don't know what I was thinking

Chorus

Oh girl, please forgive me
I know I don't deserve you
So I 'm begging you
Please forgive me

Track 06♪♪Forgive Me

Bridge

They say forgiveness will set you free
I'm hoping I am forgiven
Cause you deserve to be free

Chorus

Oh girl, please forgive me
I know I don't deserve you
So I 'm begging you
Please forgive me

Track 07♪♪♪♪♪♪♪♪♪♪♪♪♪♪♪♪♪♪♪♪♪♪♪♪♪♪♪I Don't Forgive and I Don't Forget

Verse I

How dare you asking me for forgiveness
You gotta be kidding me
Get out my face
I should've slapped you in your face
Cheating on me with your ex
Leaving our bed a mess

Chorus

Stop asking for forgiveness
Cause I don't forgive and forget (my goodness)
Better get on your knees and pray (my goodness)
'Cause only God forgives and forgets
Don't you ever forget
I don't forgive and forget

Verse II

I wish you'd stop texting me
Stop it, I ain't your babe
Save it for someone else
'Cause I'm seeing someone else
I've already crossed you out with an X
Stop with the follow requests

Chorus

Stop asking for forgiveness
Cause I don't forgive and forget
(my goodness)
Better get on your knees and pray
(my goodness)
'Cause only God forgives and forgets
Don't you ever forget, don't forget and forgive

Verse III

You thought I'd be crying and depressed
You must have forgotten
I got an S tattooed on my chest
better check yourself
Cause I've already checked myself
Just got a see thru dress for my next

Track 07♪♪♪♪♪♪♪♪♪♪♪♪♪♪♪♪♪♪♪♪♪♪♪♪♪I Don't Forgive and I Don't Forget

Chorus

Stop asking for forgiveness
Cause I don't forgive and forget (my goodness)
Better get on your knees and pray
(my goodness)
'Cause only God forgives and forgets
Don't you ever forget
I don't forgive and forget

Bridge

You should've at least cleaned your mess
Im not accepting you back in my life
Ever again, so

Chorus

Stop asking for forgiveness
Cause I don't forgive and forget
(my goodness)
Better get on your knees and pray
(my goodness)
'Cause only God forgives and forgets
Don't you ever forget, don't forget and forgive

Track 08♪♪I'm Done

Verse I

Did you ever love me?
Did you ever?
Don't you put your hands on me again
Stop with the "I love you babe"
I'm done, I'm done crying
Done covering up my scars
Done being the CoverGirl for you

Chorus

Since you can't seem to stop
I'm leaving
This time I'm leaving for good
I'm done
This time I'm done for good

Verse II

I had enough of the excuses
I'm done putting a nice smile
On my face for you
I'm done trying to please you
Nothing I do is ever good enough
I should've left a long time ago
Like yesterday, yesterday

Chorus

Since you can't seem to stop
I'm leaving
This time I'm leaving for good
I' done
This time I'm done for good

Verse III

You can't hold me hostage anymore
Cause I'm not scared of you, no more
I'm strong, beautiful and independent
I'm done living in the shower
washing away blood stains
I'm done sitting in the tub
soaking my bruises and sprains

Track 08♪♪♪I'm Done

Chorus

Since you can't seem to stop
I'm leaving
This time I'm leaving for good
I'm done
This time I'm done for good

Track 09♪♪♪ In Thin Air

Verse I

Fame, it's so overwhelming
Yet, I try to please you everyday
Even when my world's spinning
I pretend everything's okay
I've been in and out of rehab, crying

Chorus

I love the fame, being on stage
But I wish you'd get me out this cage
Before I lose my mind
Before I vanish in thin air (In thin air)
I hope you treat me fair

Verse II

We breathe the same air
Yet, you hold my expectations
So high in the air
Can't even afford a bad day
'Cause in your eyes I walk on water

Chorus

I love the fame, being on stage
But I wish you'd get me out this cage
Before I lose my mind
Before I vanish in thin air (In thin air)
I hope you treat me fair

Verse III

I've gone thru all the blood and tears
You wouldn't know
'cause you're on the outside looking in
But I think you should know
I bleed just like you, I can only take it so far

Chorus

I love the fame, being on stage
But I wish you'd get me out this cage
Before I lose my mind
Before I vanish in thin air (In thin air)
I hope you treat me fair

Track 10♪♪Never Too Late

Verse I

I should've told you
I love you from the start
Now you're in love with someone else
It's true, that I've accepted the fact
But, my heart hasn't gotten the memo
It's still chasing you, chasing you

Pre-Chorus

I wish you nothing but the best
Then again babe

Chorus

My love for you will never expire
If things don't work out, let me know
'Cause its never too late
It's never too late, oh no
It's never too late

Verse II

Even though years have gone by
My true feelings haven't died
But, I got tears in my eyes
My love for you hasn't left my heart
Even when I try to kiss it good-bye
It just won't leave, won't leave

Pre-chorus

I wish you nothing but the best
Then again babe

Chorus

My love for you will never expire
If things don't work out, let me know
'cause its never too late
It's never too late, oh no
It's never too late

Track 10♪♪♪Never Too Late

Bridge

My heart is paying the price
No one is paying attention to me
At least you have someone
Paying attention to you daily
Kissing you goodnight
Not me, it's just me, myself and I

Pre-chorus

I wish you nothing but the best
Then again babe

Chorus

My love for you will never expire
If things don't work out, let me know
'Cause its never too late
It's never too late, oh no
It's never too late

Track 11♪♪♪Seasonal Love (Part I)

Verse I
I'm so thirsty of your love
With all due respect
I'm not looking for enduring love
Just looking for seasonal love
'Cause deep down
I know our love won't last long
And the season is too short

Chorus
So babe give and take
I'll give you all my loving
I hope you take it for what it is
Before I leave for the season
'Cause this is seasonal love

Verse II
We can plant our relationship
Like those flowers in the garden
And let it grow under the full moon
As our love is beginning to bloom
I wanna remind you babe

Chorus
So babe give and take
I ll give you all my loving
I hope you take it for what it is
Before I leave for the season
'Cause this is seasonal love

Bridge
Enduring love is an enigma
I hope you understand
Seasonal love

Chorus
So babe give and take
I ll give you all my loving
I hope you take it for what it is
Before I leave for the season
'Cause this is seasonal love
I'll be leaving soon

Track 12♪♪Seasonal Love (Part II)

Verse I

Babe as the leaves start fall-ing
Let's make love till we fall in love
Let's season our love with apples
And make love under the tree
But, I don't see a future beyond fall

Chorus

This is seasonal love, this is seasonal love
Give me all your seasonal loving
Cause this love is seasonally seasoned

Verse II

We have nothing but this season
Let's not think about next season
I just can't
'Cause as the leaves start changing
My love will start fading
I'll be falling out love

Chorus

This is seasonal love, this is seasonal love
Give me all your seasonal loving
Cause this love is seasonally seasoned

Verse III

You look so incredible
Too bad I'll be gone after winter
Let's enjoy it while it lasts
It's a cold world
Let me feel the heat of your body
Let's make love under the blankie

Chorus

This is seasonal love, this is seasonal love
Give me all your seasonal loving
Cause this love is seasonally seasoned

Bridge

True love is an enigma
I hope you understand
Seasonal love babe

Track 12♪♪Seasonal Love (Part II)

Chorus

This is seasonal love, this is seasonal love
Give me all your seasonal loving
Cause this love is seasonally seasoned

Behind the Lyrics

Between the end of 2018 and early 2019, after completing "Seize the Moment," I felt more prepared than ever, as far as improving and enhancing my lyrics, though I still felt skeptical. After several days and weeks of reflecting on whether to resume the submission process, I inhaled and grasped a deep breath of fresh air. Finally, I clicked the send button to submit the tracklist of "Seize the Moment" for review.

Following that, I returned to my usual writing routine, balancing work and spending quality time with my family. Personally, I dislike the idea of interrupting my daily routine, as it can negatively affect my consistency. However, when life seems to be racing by at a hundred miles per second, you may find it necessary to slow down or pause for inexplicable or unjustifiable reasons, in order to get back on track. You have to choose: either slow down or risk burning out and crashing. I opted for the first option. While I completely slowed down, I did not stop writing altogether. Instead, I entered a phase of revisiting and revising unfinished songs. I sifted through sticky notes and receipts to see if I had inadvertently overlooked anything, taking the time to transcribe existing lyrics into Word documents.

As I drove down memory lane, revisiting old materials and reflecting on my journey as a lyricist, I had a Kodak moment of clarity. With a million dollar-smile and a sense of gratitude on my face, I felt a deep sense of joy—not just lyrically, but academically as well. However, in the end, I realized that I had no tangible rewards or recognition to show for my efforts—nothing at all, zero, zip.

All I have ever wanted as a lyricist is to see either my first and last name, Manley Petit or my alias "Patience The Ghostwriter," included in the song credits section. Nothing more, nothing less. Until that day arrives, I can only pray and hope for a breakthrough, just a break to get through the next phase.

As a result, I constantly battled the voices in my mind that told me I wasn't good enough and that it was time to wake up and stop dreaming. Meanwhile, Rachel, the Writer Relations Coordinator, continued to provide feedback that was often unhelpful and constructive.

After countless exchanges—email after email, revision after revision—my revision history grew so extensive that I felt like I needed a two-story house just to store and organize it all. However, I maintained my composure and continued to resubmit my revisions.

This process became a burden, and I found myself contemplating giving up once again. This time, though, it seemed like the best option, if not the only option I had at that moment. I was mentally drained and physically exhausted from traveling down this seemingly futile path. There were no signs of success, only potholes, speed bumps, and guardrails that made it feel like something was constantly holding me back.

I even considered letting go of what I called the "rope of hope." However, when I thought about abandoning the journey I began 14 years ago in 2005, in the cellar at 112 Methuen Street, something unimaginable happened. I received the correspondence below, which made me believe not only that dreams do come true, but also that they are built on patience, consistency, and perseverance. I deeply believe in every sense of these words. More importantly, this email reinforced my belief that "Man proposes, but God disposes," in a religious sense.

Feedback I

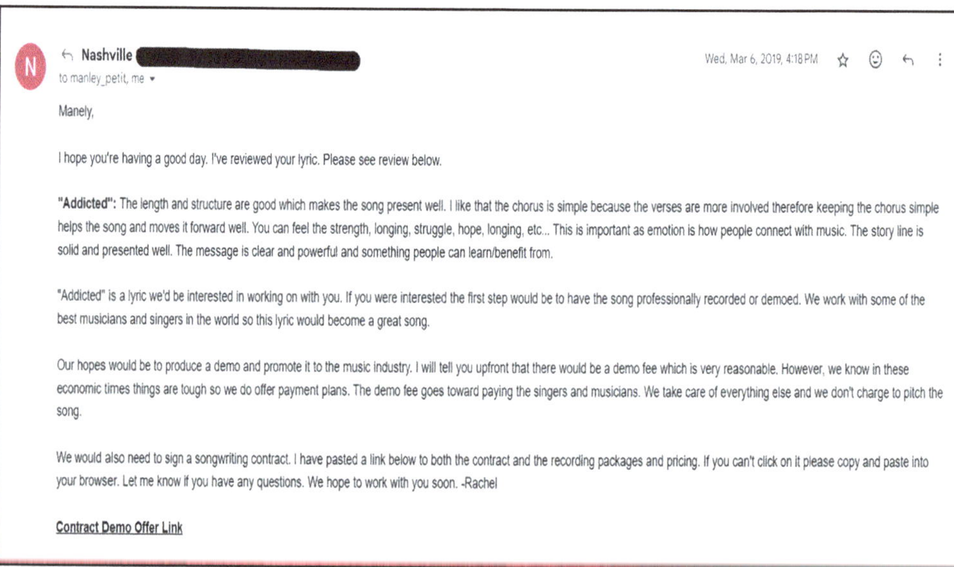

Nashville

to manley_petit, me

Wed, Mar 6, 2019, 4:18 PM

Manely,

I hope you're having a good day. I've reviewed your lyric. Please see review below.

"Addicted": The length and structure are good which makes the song present well. I like that the chorus is simple because the verses are more involved therefore keeping the chorus simple helps the song and moves it forward well. You can feel the strength, longing, struggle, hope, longing, etc... This is important as emotion is how people connect with music. The story line is solid and presented well. The message is clear and powerful and something people can learn/benefit from.

"Addicted" is a lyric we'd be interested in working on with you. If you were interested the first step would be to have the song professionally recorded or demoed. We work with some of the best musicians and singers in the world so this lyric would become a great song.

Our hopes would be to produce a demo and promote it to the music industry. I will tell you upfront that there would be a demo fee which is very reasonable. However, we know in these economic times things are tough so we do offer payment plans. The demo fee goes toward paying the singers and musicians. We take care of everything else and we don't charge to pitch the song.

We would also need to sign a songwriting contract. I have pasted a link below to both the contract and the recording packages and pricing. If you can't click on it please copy and paste into your browser. Let me know if you have any questions. We hope to work with you soon. -Rachel

Contract Demo Offer Link

I had written "Addicted" based on NFL player Josh Gordon (WR), someone I had never met and likely never would meet. At the time, I did not think much of the song I was writing as I sat in the den composing the first two verses:

Verse I
I wasn't born sick, I'm just an addict **(Line 1)**
I'm just an alcoholic **(Line 2)**

When I should have gone to bed, when I should have called it a night, these song lyrics answered the call, putting my dream back in the right direction, or pushing it forward after fourteen years of writing, countless used pens, and countless notebooks filled with chicken scratch or messy notes. I sat in the basement, regardless of how cold it was, scratching my hair for ideas as if trying to remove dandruff.

Moments like this are truly inexplicable and unforgettable. They must be embraced. When I opened my email inbox and saw the positive feedback—boy! It was priceless and left me breathless, and needed oxygen. I was so taken aback that I needed to take a moment to catch my breath. I must have read that email three or four times that day. Who would have thought? Addicted would be so dope (as they say in urban slang), without the needle.

I couldn't believe it when I thought to myself, "Holy cow! I actually did it!" I forwarded the email to a few of my supporters and believers who think I have a talent for writing. As I mentioned before, I was born on Tuesday, April 8, 1982. The truth is, after 14 years of patiently honing my craft, musically and lyrically, I can confidently say that **"A Lyricist Was Born."**

- **Date of Birth:** On Wednesday, March 6, 2019 at 4:18 PM, EST
- **Name at birth:** Patience The Ghostwriter
- **Place of birth:** The basement

That afternoon, I felt as if I was driving along Hope Road and promised myself that I would not give up on this dream. I must persevere and seize the moment.

As a result of Rachel's positive review, the recording studio began discussing the possibility of recording "Addicted" and signing a formal contract, something I had never done before. However, I was aware of the stigma surrounding the mistreatment and exploitation of artists by recording studios and labels. I had heard numerous stories in the media about famous artists expressing dissatisfaction, disputing terms, and even filing lawsuits against their labels. So, I thought carefully before proceeding.

After reviewing the contract agreement, my lawyer advised me to proceed with caution and highlighted a few areas that needed clarification. revised key points and language within the proposed document, and I paid the standard production fee.

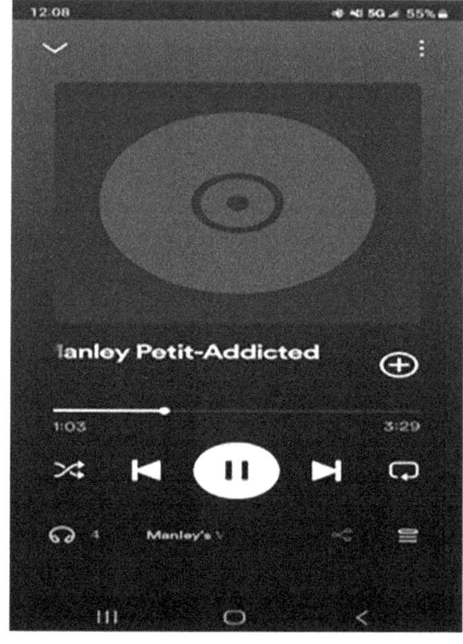

On March 27, 2019, I signed my first recording contract and allowed the recording of "Addicted." More importantly, the contract included a clause stating that once "Addicted" is fully completed and recorded, the recording company can add it to its catalog to pitch to artists.

The process was both educational and inspiring, as it was my first time negotiating and engaging in contract discussions. Honestly, I wouldn't recommend any artist to represent themselves legally; it's best to hire a lawyer. From a legal standpoint, having those back-and-forth discussions could derail your creative thought process and, more importantly, disrupt the moment.

Two and a half weeks passed, and I anxiously anticipated hearing from the recording company. Waiting for the demo or a sneak preview felt like waiting for the release of one of the most anticipated studio albums, "The Blueprint" by Jay-Z.

A few days later, I received some unpolished samples and instrumentals.

On Monday, May 20, 2019, I was notified via email that the demo was completed and attached. I hesitated to download it; after a few agonizing minutes of debate, I finally clicked the download button. With a mix of excitement and anxiety, I pressed play.

Listening to the words I had written set to music was an incredible feeling; it meant so much to me and represented my growth.

However, there always seems to be a "but" or caveat. Initially, I wasn't drawn to "Addicted" because of its beat; I was expecting it to be recorded in a pop or R&B style, which wasn't the case. Instead, "Addicted" was recorded as a country song. It seems the angels above had different plans for this track, wanting listeners to experience something new. As a result, this became my crossover moment—I transitioned into another genre. I didn't dislike the song; in fact, I appreciate country music, recognizing its significance like that of Hip-Hop. However, I'm referring to the classic hip-hop that made us move, like when Lauryn Hill had us grooving to "Doo Wop." I mean the hip-hop that thrived before Nas declared "Hip-Hop Is Dead" in December 2006.

Everything happens for a reason. I listened to "Addicted" repeatedly, and eventually, it grew on me both lyrically and musically. Of course, the lyrics resonated with me because I wrote them, after all! This was my first experience hearing my own words in a song. As I've mentioned before, I wasn't blessed with a musical tone or a natural singing voice. However, I became genuinely addicted to the song, and I shared it with some of the "people" who have supported me throughout this journey—through thick and thin—who had been eagerly awaiting a glimpse of my sound. I finally delivered my first single, which I call "Addicted." This isn't a song for romantic mingling; rather, it's a record meant to uplift those who struggle with addiction. As I write this section of the book, it feels sine qua non to play "Addicted." I'm reminded of the profound power of words.

By the way, I reached out to the recording company to express my concerns about the sound and vibe of "Addicted." They informed me that a song can be demoed in any genre and reassured me that I shouldn't be too worried. The music is being pitched to artists, and if chosen, it could be re-demoed in a completely different genre depending on the artist's style. After considering their explanation, my indecisiveness faded, and I decided their clarification was valid. Once again, I seized the moment.

After birth or a time of naivety, one must grow. I found joy in the success of "Addicted" primarily because I never anticipated it would capture anyone's attention. The lyrics were neither complicated nor straightforward; they consisted of a few verses, a three-line chorus, and a bridge. Nonetheless, it felt like an achievement, albeit I considered it to be very minuscule as I had bigger goals and more growth ahead of me. Thus, I continued my journey along the path to my dreams; I kept writing as if I were dreaming all over again, sitting in front of my computer and pouring my life into my work.

Following "Addicted," I felt that my lyrics needed a form of rehabilitation, as if they were lacking substance—not in an illegal way. They were missing something essential to elevate my work, something that would provide the "it" factor needed to engage the audience and set me apart from other upcoming or established lyricists.

When you truly love something, you must lose yourself in it, even if it means driving miles away or all the way to 8 Mile Road to reach your goal. I was determined and willing to do whatever it took, just as Imagine Dragons reminds me to do in their song, "Whatever It Takes." Writing song lyrics feels like my true calling." As I was made to write song lyrics. This was the moment I had been praying for; this was the moment I had been hoping for—a moment of clarity.

Subsequently, that's when I chose a lane. In terms of music genre, I told myself I would write solely Pop and R&B song lyrics but not eradicate the idea of writing in other genres such as country song lyrics or keep Country song lyrics in my rearview mirror in case an opportunity appears. Until then, I will be driving in my lane, and I have been writing in those two genres ever heretofore.

After reviewing and demonstrating Addicted, I noticed that the positive feedback poured in abundantly. It seems true that when it rains, it pours; my inbox was flooded with positive reviews, along with a few mixed ones. Even Rihanna's umbrella wouldn't be enough to shield me from this deluge!

Feedback II

On Fri, Apr 19, 2019 at 2:21 PM Nashville [redacted] wrote:

Manley,

I hope you're having a good day. I've reviewed your lyric. Please see review below.

"I am Done": The first thing that stands out about the lyric is the emotion that has been captured and expressed. You can feel the fear, exasperation, strength, longing, anger, conviction, etc... This is important as emotion is how people connect with music. The imagery is strong with lines like "Don't you put your hands on me again Stop with the I love you babe I'm done, I'm done crying done covering up my scars", "I'm done putting a nice smile on my face for you I'm done trying to please you Nothing I do is ever good enough", "I'm strong, beautiful & independent I'm done living in the shower washing away blood stains I'm done sitting in the tub soaking my bruises and sprains" which paints the scenes and brings the song to life. Posing questions is good as this engages your listener and makes them think about what you're saying. The story line is powerful.

I like the lyric. -Rachel

Feedback III

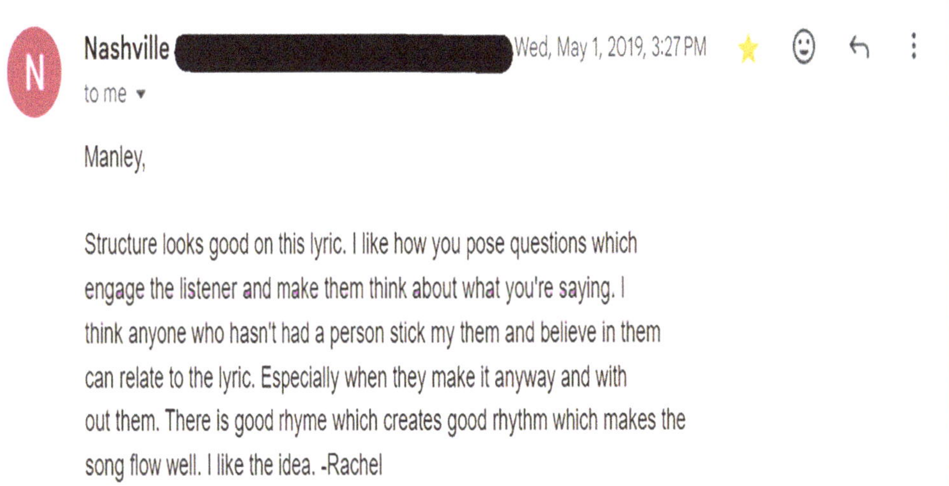
Nashville Wed, May 1, 2019, 3:27 PM

to me

Manley,

Structure looks good on this lyric. I like how you pose questions which engage the listener and make them think about what you're saying. I think anyone who hasn't had a person stick my them and believe in them can relate to the lyric. Especially when they make it anyway and with out them. There is good rhyme which creates good rhythm which makes the song flow well. I like the idea. -Rachel

Feedback IV

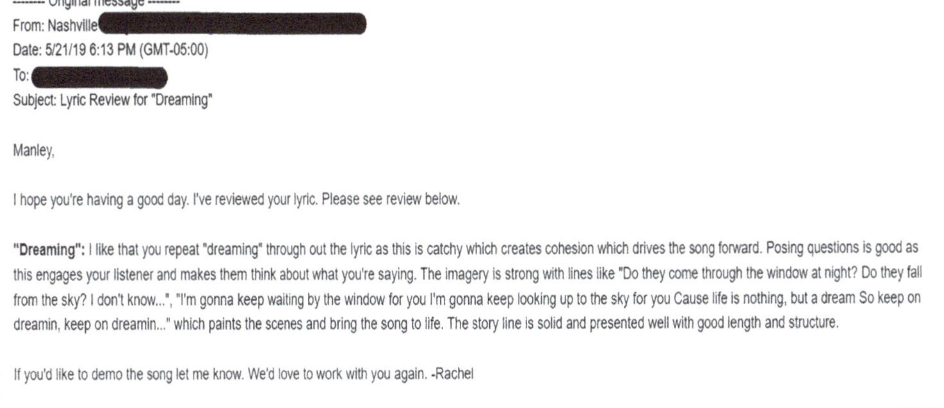
-------- Original message --------

From: Nashville

Date: 5/21/19 6:13 PM (GMT-05:00)

To:

Subject: Lyric Review for "Dreaming"

Manley,

I hope you're having a good day. I've reviewed your lyric. Please see review below.

"Dreaming": I like that you repeat "dreaming" through out the lyric as this is catchy which creates cohesion which drives the song forward. Posing questions is good as this engages your listener and makes them think about what you're saying. The imagery is strong with lines like "Do they come through the window at night? Do they fall from the sky? I don't know...", "I'm gonna keep waiting by the window for you I'm gonna keep looking up to the sky for you Cause life is nothing, but a dream So keep on dreamin, keep on dreamin..." which paints the scenes and bring the song to life. The story line is solid and presented well with good length and structure.

If you'd like to demo the song let me know. We'd love to work with you again. -Rachel

Feedback V

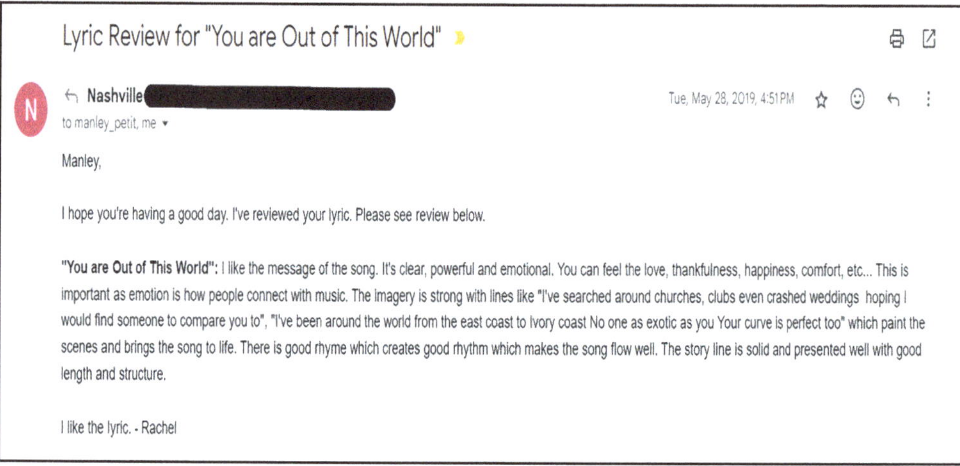

Lyric Review for "You are Out of This World"

Nashville [redacted]
to manley_petit, me

Tue, May 28, 2019, 4:51 PM

Manley,

I hope you're having a good day. I've reviewed your lyric. Please see review below.

"You are Out of This World": I like the message of the song. It's clear, powerful and emotional. You can feel the love, thankfulness, happiness, comfort, etc... This is important as emotion is how people connect with music. The imagery is strong with lines like "I've searched around churches, clubs even crashed weddings hoping I would find someone to compare you to", "I've been around the world from the east coast to Ivory coast No one as exotic as you Your curve is perfect too" which paint the scenes and brings the song to life. There is good rhyme which creates good rhythm which makes the song flow well. The story line is solid and presented well with good length and structure.

I like the lyric. - Rachel

Feedback VI

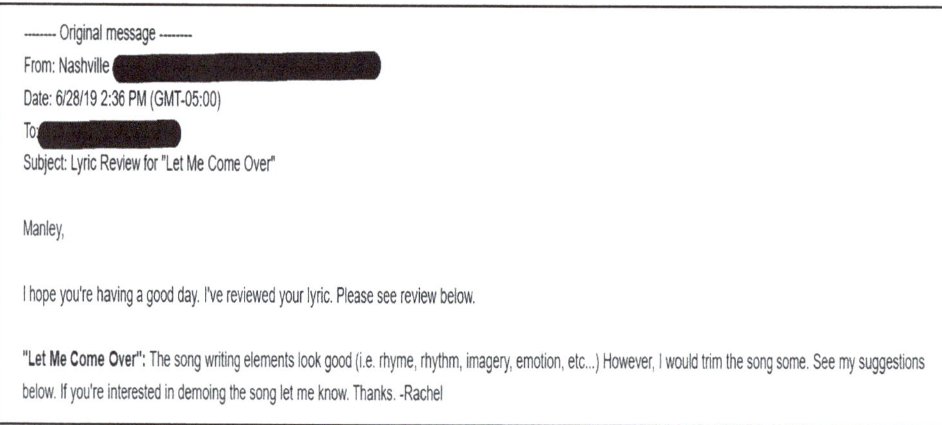

-------- Original message --------
From: Nashville [redacted]
Date: 6/28/19 2:36 PM (GMT-05:00)
To: [redacted]
Subject: Lyric Review for "Let Me Come Over"

Manley,

I hope you're having a good day. I've reviewed your lyric. Please see review below.

"Let Me Come Over": The song writing elements look good (i.e. rhyme, rhythm, imagery, emotion, etc...) However, I would trim the song some. See my suggestions below. If you're interested in demoing the song let me know. Thanks. -Rachel

Thank you for your order!

Your order #466006 (May 15, 2020) at American Songwriter has been completed

ORDER DETAILS

Order Number: 466006 Order Date: May 15, 2020

PRODUCT	QUANTITY	PRICE
Lyric Contest Entry	3	$45.00

SUBTOTAL: $45.00
PAYMENT METHOD: CREDIT CARD
TOTAL: $45.00

Billing address:
Manley Petit

I guess you could say that 2019 was not only the year of my birth but also a period of significant development for me. I was experiencing growth while still putting in the hard work. I continued to write early in the mornings, around 5 or 6 AM, before the world woke up.

I was feeling good about myself. In other words, I was becoming comfortable as a writer. Even though I hadn't topped the music charts or had my name in the credits of a song, I was still confident in my abilities. When it comes to creativity and ambition, my mind is like a New York subway—ideas are constantly running through my mind non-stop. One idea, in particular, enchanted me: I should participate in song or lyric contests. Voila!

After taking this idea to heart, I began browsing the internet for various lyric and song contests. My search yielded several options, but after careful consideration, I decided to enter the monthly American Songwriter Lyric Contest, which has been established since 1984. Before submitting, I thoroughly read the FAQ section of the contest.

Here are the answers to four common questions:

1. How much does it cost? $15 per song.
2. How do I submit my lyrics? Simply copy and paste your lyrics into the form provided.
3. Do I maintain ownership of my lyrics? Yes! We do NOT claim ownership of the materials you submit to the contest.
4. Is the contest international? Yes! The contest is open to anyone in the world.

In the first month, I submitted at least two to three songs, which amounted to forty-five dollars. While it wasn't a significant sum, forty-five dollars is valuable, especially in today's unpredictable economic climate. I viewed it as an investment in my craft, so I didn't lose sleep over it. When the results for that month were announced in the monthly issues of American Songwriter, I learned that I wasn't a winner but a contender. I was okay with this, but after reading the winner's lyrics, I felt a mix of jealousy and envy. I can't say which emotion came first. At the same time, I felt underappreciated and undervalued, convinced that my lyrics deserved recognition

The following month, I entered another set of song lyrics, but the results were the same: I didn't win. However, I didn't get discouraged or stop writing because of the contest losses, although there was a tiny hair follicle of disappointment on my head. I have learned in life you have to pull it, so I plucked it.

The following month was the last time I submitted my song lyrics; they were the same lyrics I had submitted previously. Once again, I did not see my name or my lyrics in the magazine. Although I never became a finalist and my lyrics were never published, I did read many of the winning songs. Some of those songs were indeed impressive in terms of their lyrics.

As the saying goes, I moved on, but the fire within me only bolstered. Honestly, I hated quitting because it's not in my nature. While I no longer participate in those songwriting contests, I recognize their value; they provide artists, including lyricists, a platform to showcase their talents. However, I prefer to pursue my craft in my own way. I estimate I lost about one hundred five dollars in entry fees. The only thing I gained from participating in the American Contest was a free issue of American Songwriter magazine in June or July. In the end, I told myself that one day, I would be on the cover page. Until then, I've moved on, but this time, with a sense of happiness.

ALBUM X
HAPPINESS

"Happiness is like a butterfly, the more you chase it, the more it will elude, but if you turn your attention to other things, it will come and sit softly on your shoulder." Henry David Thoreau.

How do you define happiness? Better yet, can it truly be defined? Is it possible for someone to be perpetually happy? For the past decade, I have been trying to understand what happiness really is. As I approached my mid-thirties and got closer to turning 35, I believed I had figured it all out. I thought that being successful and having everything I ever wanted in life would lead to happiness. All the dreams I had as a child seemed to come true, but I soon realized how wrong I was. I quickly learned that happiness is difficult to define. However, I discovered that my happiest moments occur when I can put a smile on the face of someone I care about deeply and genuinely.

Over the years, I have experienced moments of happiness. My first true encounter with happiness occurred in February 2010, less than a month after the 7.0 magnitude earthquake devastated much of western Haiti. Three weeks later, I flew from Logan Airport in Boston to Santiago, Dominican Republic, as there were no direct flights available to Port-au-Prince, Haiti, due to Toussaint Louverture International Airport being closed in the aftermath of the earthquake.

When I arrived in Santiago late that afternoon, I found that I could not take the bus to Port-Au-Prince because the last bus of the day had already left. As a result, I decided to spend the night in Santiago and catch the bus to Port-Au-Prince the following morning.

As sad as I was, I didn't resist the idea of staying overnight because I was exhausted—not physically, but mentally. I was anxious about what physical condition I would find my mother in. I knew she was alive but had been wounded while being pulled from the rubble of our family's two-story house. Those long, sleepless nights were spent praying in my bed, cuddling with a framed picture of my mother that I had taken off the wall on Wednesday,

January 13, 2010. I kept that picture with me for days, unsure if she had survived. Miraculously, she made it out alive. Thank God for that.

The entire trip felt like a rescue mission. I had one goal: to go to the U.S. Embassy the following day to request a humanitarian visa for my mother so she could relocate to Massachusetts. As night fell, I couldn't sleep; I felt a mix of excitement and nervousness since I hadn't seen her since the spring of 2007. The next day, I hopped on the first bus heading to Port-au-Prince, which was about a five-hour ride. I remember the bus stopping for 15 minutes so people could eat. I don't recall what I ate, but I ended up with an upset stomach, and the heat didn't help, as I was also dehydrated. Fortunately, I was sitting in the back of the bus, right next to the restroom, which meant I didn't have to take a bus trip to take care of business; I mean number two. I must have made at least three trips to the restroom in the first two hours of the journey; my stomach was certainly not cooperating that day.

As we approached the border between Haiti and the Dominican Republic (DR), I witnessed something I could hardly comprehend: Haitians—children, mothers, and babies—were living in conditions that were unimaginable to me. My jaw dropped in disbelief, and I felt sick to my stomach; I had to find a restroom once again because my nausea was overwhelming.

The process took some time, and when I returned to my seat, I noticed the happy faces around me, which puzzled me. How could anyone be happy living in such conditions? As the bus continued its route, I tried to comprehend what I had just witnessed. It was then that I realized that happiness cannot be defined without the word "pursuit."

I reluctantly came to a conclusion. I kept thinking, trying to find an answer, and the only explanation I could come up with was that those faces reflected hope—hope that they might cross the border. Despite living in unbearable conditions, they were engaged in the very human endeavor of pursuing happiness.

The second memorable moment was the smile on my mom's face when the Ambassador approved her visa application to become a permanent resident of the United States. You can't put a price on that. This album is about my pursuit of happiness.

Tracklist

01. **Broken Record**
02. **Take Me Back**
03. **Winner**
04. **Let Him Go**
05. **Miles Away**
06. **All Season**
07. **Deja Vu**
08. **Fire Of Love**
09. **We Gonna Have Fun**
10. **Every Day**

Track 01♪♪♪Broken Record

Verse I

Listen, I don't do well with farewell
Between me and you, I'm sad, mad
At the same time, I'm fine
To tell you the truth boo
My heart is traveling, traveling
All over the place in a suitcase
Like a nomad searching, searching
For anything to hold onto you

Pre-chorus

Here you are, telling me, you love me
Telling me "it's not you, it's me"
Telling me, I just need some time
For the record, if you mean it this time

Chorus

Promise me you'll let the melody
Of our first kiss
Plays in your mind over and over
Like a broken record
Like a broken record
Put me on repeat, so you hear
The sound of my heartbeat
Beating for you over and over
Like a broken record

Verse II

But listen, while you're out there
Hope you stay faithful, fair
And be aware, aware
If you kiss Becky with the good hair
I won't be waiting in my bedroom
Like a patient in a waiting room
Hoping, you'll call me soon
To take my body to the moon

Track 01♪♪Broken Record

Pre-chorus

Here you are, telling me, you love me
Telling me "it's not you, it's me"
Telling me, I just need some time
For the record, if you mean it this time

Chorus

Promise me you'll let the melody
Of our first kiss
Plays in your mind over and over
Like a broken record
Like a broken record
Put me on repeat, so you hear
The sound of my heartbeat
Beating for you over and over
Like a broken record

Bridge

It's not like I don't trust you
But, you've broken my heart before
with broken promises
So, before you walk out that door
Out that door, out that door

Chorus

Promise me you'll let the melody
Of our first kiss
Plays in your mind over and over
Like a broken record
Like a broken record
Put me on repeat, so you hear
The sound of my heartbeat
Beating for you over and over
Like a broken record

Outro

Oh, oh, that Beep! Beep!
You hear in your ear
Is the sound of my heartbeat
Playing for you over and over
Like a broken record, broken record

Behind the Lyrics

Here we are again with another session of "Behind the Lyrics." This song tells the story of a brokenhearted woman who is setting her boyfriend free. Although she still loves him deeply, she encourages him to explore the world, take some time for himself, and find self-love. Ultimately, she hopes he will return, not as someone heartbroken or looking for a rebound, but fully committed to a long-term relationship. Despite the pain and sadness of the situation, she is willing to wait for him, with one condition: that he makes a promise to her.

Verse I

I wrote from the perspective of this brokenhearted woman. While the verse does not explicitly capture her boyfriend's side of the conversation or the events that led to her reaction, it reflects her response to his sudden change of heart. Once again, he tells her that he loves her but wants to take another break, which is a pattern he has established. Her first response is:

Listen, I don't do well with farewell **(Line 1)**
Between you and me, I'm sad, mad **(Line 2)**
At the same time, I'm fine **(Line 3)**

Since I chose "Broken Record" as the title of the song, with "broken" derived from the adjective "brokenhearted," I decided to start the song with the word "listen." When I hear the term "broken record," the first thing that comes to mind is those vinyl records my family used to play repeatedly during my adolescence. I believe this is a catchy way for the artist to express her emotions and capture the attention she deserves. Additionally, I see the introduction of any song as akin to a first date; you want to impress your date and leave a positive first impression. Moreover, she is emotionally drained, expressing all her feelings upon hearing the news of his departure, as outlined in Lines 2 and 3.

As I mentioned earlier, this is the introductory or background phase of the song. I wanted to avoid revealing too much, as I aim to keep the audience engaged and intrigued. By providing minimal information, I hope to build anticipation. We will explore the concept of anticipation in more depth as we approach the Pre-Chorus, which is one of my favorite sections of this song.

As a writer and lyricist, I often struggle with connecting to my audience and listeners. At this stage, all I have are words. In the past, I would write without a clear understanding of the emotions or feelings I wanted to convey. I still face this challenge because I have never performed on stage in front of an audience, meaning I haven't had the opportunity to witness live reactions. This is why I must be very creative and imaginative when illustrating the girl's emotions, particularly her mixed feelings. I have no idea how an audience would react during a live event like Coachella or the Grammys. One reason I specifically chose the three emotional words "sad," "mad," and "fine" is to express the girl's feelings, highlighting her mixed emotions as she realizes that her relationship is coming to an end. She might be in denial or perhaps just confused. At one point, I was unsure how to write this line, so I took a fifteen-minute break to reflect on my past relationships. I hoped to find a specific scenario that could inform the song and make it more relatable.

To tell you the truth boo **(Line 4)**
My heart is traveling, traveling **(Line 5)**
All over the place in a suitcase **(Line 6)**

Line 4 resonates deeply with me as a man because "truth" is a vital element in any relationship—be it friendship or partnership. Historically, we men have often been criticized for lacking communication and trust. Ultimately, one cannot have a healthy and honest relationship without truth. I wanted to illustrate how trustworthy and transparent she is as a woman, even though her boyfriend is about to leave her. Despite this, she expresses herself with no restraint.

Her heart is "traveling, traveling." I could have chosen a different word, but I wanted each line to intertwine metaphorically. If I had used the word "leaving" instead—"Boo, my heart is leaving, leaving"—it would have turned into a mundane and hopeless story.

I then continued with, "all over the place in a suitcase." This line came to me during a run in June 2020, when the world was still grappling with the COVID-19 pandemic and health authorities were drafting and implementing new policies and protocols. Local agencies were also adapting to the new reality. I vividly remember that early morning when I was returning from my fifteen-minute run. As I stopped near the football field to catch my breath, I noticed the birds chirping and wandering around the college campus. I wished I could travel like them. At that time, our society felt trapped; COVID-19 had stripped away our freedom, and we were living in isolation.

Like a nomad searching, searching **(Line 7)**
For anything to hold onto you **(Line 8)**

Regardless of the circumstances, a grain of hope remains in her mind, as reflected in the above lines.

Pre-Chorus

Telling me "it's not you, it's me" **(Line 2)**
Telling me, I just need some time **(Line 3)**
For the record, if you mean it this time **(Line 4)**

This is an extension of Verse I, where she reflects on what he typically says to her before each breakup. For example, he often uses a familiar phrase to try to alleviate the pain, but the question remains: will it be effective? That is yet to be determined or written. Line 4 is written with a different tone to set the stage for the anticipation leading up to the Chorus. She wants to clarify that if he intends to return, he must...

Before I dive into the chorus, allow me to provide a history of the pre-chorus. Initially, the pre-chorus was written as follows:

Original Version

I love you, I really do boo
But I understand you want a break
Take the time to love yourself
'Cause I want what we have to work
Even on Labor day, but for the record

Final Version or Edited Version

Here you are, telling me, you love me
Telling me "it's not you, it's me"
Telling me, I just need some time
For the record, if you mean it this time

Which version do you prefer? Do you have any suggestions? Please speak now or forever hold your breath.

Chorus

Up to this point, I have not disclosed her request. First and foremost, she wants him to remain faithful. Secondly, she wants him to recall their good days and replay those memories in his mind like a broken record, as described below:

Promise me you'll let the melody **(Line 1)**
Of our first kiss **(Line 2)**
Plays in your mind over and over **(Line 3)**

Like a broken record **(Line 4)**

Verse II

Hope you stay faithful, fair **(Line 2)**
And be aware, aware **(Line 3)**
If you kiss Becky with the good hair **(Line 4)**

She seizes the opportunity to remind him not to mess up: "Kiss Becky with the good hair." This line is a reference to "Sorry" by Beyoncé. It came to me naturally as I had been thinking about the words "aware" and "fair," and then the word "hair" popped into my mind.

I won't be waiting in my bedroom **(Line 5)**
Like a patient in a waiting room **(Line 6)**
Hoping, you'll call me soon **(Line 7)**
To take my body to the moon **(Line 8)**

These lines, outlined above, are probably my favorite lines because they contain some sexy, beautiful, and romantic rhymes at the end. Just so you know, I used the word "moon" as a metaphor for reaching climax or orgasm to spice things up in the bedroom.

Bridge

With broken promises **(Line 3)**
So, before you walk out that door **(Line 4)**
Out that door, out that door **(Line 5)**

Lastly, we have not crossed the bridge yet, so let's cross over the bridge. She elaborates on why she has given him an ultimatum: it's not a coincidental; it stems primarily from his past behavior of frequently breaking up and always promising that each time would be the last. This pattern is reflected in the last three lines above.

Outro

For the "record," most of my songs do not include an outro, but this particular song would feel "broken" without one.

Oh, oh, that Beep! Beep! **(Line 1)**
You hear in your ear **(Line 2)**
Is the sound of my heartbeat **(Line 3)**

Therefore, I added five additional lines that the listeners, especially her boyfriend, could listen to as the music fades out; reminding him that her heart still beats for him in the succeeding lines.

Track 02♪♪♪Take Me Back

Verse I

Sadly, I am writing this letter
Trying to repair love that I impaired
And as a friendly reminder
Just so you're aware, leaving you
Without saying goodbye wasn't fair
Lately, wish you were here
In my snuggle chair, rubbing my hair
But you way over there to even care

Pre-Chorus

There's no secret, I regret
Choosing someone new, over you
Now that I've learned love ain't sweeter
On this side of town, without you honey

Chorus

Would you take me back?
If I come back to make it right?
If I swallow my pride to be by your side?
Would you take me back?
Would you take me back?
With a broken heart try to win your heart?
If I pour my heart out?
Would you take me back?
Please reply, you'll take me back

Verse II

Since I'm asking for forgiveness
Must confess, getting pain of my chest
One night I miss you so much, rushed
To your home uninvited, there I was
Knees on the floor, knocking on door
Hoping you'd open up, to my surprise
You were there with someone
So I couldn't tell you face to face

Track 02♪♪Take Me Back

Pre-Chorus

There's no secret, I regret
Choosing someone new, over you
Now that I've learned love ain't sweeter
This side of town, when you ain't around

Chorus

Would you take me back?
If I come back to make it right?
If I swallow my pride to be by your side?
Would you take me back?
Would you take me back?
With a broken heart try to win your heart?
If I pour my heart out?
Would you take me back?
Please reply, you'll take me back

Bridge

I wish I had stayed
Then again, had I stayed who's to say
I'd feel this love I'm feeling, feeling
I guess, I had to burn bridges to learn
The road to true love is back to you
Sooo… hon

Chorus

Would you take me back?
If I come back to make it right?
If I swallow my pride to be by your side?
Would you take me back?
Would you take me back?
With a broken heart try to win your heart?
If I pour my heart out?
Would you take me back?
Please reply, you'll take me back

Outro

Before I let go, just wanna know
You'll take me back, you'll take me back

Track 03♪♪♪Winner

Verse I

Have no fear, this ain't just a story
Open your ear, just last year
I was waiting in your lobby
For a record deal
Looked at me like an imbecile
Was told we need a better story
A hit song like a Pop song

Pre-Chorus

As I was leaving
I remember just like yesterday
Management saying
"Maybe next time, have a nice day"
Little did they know, I'd get Radio play

Chorus

Now I'm in your eardrums
Hear the sound of the drums
I ain't no quitter, I am a winner (winner)
I ain't no quitter, I am a winner (winner)
See you later naysayers
I ain't no quitter, I am a winner (winner)
I ain't no quitter, I am a winner (winner)
If you're a dreamer, be a believer
And a winner, winner (winner)

Verse II

Now I'm on stage, Coachella, Nashville
Shows in London, how do you feel?
In NYC, cause dreamers never sleep
Who knew a kid with a broken guitar?
Would make it this big and far
At the ESPYs, winning Grammys
Among so many stars, from Big easy

Track 03♪♪Winner

Pre-Chorus
As I was leaving,
I remember just like yesterday
"When you have something better
Come see me , have a nice day"
Little did they know, I'd get Radio play

Chorus
Now I'm in your eardrums,
Hear the sound of the drums
I ain't no quitter, I am a winner (winner)
I ain't no quitter, I am a winner (winner)
See you later naysayers
I ain't no quitter, I am a winner (winner)
I ain't no quitter, I am a winner (winner)
If you're a dreamer, be a believer
And a winner, winner (winner)

Bridge
Do what makes you happy
the rest is history
I ain't bragging, Record labels keep calling
Wanna sign me, "Have a nice day"
Give them a dose of their own pill,
Of their own pill, cause

Chorus
I ain't no quitter, I am a winner (winner)
I ain't no quitter, I am a winner (winner)
See you later naysayers
I ain't no quitter, I am a winner (winner)
I ain't no quitter, I am a winner (winner)
If you're a dreamer, be a believer
And a winner, winner (winner)

Outro
Hear the sound of the drums, in your eardrums
I am a winner (winner)
I'm a winner (winner)

Track 04♪♪Let Him Go

Verse I

Girl what's going on?
After all these years
Didn't think you'd call
I am sorry to hear
You guys aint getting along
I believe, you've tried your best
To make it work
But he refuses to do his part
Keeps breaking your heart

Pre-chorus

How much should a woman tolerate?
Listen to your heart
Don't be afraid

Chorus

You gotta let him go
You gotta let him go
You're too beautiful, too powerful
To let him break you down
You gotta let him go
You gotta let him go

Verse II

Don't you cry, feeling guilty
Be strong, you're not alone
Come over here, stay with me
Where never-ending love begins
I believe, one man's loss
Is another man's win
I'll take you out his misery
Your body on a journey
Where pain and fear be history

Pre-chorus

How much should a woman tolerate?
Listen to your heart
Don't hesitate

Track 04♪♪Let Him Go

Chorus

You gotta let him go
You gotta let him go
You're too beautiful, too powerful
To let him break you down
You gotta let him go
You gotta let him go

Bridge

I aint no hero
Understand, I'm just a man
Trying to rescue you
But if you believe, taking my hand
Will take you to the promised land

Chorus

You gotta let him go
You gotta let him go
You're too beautiful, too powerful
To let him break you down
You gotta let him go
You gotta let him go

Outro

Oh you, gotta let him go
You gotta let him go

Track 05♪♪Miles Away

Verse I

How could you be so selfish? I wish
You'd stop throwing dirt on my name
Tellin' everyone, I'm the reason we broke up
Go ahead, I'll shoulder the blame
Remember, you're the reason I gave up
Ended up in the wrong lane

Pre-chorus

Everything was your way or the highway
Even, when I'd go the wrong way
To save your day, you still complained
That's when I said

Chorus

It's best if we go our separate ways
'Cause the distance between us
Is miles away, miles away
Like night and day
I ain't staying, no way (no way)
It's best if we go our separate ways
'Cause the distance between us
Is miles away, miles away

Verse II

The truth is, we want the same thing
Freedom and unconditional loving
But, love is a two-way street
With speed bumps and red lights
'Cause we gotta share the road
Pay attention to someone, right?

Pre-chorus

Everything was your way or the highway
Even, when I'd go the wrong way
To save your day, you still complained
That's when I said

Track 05♪♪♪Miles Away

Chorus

It's best if we go our separate ways
'Cause the distance between us
Is miles away, miles away
Like night and day
I ain't staying, no way (no way)
It's best if we go our separate ways
'Cause the distance between us
Is miles away, miles away

Bridge

I tried to give you the world, but I failed
Feel bad till this day
At least, give me an A for effort
No wonder why we crashed

Pre-chorus

Everything was your way or the highway
Even, when I'd go the wrong way
To save your day, you still complained
That's when I said

Chorus

It's best if we go our separate ways
Cause the distance between us
Is miles away, miles away
Like night and day
I ain't staying, no way (no way)
It's best if we go our separate ways
'Cause the distance between us
Is miles away, miles away

Track 06.♪♪♪All Season

Intro

Tired of chasing you, what are we doing?
Should we just move on?

Verse I

Like the season
You never give me a reason
To fall or stay in love with you
Just like the season
You keep changing on me
Even at the four seasons
Barely turning me on (c'mon)

Pre-chorus

One day, your love's hotter
Than Haiti
One day, your love's colder
Than DC
What are we doin'? (c'mon)

Chorus

Please let me know now
'Cause I want your love
All season long
From summer till I fall
I'm listenin' (c'mon)
Please let me know now
'Cause I wanna make love
All season long
From winter till I'm sprung
I'm listenin' (c'mon)
Please let me know now

Track 06♪♪All Season

Verse II

After everything you
Have put me through
Ain't gonna stop loving you
Even though, we both know
You're usin' me like a rebound
Like crazy glue, I stick around
Let love knock me down ('c'mon)

Pre-chorus

One day, your love's hotter
Than Houston
One day, your love's colder
Than Boston
What are we doin'? (c'mon)

Chorus

Please let me know now
'Cause I want your love
All season long
From summer till I fall
I'm listenin' (c'mon)
Please let me know now
'Cause I wanna make love
All season long
From winter till I'm sprung
I'm listenin' (c'mon)
Please let me know now

Bridge

As you know
Season comes and go
Can't promise I won't say so long
After this song
So babe, come season my body
With a teaspoon of love soon

Track 06♪♪♪All Season

Chorus

Please let me know now
'Cause I want your love
All season long
From summer till I fall
I'm listenin' (c'mon)
Please let me know now
'Cause I wanna make love
All season long
From winter till I'm sprung
I'm listenin' (c'mon)
Please let me know now

Outro

'Cause all season long, is way to long
So let me know, let me know, now

Track 07♪♪Deja Vu

Intro

Hey! WYA? It's that time again. Text me. lol

Verse I (Female Singer)

Just left club Liv, I wanna leave
It's 5:22, been waitin' on you
Homegirl left without me
I'm waitin' in the lobby
Can't sleep without you
Even a melatonin won't do

Pre-chorus

Beggin' you, beggin' you
You know I never ask you
For anything, don't you?

Chorus (Duet)

Where are you boo?
I'm at the Fontainebleau
By the ocean view
Havin' déjà vu
My body surfin' on top of you
For an hour or two (oui boo)
Its a rendez vous
I'm at the Fontainebleau
By the ocean view
Havin' déjà vu
My body surfin' on top of you
For an hour or two

Verse II (Male Singer)

Wish I could tell you boo
On the phone how, bad I want you
Please stay, I'm on my way
Business as usual, black suit
Hoping you would follow suit
In your birthday suit

Pre-chorus

Beggin' you, beggin' you
You know I never ask you
For anything, don't you?

Track 07♪♪Deja Vu

Chorus (Duet)

Where are you boo?
I'm at the Fontainebleau
By the ocean view
Havin' déjà vu
My body surfin' on top of you
For an hour or two (oui boo)
Its a rendez vous
I'm at the Fontainebleau
By the ocean view
Havin' déjà vu
My body surfin' on top of you
For an hour or two

Bridge (Duet)

Didn't make it to the bedroom
Body sweepin' the lobby restroom
Like a broom (Knock! Knock!)
Security telling us to get a room
Give us another hour or two

Chorus (Duet)

Where are you boo?
I'm at the Fontainebleau
By the ocean view
Havin' déjà vu
My body surfin' on top of you
For an hour or two (oui boo)
Its a rendez vous
I'm at the Fontainebleau
By the ocean view
Havin' déjà vu
My body surfin' on top of you
For an hour or two

Outro

I don't need much time boo
Just an hour or two
So come give my body
That déjà vu, oui boo

Track 08♪♪♪Fire of Love

Verse I

Are we better as friends?
Are we friends with benefits?
Only asking 'cause our relationship
Is like a dead-end
We keep messing around and then
You go left, I go right, either way
We end up in the same place
Making love next to the fireplace

Pre-chorus

Don't want either of us to get burnt
But, if I have to let love burn to learn
So, once and for all, before we fall

Chorus

In the fire of love
Are we friends? Are we lovers?
In the fire of love
Are we friends? Are we lovers?
Please tell me
Are we friends? Are we lovers?
'Cause I am falling
In the fire of love (fire of love)
In the fire of love (fire of love)

Verse II

We had tried to be lovers
When we were younger, a disaster
Wish we could start over
I'd be better, but now we're older
You have a lover, I have a lover
Loving you is such a danger
'Cause every time we touch
We add more fuel to tinder

Pre-chorus

Don't want either of us to get burnt
But, if I have to let love burn to learn
So, once and for all, before we fall

Track 08♪♪Fire of Love

Chorus

In the fire of love
Are we friends? Are we lovers?
In the fire of love
Are we friends? Are we lovers?
Please tell me
Are we friends? Are we lovers?
'Cause I am falling
In the fire of love (fire of love)
In the fire of love (fire of love)

Bridge

Love it, when you whisper my name
Even though, I feel guilty, ashamed
Knowing you have his last name
I try to put the fire out
Like a firefighter, as it turns out
I can't, cause loving you
Burns deeper than wildfires
In southern California, woo!

Chorus

In the fire of love
Are we friends? Are we lovers?
In the fire of love
Are we friends? Are we lovers?
Please tell me
Are we friends? Are we lovers?
'Cause I am falling
In the fire of love (fire of love)
In the fire of love (fire of love)

Behind the Lyrics

Being an artist is like living in a fantasy world, where the mind can be twisted and imaginative, leading to the creation of marvelous art. Here, I'd like to share my thoughts on what inspired me to pen "Fire of Love." So, sit back and relax while you enjoy this book. Hopefully, you are near a fireplace with a glass of wine—red or white—whichever one ignites your own fire of love. Without further ado, let the "Fire of Love" burn, just as Usher sings, "Let it Burn!"

"Fire of Love" took me a full year to write. I began working on it in the early spring of 2021 and completed the bridge on April 17, 2022, which is just eight days after my birthday. You could say it was a late birthday present.

This song tells the story of a clandestine affair between two ex-lovers who remain undeniably in love. Although they are both in committed relationships, they have secretly rekindled their bond—not in a sexual way, but amicably. As their fire of love begins to ignite, the status of their relationship comes into focus, raising a multitude of unanswered questions. Consequently, one of the lovers must take action into their own hands.

Title

How do you choose a title? How can you be sure you have the "right" title? Selecting the perfect title for a song can be time-consuming. In my early years, it felt like a full-time job, often requiring overtime.

Initially, I would have a title in mind before I started writing a song. However, as the story developed, the original title often became irrelevant.

As a result, I've changed my technique over the last three years. I now focus less on titles and allow the verses, chorus, bridge, or other sections of the song to inspire the title. Initially, the song was titled "Better as Friends," which derived from the first line of Verse 1, outlined below.

Are we better as friends? **(*Line 1*)**

However, as I began to shift toward the pre-chorus and reviewing every line of Verse I, I discovered a key word embedded in the first verse that grabbed my attention. Can you guess what it is? If you answered " fireplace," you are correct. The word "fireplace" is outlined in Line 8, which rhymes with Line 7. I remember sitting in a chair and deciding to go downstairs to see the fireplace, which had been non-functioning since I purchased the house.

I was inspired to modify the title to "Fire" even though there was no fire burning in the fireplace. I could see it, I could smell the scent of wood burning through the chimney. Subsequently, I thought of the word "Love," but I could not reject the concept of excluding it from the title. Besides, who am I to say no to love?

Verse I

Let's take a closer look at the lyrics in Verse I, shall we? I wrote this verse based on a previous dating relationship. I remember often being asked those questions during my early dating years. To be honest, I never had a perfect answer; I would always try to come up with excuses.

Are we better as friends? **(Line 1)**
Are we friends with benefits? **(Line 2)**

I chose to commence the song with those two lines for these reasons:

1. Posing questions is excellent as it requires or engages the listener to heed or pay attention to what you are saying. In relationships, we often become so enamored with the positive aspects of love that we forget to question its longevity, believing it to be everlasting. The truth is that love can be perplexing. We know there are many unanswered questions that need addressing, yet we often avoid them.
2. Consider your opening line as a welcoming invitation, much like a wedding save-the-date card or an invitation that reads "Please join us." The reader should take a moment to digest the message you're conveying. Similarly, the first line of a song should create an impact, prompting the listener to explore the music more deeply.
3. This approach is communicative for a reason. In tricky or ambiguous situations, people often seek to label a relationship, leading them to ask common questions such as, "What are we?" "Are we just friends?" or "Are we friends with benefits?"

Only asking 'cause our relationship **(Line 3)**
Is like a dead-end **(Line 4)**

Lines 3 and 4 of the song play a crucial role in developing the first verse. As a lyricist, it is essential to address the first two questions within the song; otherwise, the listener may feel intrigued and confused. It's important to provide clues or hints, even if the answers are not perfect.

Pre-Chorus
This is one of my favorite pre-choruses because it feels adventurous and builds heightened anticipation, preparing listeners for the most exciting part of any song: the chorus.

Don't want either of us to get burnt **(Line 1)**
But, if I have to let love burn to learn **(Line 2)**
So, once and for all, before we fall **(Line 3)**

The first line suggests, "I don't want either of us to get caught." The second line implies that if we must get caught to understand the consequences of a clandestine affair, then so be it. But before we face that possibility, what is our relationship status?

Instead of directly asking about our relationship status, I began the chorus with the title as my opening line. This choice aligns perfectly with the end of the pre-chorus. Grammatically, it forms a complete sentence if I combine the two dependent clauses, as illustrated below:

Pre-chorus	**Chorus**
So, once and for all, before we fall **(Line 3)** +	*In the fire of love* **(Line 1)**

Chorus
Are we friends? Are we lovers? **(Line 2)**
In the fire of love **(Line 3)**
Are we friends? Are we lovers? **(Line 4)**
Please tell me **(Line 5)**
Are we friends? Are we lovers? **(Line 6)**

As anticipated with most clandestine relationships, decisions must be made; thus, it should be no surprise that I repeated the lines, "Are we friends? Are we lovers?" three times in the chorus.

'Cause I am falling **(Line 7)**
In the fire of love (fire of love) **(Line 8)**

Line 7 is highly significant because the word "falling" symbolizes falling in love.

Verse II

We had tried to be lovers **(Line 1)**
When we were younger, a disaster **(Line 2)**
Wish we could start over **(Line 3)**

The second verse recalls the history of their relationship before the clandestine affair.

I'd be better, but now we're older **(Line 4)**
You have a lover, I have a lover **(Line 5)**
Loving you is such a danger **(Line 6)**

Lines 4 and 5 emphasize themes of remorse and reflection in the song. As reality sinks in, the characters confront the fact that their romance is becoming increasingly risky and unstable. This intensity could further complicate their already passionate relationship, described as the "Fire of Love."

'Cause every time we touch **(Line 7)**
We add more fuel to tinder **(Line 8)**

Line 8 initially ended with the word "fire," but I changed it to refer to the app Tinder, of which I have never used.

Bridge

In this bridge, my goal was to take a contrasting approach, season the song with more spice, and maintain an atmosphere as hot as an oven, similar to Marvin Gaye's "Sexual Healing."

Love it, when you whisper my name **(Line 1)**
Even though, I feel guilty, ashamed **(Line 2)**

I decided that Line 1, "I love it when you whisper my name," would highlight their intimacy.

Burns deeper than wildfires **(Line 7)**
In southern California, woo! **(Line 8)**

Finally, despite the danger, the last line indicates that their romance will continue unabated, as it "burns deeper than wildfires."

Track 09♪♪We Gonna Have Fun

Verse I

I heard you got dumped, is it really true?
For your best friend, he's such a fool
I know you're hurting and
Can't wait for the night to end
I might not have all the answers
But, I know going to bed with a broken heart
Will hurt even more, even more

Pre-Chorus

Girl let me, let me come over
Before the weekend's over
If you'd like

Chorus

We can go from friends to best friends
From friends to lovers
Whatever pleases you, I promise you
We gonna have fun
Oh yeah, we gonna have fun

Verse II

You don't have to be alone
Let me help you bounce back
I can help you put the pieces
Of a broken heart back together
'Cause' I have learned
One man's loss is another man's treasure
I'll treasure you, like a piece of fine art

Pre-Chorus

Girl let me, let me come over
Before the weekend's over
If you'd like

Chorus

We can go from friends to best friends
From friends to lovers
Whatever pleases you, I promise you
We gonna have fun
Oh yeah, we gonna have fun

Track 09♪♪♪We Gonna Have Fun

Bridge
I've been calling you, can't seem to get thru
Everyone's calling, trying to console you
You prolly debating on what to do
Girl take your time, but remember
You deserve a night to get even, right?
I bet he's having a helluva nite

Pre-Chorus
Girl let me, let me come over
Before the weekend's over
If you'd like

Chorus
We can go from friends to best friends
From friends to lovers
Whatever pleases you, I promise you
We gonna have fun
Oh yeah, we gonna have fun

Track 10♪♪Every Day

Intro

Ay, just so you know

Verse I

It's not easy to find a lover
Let alone find someone like you
Who vows loving forever
Good or bad, you're heaven-sent
You're my angel walking on water
Couldn't ask for a better rescuer

Pre- chorus

I'd never be able to repay you
And buy your heart
But, I can promise you, until you depart

Chorus

I'm gonna make love to you
Every day
Not just on our anniversary day
But every day, every day
Kiss your lips like Hershey's kisses
Not just on valentine's day
But every day, every day
Lift you up like a Superbowl trophy
Not just on your birthday
But every day, every day, every, day

Verse I

Can't believe after all these years
Your love for me is still intact, in fact
Even with a broken back, got my back
Even in a leap year
Always got one day left
To make me smile from ear to ear

Pre- chorus

I'd never be able to repay you
And buy your heart
But, I can promise you, until you depart

Track 10♪♪Every Day

Chorus

I'm gonna make love to you
Every day
Not just on our anniversary day
But every day, every day
Kiss your lips like Hershey's kisses
Not just on valentine's day
But every day, every day
Lift you up like a Superbowl trophy
Not just on your birthday
But every day, every day, every, day

Bridge

As we grow old like yesterday
We may not get another day
Its gonna be hard to say, every day
So today its fair to say

Chorus

I'm gonna make love to you
Every day
Not just on our anniversary day
But every day, every day
Kiss your lips like Hershey's kisses
Not just on valentine's day
But every day, every day
Lift you up like a Superbowl trophy
Not just on your birthday
But every day, every day, every, day

Outro

Not just today, but every day, every, day
Ay, ay, ay, every day

More Positive Feedback

As I was completing the Happiness album, I received a steady stream of positive reviews. I took my sweet time reading each one, appreciating them so much that I could have developed cavities from the sweetness of their words. Each review felt like the heartbeat of my dream; nurturing this dream was crucial. Any joyful feedback I received resonated with me in ways I couldn't fully understand, but I knew that just one line, one verse, or one pre-chorus could be transformative and lead me to my final destination. Therefore, I firmly believe that one day everything will make sense through my six senses. For example, the reviews I received, such as the one illustrated below, demonstrated my growth as a lyricist.

Feedback I_ He Can't

N Nashville [redacted] Thu, Oct 17, 2019, 4:10 PM

to me

You have structure and length down. So now it's about writing unique and different ideas. Something that sets your lyric apart. That different twist on an old idea or a brand new idea. Or a great moving love, etc...

- Rachel

Feedback II_ The Old Days

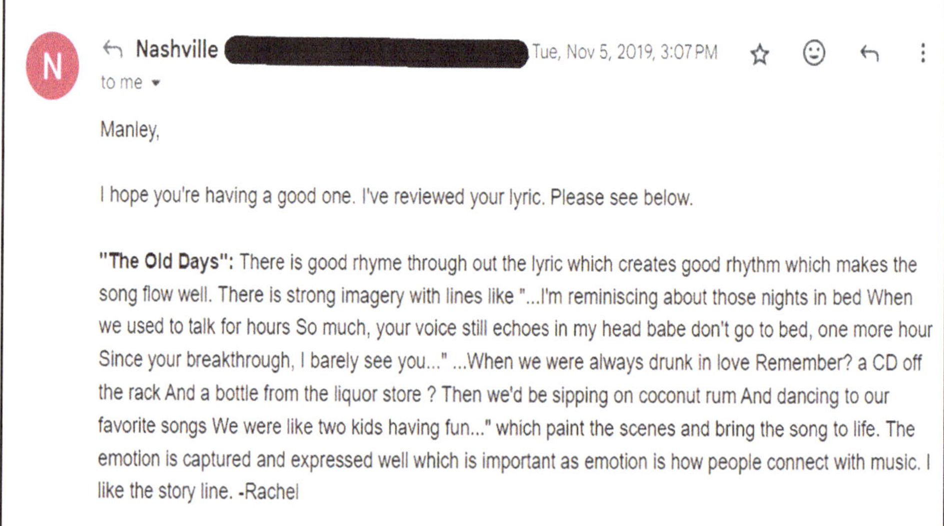

N Nashville [redacted] Tue, Nov 5, 2019, 3:07 PM

to me

Manley,

I hope you're having a good one. I've reviewed your lyric. Please see below.

"The Old Days": There is good rhyme through out the lyric which creates good rhythm which makes the song flow well. There is strong imagery with lines like "...I'm reminiscing about those nights in bed When we used to talk for hours So much, your voice still echoes in my head babe don't go to bed, one more hour Since your breakthrough, I barely see you..." ...When we were always drunk in love Remember? a CD off the rack And a bottle from the liquor store ? Then we'd be sipping on coconut rum And dancing to our favorite songs We were like two kids having fun..." which paint the scenes and bring the song to life. The emotion is captured and expressed well which is important as emotion is how people connect with music. I like the story line. -Rachel

However, I occasionally received mixed reviews—comments like "you are good, but not that good," which were outlined in reviews such as this one.

Feedback III_ The Way You Dance

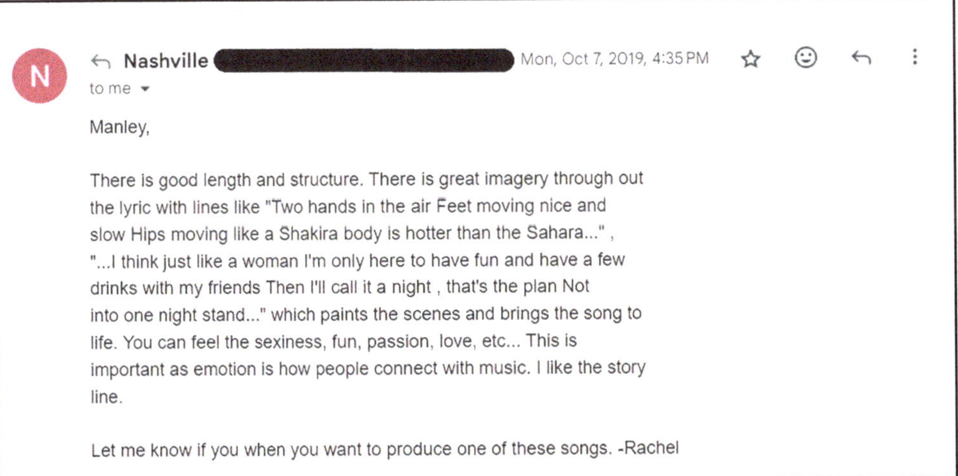

Nashville [redacted] Mon, Oct 7, 2019, 4:35 PM
to me

Manley,

There is good length and structure. There is great imagery through out the lyric with lines like "Two hands in the air Feet moving nice and slow Hips moving like a Shakira body is hotter than the Sahara..." , "...I think just like a woman I'm only here to have fun and have a few drinks with my friends Then I'll call it a night , that's the plan Not into one night stand..." which paints the scenes and brings the song to life. You can feel the sexiness, fun, passion, love, etc... This is important as emotion is how people connect with music. I like the story line.

Let me know if you when you want to produce one of these songs. -Rachel

Feedback IV_ Miles Away

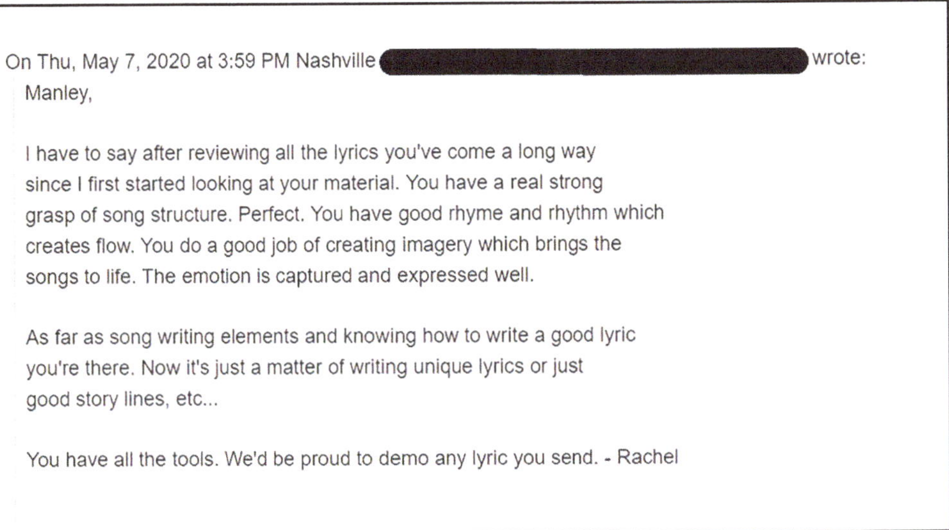

On Thu, May 7, 2020 at 3:59 PM Nashville [redacted] wrote:

Manley,

I have to say after reviewing all the lyrics you've come a long way since I first started looking at your material. You have a real strong grasp of song structure. Perfect. You have good rhyme and rhythm which creates flow. You do a good job of creating imagery which brings the songs to life. The emotion is captured and expressed well.

As far as song writing elements and knowing how to write a good lyric you're there. Now it's just a matter of writing unique lyrics or just good story lines, etc...

You have all the tools. We'd be proud to demo any lyric you send. - Rachel

At this point, I had become unsusceptible to their reviews—whether positive, mediocre, or constructive; I no longer took offense. I welcomed every comment warmly, both musically and lyrically, as long as the reviewer's observations were not intended to undermine my character or integrity. As long as the feedback came from a respectful place, I confidently accepted each one, knowing that I, Patience The Ghostwriter, would create better song lyrics than my previous ones. This became my strategy.

“How can I top my last song? How can I outdo myself? How can I surpass my lyrical intellect?” These were questions I frequently asked myself. Most of the time, I had no clear path forward; however, I knew my pen and notebook would deliver or rescue me.

Honestly, Rachel’s assessment of my songs was spot on, particularly her evaluation of the song “Miles Away,” which is ironically unrelated to distance or mileage. She noted, “You’ve come a long way” (Refer to Feedback IV).

I wholeheartedly agree that I have come a long way, but as the title suggests, I am still “miles away” from my ultimate destination.

Nevertheless, these four reviews meant the world to me, making me feel like I could set the world on fire.

At that moment, no song felt too big or challenging for me to write. I felt capable of conquering the lyrical landscape of Pop, R&B, and even Country music. I had an uncanny feeling, a colossal desire, to promote more songs and share new material because I believed my song lyrics were uniquely different in terms of storyline, rhyme, flow, wordplay, metaphors, and similes. I envisioned better bridges, more engaging intros, and vivid imagery—the whole nine yards—to distinguish my work from other lyricists in the music industry.

I was at peace with my current lyrical progress, so I coincidentally named my next project or album "Peaceful," as serene as the morning breeze on the first day of spring.

ALBUM XI
PEACEFUL

I love each album or chapter of my life like a parent unconditionally loves all their children. However, one cannot refute or deny the existence of nepotism, even though I dislike playing the favorite child game in this context. Yet, I have to choose, and the truth is that this chapter of my life is arguably my favorite for several reasons

- This is where I went from being born as a lyricist to a toddler lyricist
- This album is the fruit of hard labor, dedication, and internal reflection
- I gained a clearer understanding and acceptance of my lyrical, mental, and physical state.
- I abandoned the chase for happiness and found myself once again reaching for peace.

If you often find yourself battling voices, distractions, and nuisances in your head, especially in life, this album is designed to ease those struggles, soothe your mind, and help you feel at peace and **alive**. More importantly, it serves as a reminder that **giving up** is not an option. Even when the road ahead looks unclear and treacherous, and you are **blinded** by the lights every weekend, you must **keep going** because you have the **heart of a champion.** You should continue **dreaming** and taking action, as God will always take care of the impossible. I assure you that everything will be alright one day, and you'll be celebrating **with a bottle of wine,** having the **best time** of your life. In the end, **the way you dance** will not only be a celebration but also a moment of rebirth. And just because your friend says **he can't** achieve something doesn't mean you should stop pursuing your dreams or goals. In reality, those closest to you may unknowingly impart their fears onto you; sometimes, it's intentional, and other times it isn't. To all women, be cautious about who you let into your life; do not let any man **in your bedroom,** even if someone seems down to earth, they might not have your best interests at heart.

Before I continue, what is your favorite song or album thus far? Share it now or **forever hold your peace.**

Tracklist:

01. Ain't Giving Up
02. Alive
03. Best Time
04. Blinded
05. Dreaming
06. Forever Hold Your Peace
07. He Can't
08. Heart of a Champion
09. I'll Be Fine (With A Bottle of Wine)
10. In Your Bedroom
11. Keep Going Back
12. The Way You Dance

Track 01♪♪Ain't Giving Up

Verse I

Everyone's looking for a come up
been patiently waiting for a miracle
Something to get me on top
I'm on the sidewalk looking up
People having fun on the rooftop
They have made it, so bottoms up
I'm still on the bottom, so head down

Pre-chorus

I am hearing don't quit your day job
This ain't for you
You should change a few things here and there
I hear you

Chorus

But I ain't giving up, I ain't giving up
I'm gonna keep coming back
Till you listen to this track
I'm gonna keep knocking
Till I'm invited on top
'Cause I ain't giving up
I ain't giving up
One day I'll be on top

Verse II

I keep knocking on closed doors
Like I'm knocking on heaven's door
The key is to never lose hope and patience
Destined for a breakthrough
Some people helped for a few
But gave up, couldn't wait much longer
'Cause success is taking too long

Pre-chorus

I am hearing don't quit your day job
This ain't for you
You should change a few things here and there
I hear you

Track 01♪♪♪Ain't Giving Up

Chorus

But I ain't giving up, I ain't giving up
I'm gonna keep coming back
Till you listen to this track
I'm gonna keep knocking
Till I'm invited on top
Cause I ain't giving up
I ain't giving up
One day I'll be on top

Bridge

Maybe I should listen
Do something else
Stop wasting my time
Maybe I should do it all by myself

Pre-chorus

I am hearing don't quit your day job
This ain't for you
You should change a few things here and there
I hear you

Chorus

But I ain't giving up, I ain't giving up
I'm gonna keep coming back
Till you listen to this track
I'm gonna keep knocking
Till I'm invited on top
'Cause I ain't giving up
I ain't giving up
One day I'll be on top

Behind the Lyrics

While reflecting on my journey, I found inspiration for a storyline that encapsulates my current state—"Peaceful." I wrote this song to uplift myself. It is an uplifting and motivational piece that starts with themes of beginning at the bottom and facing disappointment. However, the heart of the song, especially the chorus, emphasizes patience, perseverance, and ultimately, confidence.

Verse I

Everyone's looking for a come up **(Line 1)**
Been patiently waiting for a miracle deal **(Line 2)**
Something to get me on top **(Line 3)**

The opening line came to me while reflecting on how social media platforms like Instagram, YouTube, and Facebook have transformed the way goods are promoted and marketed. We are living in a unique time where many people are seeking success through social media, often taking shortcuts without putting in the necessary effort or experiencing life's struggles. They expect to become famous without the hard work that typically accompanies achievement. As a society, we need to remember the fundamentals of life: there is no true success without working toward something valuable. Social media continues to evolve and permeate households in America and around the world. Consequently, we become wounded or unwell to what I call " Entitlement Syndrome" and "Easy way out," where one is expecting to get on top of that mountain without ever climbing or holding one rock. In Line 2, I wanted to convey this message through a song about an artist who struggles for success, yet still holds on to the hope that a miracle may happen.

I'm on the sidewalk looking up **(Line 4)**
People having fun on the rooftop **(Line 5)**
They have made it, so bottoms up **(Line 6)**
I'm still on the bottom, so head down **(Line 7)**

In Lines 4 through 7, I envisioned the setting as a rooftop party filled with A-list celebrities and well-known stars, including artists who have already achieved breakthroughs and become established in the music industry. The protagonist walks around the venue and observes that everyone is having a great time, drinking and celebrating—hence the phrase "so bottoms up" in Line 7. Although he knows he deserves to be there, his moment has not yet arrived, and he feels uninvited. He experiences feelings of jealousy, envy, and, most importantly, disappointment, as implied in Line 7: "Still on the bottom, so head down."

Pre-Chorus

I am hearing don't quit your day job ***(Line 1)***
This ain't for you ***(Line 2)***
You should change a few lines here and there ***(Line 3)***

Line 1: I aimed to build anticipation for the chorus. Instead of jumping straight into it, I wanted to create a sense of progression. I enjoyed how the artist interacts with someone, giving the song an approachable and conversational vibe. In the pre-chorus, I often hear phrases that one might say to someone when they don't believe that person is capable of achieving something. Line 2: In this part, I describe the interaction the artist is having with a potential recording company while discussing a contract agreement and reviewing his work. He is currently in a meeting with a Major Label A&R Executive. The executive suggests making "a few changes here and there," but the artist senses that they are not interested in signing him, even if it's not stated outright. The meeting concludes without any clear path forward, and he leaves without a contract. As he exits the building, he tells himself, "I am not giving up." This motivates him to write a song titled "Ain't Giving Up" as a way to express his frustrations and keep himself motivated.

Chorus

I'm gonna keep knocking ***(Line 4)***
Till I'm invited on top ***(Line 5)***
Cause I ain't giving up ***(Line 6)***
I ain't giving up ***(Line 7)***

I aimed to craft a chorus that encapsulates the various moods and emotions one experiences when facing rejection. Since the chorus is the most memorable part of a song for most listeners, I wanted to highlight the phrase "Ain't giving up." This is why it is repeated four times. Typically, a song's title is included in the chorus at least twice. he final line, "One day I'll be on top," carries the most weight, as it conveys the artist's exasperation towards the A&R executive who chose not to sign him.

Verse II

But gave up, couldn't wait much longer ***(Line 6)***
'Cause success is taking too long ***(Line 7)***

As he struggles to achieve a breakthrough, those closest to him—his friends, who once supported him on this journey—begin to lose patience. They helped for a while, but now they are giving up on him and rejecting him. His dream is taking too long to realize, and as a result, his friends are becoming increasingly impatient with his lack of success.

Bridge
This is a moment of doubt and acceptance. He starts to look at himself in the mirror, questioning his self-worth and contemplating giving up on his dream. Additionally, I want the artist to express philosophical lyrics that reveal his acceptance of the possibility that he may never achieve a breakthrough.

Do something else **(Line 2)**
Stop wasting my time **(Line 3)**
Maybe I should do it all by myself **(Line 4)**

In Line 1, there's a sentiment expressed: "Maybe I should listen." In Line 3, the statement "Stop wasting my time" conveys frustration. Line 4 reflects a desire for independence: "Maybe I should do it all by myself." This suggests a motive for promoting independent or "indie" music, as the artist contemplates going independent and gaining complete control over distribution, marketing, artwork, and more. Who could blame him? As I mentioned earlier in this book, the music industry can be unpredictable. If I had signed with a label, I would have lost the freedom to dictate my creative vision, including the ability to include those lyrics in a book, which would have been prohibited.

Track 02♪♪Alive

Verse I

I keep hearing the good die young
The good die young, might feel like
You don't have much to live for
Rich or poor, who's been there before?
Yeah, I've been there before
Living with regrets and unpaid debts
Dream hasn't come true yet
No breakthrough yet, I bet
To top off 2020 got us sick, upset

Pre-chorus

Listen, despite what we 've been through
We've become one, stronger than ever
Let's celebrate what we've overcome
till kingdom come, so bottoms up, hands up

Chorus (as we sing)

We are alive, we are (we are alive)
Yeah, we are alive (we are alive)
Turn it up (way up)
As we sing one more, one more time
We are alive, we are, (we are alive)
Yeah, we are alive (we are alive)

Verse II

Shine the night, beautiful star, we are
Let's go all out tonight, with a fight
Don't matter the weather, have no fear
I feel free like a bird, that's right
Spread our hands like we're flying
'Cause when our numbers are called
There be no voicemail with a number

Pre-chorus

Listen, despite what we 've been through
We've become one, stronger than ever
Let's celebrate what we've overcome
Till kingdom come, so bottoms up, hands up

Track 02♪♪♪Alive

Chorus (as we sing)

We are alive, we are (we are alive)
Yeah, we are alive (we are alive)
Turn it up (way up)
As we sing one more, one more time
We are alive, we are, (we are alive)
Yeah, we are alive (we are alive)

Bridge

Even when we fall, hit a wall, lose control
Don't give up, stand up, dance it off
Cause we're strong and the night is young
So bottoms up, hands up

Chorus (as we sing)

We are alive, we are (we are alive)
Yeah, we are alive (we are alive)
Turn it up (way up)
As we sing one more, one more time
We are alive, we are, (we are alive)
Yeah, we are alive (we are alive)

Outro

Oh yeah, we are alive, we are (we are alive)
Yeah, we are alive (we are alive)
To call back, we'll be gone forever
Until then the party ain't over

Behind the Lyrics

Are you alive? If you are reading this, then yes, you are alive. Let's dive in. This song is probably one of the most memorable pieces I have penned, if not the most significant one I have authored, as it celebrates life after overcoming fear, sorrow, uncertainty, tragedy, and death.

The first verse was written in the winter of 2019. After sitting on the song concept for a few months and feeling unsure about how to proceed, the unprecedented tragedy of the COVID-19 pandemic and the horrific murder of George Perry Floyd Jr. on May 25, 2020, emerged.

I remember, in the midst of it all—probably around June or July of 2020—thinking, "The world is falling apart; so many people have died without a proper burial." The streets of America became unsafe as the pandemic spread through every city and corner like a speeding bullet. The virus did not discriminate; everyone was impacted, regardless of wealth, race, or background.

Furthermore, the killing of George Floyd captured media attention, including on social media, going viral and reminding us once again, "This is America," as highlighted in the song by Childish Gambino. As a result, many Black Americans took to the streets to protest. The danger shifted; this time, the pervasive virus was not just COVID-19, but the endemic virus of racism, which disproportionately affects Black individuals. We were left to grapple with fighting two types of viruses: Coronavirus and Racism. In that moment, I shouted, "Thank God I am alive," even though I could not fully understand it all. Staring at the wall, I envisioned the lyrics forming in my mind, and I grabbed my pen and pad to let the song flow. I poured my emotions into this piece; every line felt like teardrops as the song answered the call.

A couple of months later, I attended a Black Lives Matter protest just outside Boston. The painful memory of George Floyd's cruel murder still resonated deeply within us, and we sought answers from the police about how an officer could commit such an act.

As a Black man, I am constantly reminded that racism occurs every day, often in silence. However, this time, the true nature of pure hate and racism was exposed for all to see. Anyone with a sense of common decency who witnessed an officer kneeling on another human being would agree that the incident was inhumane; even animals should not be subjected to such monstrous treatment. Yet, such acts of brutality happen all too often in America.

Processing all of this while the world battled the pandemic was overwhelming. The reality for Black individuals in America has been a daily struggle of fighting against discrimination, stereotypes, inequality, and racism. As 2020 came to a close, the idea of capturing these experiences in a song gained momentum in my mind. By 2021, I knew I had something special to write about, and the rest of the song's concept flowed into my head freely.

Verse I

I keep hearing the good die young	***(Line 1)***
The good die young, might feel like	***(Line 2)***
You don't have much to live for	***(Line 3)***

Line 1, I wanted to be very transparent and honest about the current state of society and the world at this time. It felt essential to use the word "die," as that is what was happening in every ghetto, every corner, and every community—people were dying.

Line 3, This realization came to me while listening to people's stories about how COVID-19 was impacting their mental health. Many individuals were struggling with depression and loneliness as the pandemic forced them to stay sheltered or socially distanced from loved ones. For some, mental health deteriorated further because they did not have close family members to interact with even before the pandemic, leading to a decline in their overall well-being.

Rich or poor, who's been there before?	***(Line 4)***
Yeah, I've been there before	***(Line 5)***
Living with regrets and unpaid debts	***(Line 6)***
Dream hasn't come true yet	***(Line 7)***
No breakthrough yet, I bet	***(Line 8)***
To top off 2020 got us sick, upset	(Line 9)

In Line 9, the phrase "to top off 2020, get us sick, upset" includes the word "upset" for two reasons. First, it rhymes with "yet" and "bet," which I used in Line 8: "No breakthrough yet, I bet." Second, the word "upset" evokes the emotional state of predominantly Black communities in relation to their experiences with the police, particularly the incident involving a white officer kneeling on a Black man's neck. I believe that without expressing these emotions at the beginning of the song, "Alive" would have been overlooked; Line 9 significantly enhanced the message.

Pre-Chorus

Listen, despite what we've been through **(Line 1)**
we've become one, stronger than ever **(Line 2)**

The opening line is about hope and serves as a reminder for everyone to take a deep breath as we unite as a nation to combat both the pandemic and racism. In Line 2, it is stated, "We've become one, stronger than ever." Historically, I have witnessed that when tragedy and sorrow strike, humanity and communities come together to fight for a common cause. I believe that the events surrounding COVID-19 and the torture of George Floyd sparked a significant movement, with residents marching in the streets and on every corner of America to express their true feelings and their ongoing frustration with a system that has repeatedly failed Black and Brown people. They demanded change, particularly in police reform. Although I felt deep down that real change would never come—just as it didn't after what happened to Sam Cooke—the audacity of hope encouraged me to sing, "It has been a long, a long time coming, but I know a change is gonna come."

I knew I was lying through my teeth, and it was wishful thinking on my part. However, the reality is that in a world filled with sorrows and sadness, my pen wouldn't allow me to contribute more sorrow and sadness. Thus, I wrote the following lines:

Lets celebrate what we've overcome **(Line 3)**
Till kingdom come, so bottoms up, hands up **(Line 4)**

These messages are aimed at all survivors of racism and COVID-19, reminding everyone to celebrate life to the fullest because everything can change in an instant. Despite the challenges one has faced, that is the intent of the pre-chorus. Additionally, using the word "listen" in the opening line is a powerful way to ensure that listeners pay thoughtful attention and feel the anticipation for the heightened lyrics that come before the chorus.

Chorus

After the Pre-chorus, I had no reason to hold on to the song's heart, which is the central idea: the chorus. So, I began the chorus with the following lines:

Yeah, we are alive (we are alive) ***(Line 2)***
Turn it up (way up) ***(Line 3)***
As we sing one more, one more time ***(Line 4)***
We are alive, we are, (we are alive) ***(Line 5)***

The line, "We are alive, we are (We are alive)," delivers a powerful message filled with joy, resilience, and hope during a time marked by uncertainty, sadness, and fear, especially in the years 2020, 2021, and even 2022 when the world faced a surge of racism and the COVID-19 pandemic, which resulted in a high mortality rate. The title of the song is repeated numerous times because I wanted to ensure it didn't go unnoticed; I envisioned a crowd of thousands of fans chanting and celebrating as this song played. Therefore, it was essential to use catchy and simple words so the entire crowd could easily sing along.

Moreover, as you can see at the end of Line 1, "(we are alive)" appears in parentheses. This is a perfect example of inserting "ad-libs," a term derived from the Latin phrase "ad libitum," which translates to "one's liberty." The phrase "(we are alive)" can be interpreted differently by each artist or singer. These ad-libs add a unique emotional vibe to the song and enhance both the chorus and the melody. Each fan in the crowd will interpret the ad-libs in their own way, which highlights the beauty of incorporating them into the music.

As a lyricist, I never know when I will add an ad-lib; it often comes to me spontaneously. Some songs seem to have a life of their own, dictating every aspect of the lyrics, from the chorus to the verses, guiding specific lines that need to be written. As a writer, you have two choices: let the song guide you or allow it to take the lead while you remain obedient. If you try to take control, you may end up empty-handed.

Before I started writing this book, I had told myself that each "Behind the Lyrics" section would be short and sweet, about one page long. I didn't think I would be able to remember the rationale and background behind every song. However, as I narrate these sections, especially for "Alive," I find I have so much to say, share, and purge. It feels unfair to conceal the authenticity, the true story, the true nature of every song I ever penned or written. therefore, Behind the Lyrics would be rolling like the rolling stone in this book; freely, allowing you to experience my lyrical mind an connect with line I have created, without limitations. So, let's proceed with Line 3, shall we?

In Line 3, the phrase "Turn it up (way up)" was added for several musical reasons. Firstly, it gives fans or the live audience a sense of control over the performance, allowing them to express their dissatisfaction loudly and request that the music be turned up, as suggested by rappers Fat Joe and Remy Ma.

If their request is not met promptly, I imagine the lead singer or performer stopping the show to repeat or echo Line 3, urging the DJ to turn the music up, specifically "(way up)." Meanwhile, the fans or audience, along with the performer, would continue to chant, "Turn it up, turn it up, turn it up," in unison. Line 4 explains why the music should be turned up, or in this case, way up. And there you have it.

Verse II
My main focus was to write something relatable that highlights positive attributes, aiming to unify those who have survived either the pandemic or racism. At this point, Covid-19 had claimed millions of lives, and Black or brown individuals were facing significant challenges. I'll leave the rest for you to fill in.

Shine the night, beautiful star, we are **(Line 1)**
Let's go all out tonight, with a fight **(Line 2)**
Don't matter the weather, have no fear **(Line 3)**

In line 2, "Let's go all out tonight, with a fight," I encourage everyone to go outside and celebrate life after experiencing isolation, distancing, quarantines, and sheltering in place. At the time I was writing this verse, the virus hadn't disappeared entirely, but I wanted to convey a sense of hope; life would return to normal as there were signs of progress on the horizon. Pharmaceutical companies were developing vaccines, which offered some control over the spread of the virus. Nonetheless, many people were still afraid to go outdoors, and it was understandable given the virus's lethality.

The primary purpose of line 3 is to empower people to confront their fears. Despite the frightening and threatening nature of the world, I wanted to include empowering words for those struggling with fear—whether it's the fear of losing someone, the fear of the future, or the fear of socializing without masks. These are all fears that many accumulated during the pandemic. Furthermore, fear of being black or brown in America could not be ignored as white Police Officers were spraying our melanin with bullets.

'Cause when our numbers are called **(Line 6)**
There be no voicemail with a number **(Line 7)**
To call back, we'll be gone forever **(Line 8)**
Until then the party ain't over **(Line 9)**

Lines 6, 7, and 8 serve as a reality check. While it's possible to be fearless and hopeful that the future will be better than yesterday, we must remember that when our numbers are called, we will be gone forever. Therefore, the key takeaway is to seize the moment. As emphasized in Line 9, "until then, the party ain't over."

Bridge
Even when we fall, hit a wall, lose control **(Line 1)**
Don't give up, stand up, dance it off **(Line 2)**
Cause we're strong and the night is young **(Line 3)**
So bottoms up, hands up **(Line 4)**

The first line of the song is arguably the most profound, as it reflects the journey of life. I have experienced setbacks, faced obstacles, and struggled to maintain control, yet I have never given up. It was essential for me to share this personal insight. Moreover, the first line features some rhymes that I take great pride in, as they create a smooth transition into the chorus.

In line four, my intention was to evoke imagery of the crowd enjoying themselves after a long and challenging journey. They were finally able to stand up and see unmasked faces after enduring at least a year of battling COVID-19. Some might suggest that experts and scientists should have referred to it as COVID-20, as 2020 was the deadliest year. Did they get it right? Well, what do I know?

Track 03♪♪Best Time

Verse I

Babe, it's okay, you wanna call it quits
I'd been in so many relationships
So many heartbreak
And cried many tears my eyes ached
Been cheated on, been lied to
Some girls never called me back
'Cause I had only pocket change
Lookin' for guys into stocks exchange

Pre-chorus

Babe, if today is our last day together
I couldn't be happier and prouder
'Cause when I was with you

Chorus

Babe, I had the best time of my life
Best time of my life
Babe, I had the best time of my life
Best time of my life
Even though, we're about to go
Separate ways, want you to know
Babe, the best time of my life
Was with you
No doubt, I had the best time, with you

Verse II

I usually do well with farewell
Like most guys I don't get mad, sad
I just move on and say, oh well
For breaking my heart, believe or not
Everything about you will be missed
Taste of your lips when we kissed
Even though, now its bittersweet
I ain't sad, 'cause from all the exes I had
You' the best lover I've ever had

Pre-chorus

Babe, if today is our last day together
I couldn't be happier and prouder
'Cause when I was with you

Track 03♪♪♪Best Time

Chorus

Babe, I had the best time of my life
Best time of my life
Babe, I had the best time of my life
Best time of my life
Even though, we're about to go
Our separate ways
Believe me, babe, best time of my life
Was with you
No doubt, I had the best time, with you

Bridge

Please don't leave me
I need you in my life babe
I can't go through this again, but

Pre-chorus

Babe, if today is our last day together
I couldn't be happier and prouder
'Cause when I was with you

Chorus

Babe, I had the best time of my life
Best time of my life
Babe, I had the best time of my life
Best time of my life
Even though, we're about to go
Our separate ways
Believe me, babe, best time of my life
Was with you
No doubt, I had the best time, with you

Outro

I had the best time of my life
With you, yeah with you

Behind the Lyrics

For a long time, I have wanted to write a song about men's vulnerability, showcasing our softer, teddy bear sides. This is a story about expressing true feelings as men, something I know I am guilty of avoiding. We often feel confined by our emotions, but I wanted to create a song that not only reveals those hidden feelings but also addresses coping with them. The message is that when men free their sensitive side, it can be a powerful experience.

He continues by saying, "I've been there before." As she processes his unexpected reaction, the atmosphere in the room shifts, and she begins to question him, asking, "Do you even care? You could at least pretend to care." His response doesn't sit well with her; she perceives his indifference as a lack of concern. As the song progresses, he gradually reveals his true feelings, admitting that she will be missed because she is the best thing that ever happened to him. However, as the bridge approaches, he gathers himself, ultimately expressing sadness and pain as he realizes she is truly leaving him for good. In a moment of vulnerability, he begs her not to go.

Verse I

Babe, it's okay, you wanna call it quits **(Line 1)**
I'd been in so many relationships **(Line 2)**

These two lines continue the conversation between the characters, which is not well documented in Verse 1. However, Line 1 and Line 2 beautifully establish the song's background, allowing the audience to understand the rationale behind the situation without having to guess. I intentionally used the word "babe" to soften the delivery of the news; I wanted to avoid creating a scandalous or confrontational scene. My aim was to control the intensity and emotions in the room as cordially as possible. Breakups can often turn nasty, but not every breakup has to end with a broken heart. I wanted to challenge that norm in this song, as demonstrated in the following lines.

Some girls never called me back **(Line 6)**
'Cause I had only pocket change **(Line 7)**
Looking for guys into stock exchange **(Line 8)**

Lines 5 through 8 provide a detailed history of his relationships, so ending things is nothing new for him. I then wanted to logically explain why some girls never call him back. Additionally, I wanted to be creative, so I decided to incorporate a playful element: I used the phrase "pocket change," which rhymes with "exchange," to illustrate my point. Originally, the song was titled "Time," but I felt that was too vague, so I renamed it to make it more appealing and mysterious. As a writer, I strive to ensure that my audience engages with my work beyond just the title; therefore, I aim to choose titles that evoke curiosity and intrigue, something I have worked on mastering over the years.

Pre-Chorus
Babe, if today is our last day together **(Line 1)**
I couldn't be happier and prouder **(Line 2)**
'Cause when I was with you **(Line 3)**

The opening line starts with the same word, "Babe," as I previously mentioned. My aim was to maintain the amicable and respectful tone of their conversation to prevent any escalation. I chose to keep the word "babe" for consistency, at least for now, until later in the song when I would take the audience on a brief journey, saving the best line(s) for last.

For Lines 2 and 3, I kept the pre-chorus short—just three lines with new lyrics. This section of the song is crucial for harmonizing and building up to the chorus, so I used the word "'cause" as a shortened form of "because" to ensure it flows musically.

Chorus
"Cause when I was with you **(Line 1)**
Babe, I had the best time of my life **(Line 2)**

In songwriting 101, it's important for the last line of the pre-chorus to flow smoothly into the first line of the chorus, creating the feel of a complete sentence. Academically, you might phrase it as, "Because when I was with you, I had the best time of my life," which is grammatically correct but may not work musically. Since the singer is performing rather than simply reading, I needed to shorten and modify the line to ensure it flows well. Additionally, I wanted the audience to enjoy singing the chorus like an anthem, so a key strategy was to repeat the title "Best time" five times throughout the song.

Verse II
Everything about you will be missed **(Line 4)**
Taste of your lips when we kissed **(Line 5)**
Even though, now its bittersweet **(Line 6)**

I thoroughly enjoyed writing the three lines above. They reflect what I refer to as textbook lyricism, as they include wordplay, metaphor, and rhyme.

Whenever I compose a line that impresses me, it brightens my day and fills me with happiness and joy. I truly had one of the best writing sessions of my life while creating this part of the song. So, why do you think I titled it "Best Time"? It wasn't by chance—just ask Chance the Rapper!

Bridge
Please don't leave me **(Line 1)**
I need you in my life babe **(Line 2)**
I can't go through this again, but **(Line 3)**

Similarly, the bridge consists of three lines to mirror the pre-chorus. I considered extending the bridge, but for the sake of consistency, I opted to keep it short. After all, consistency builds trust in life, and in music, it keeps the audience engaged and loyal. Before I finish, I must point out that conjunctions like "but," "because," or "'cause" are excellent tools for connecting every section of a song structurally. Some may think these minor details are unnecessary or tedious—like making your bed every morning—but believe me, their value is significant. This is especially true for someone like me, a lyricist who doesn't have a singing voice. You need to think like a singer; otherwise, working or collaborating with an artist as a sole lyricist can be very challenging.

Track 04♪♪Blinded

Verse I

Hey, sorry I am late
After all its only on a blind date
You look me straight in the eye
I wonder why?
You look just like the other girls
But when you take your shades off
You don't look the same

Pre-Chorus

I've been waiting for this moment
Since I was eight
Can't let it go to waste, be patient with me

Chorus

Babe you got me blinded
I can't see
Kiss me, so I can tell
Touch my body, so I can tell
Don't worry, I don't kiss and tell
Babe I am sorry, I'm blinded

Verse II

You look so good in daylight
I got to see you at night
Come a little closer so you and I
Can see an eye for an eye
But babe I ain't trying to be blind
Let's go in the dark
And close the blinds

Pre-Chorus

I've been waiting for this moment
Since I was eight
Can't let it go to waste, be patient with me

Track 04♪♪Blinded

Chorus
Babe you got me blinded
I can't see
So kiss me, so I can tell
So touch my body, so I can tell
Don't worry, I don't kiss and tell
Babe I am sorry, I'm blinded

Bridge
They say love is blind
But I'm not
Not sure if you're the one for me, but

Pre-Chorus
I've been waiting for this moment
Since I was eight
I can't let it go to waste, be patient with me

Chorus
Babe you got me blinded
I can't see
So kiss me, so I can tell
So touch me, so I can tell
Don't worry, I don't kiss and tell
Babe I am sorry, I'm blinded

Outro
Oh yeah, I am sorry, babe
Can't you tell, I'm blinded

Behind the Lyrics

First and foremost, this song was written in early 2019. Fast forward to Friday, February 16, 2024, and there I was, sitting in my workplace cubicle, inattentively listening to a 9 o'clock Zoom meeting. I tried to recall why I wrote this song, so please bear with me as I narrate and jog my memory.

For the longest time, I wanted to write a song about blind dates—not just any blind date, but one that is flirtatious, realistic, exciting, and spontaneous. One of my goals was to highlight the dangers of blind dating and online dating, as we live in a society where trust can be risky. Although I have never been on a blind date myself, I aimed to create compelling imagery that would make it feel as if Manley was experiencing my first blind date.

Feel free to use these lines on your first blind date—just kidding!

Verse I

As I was developing the first verse in my mind, I thought to myself, How would I handle a blind date? What would I say? Should I close the deal on the first date? Well, I have never been on a blind date, so allow me to fantasize. On my first blind date, I would probably run late in Haitian time. It is sad but true as Haitians generally disobey this fundamental law of physics and time and are notorious for showing up late to events. I am guilty as charged, so it's only fitting to start Verse I as outlined below.

Hey, sorry I am late **(Line 1)**
After all its only on a blind date **(Line 2)**
You look me straight in the eye **(Line 3)**
I wonder why? **(Line 4)**
You look just like the other girls **(Line 5)**
But when you take your shades off **(Line 6)**

Line 1 highlights one of my flaws—tardiness, which many people would consider a bad habit. However, I have made tremendous improvements lately (get it, "as of late"?). Line 2 downplays the significance of an actual blind date, suggesting that being late isn't such a big deal. In reality, though, in this situation, being tardy is significant, as the following line indicates. As I approach the table, I imagine she will look away in annoyance.

Lines 4 and 5 expand the conversation from a male perspective. Additionally, I intentionally used the phrase "shade off" in Line 6 to refer to the blind date, as the woman is wearing sunglasses, making it impossible for me to see her face behind them.

Pre-Chorus

I've been waiting for this moment ***(Line 1)***
Since I was eight ***(Line 2)***
Can't let it go to waste, be patient with me ***(Line 3)***

The first two lines introduce new lyrics that take the song in a fresh direction. When she takes off her sunglasses, I suddenly realize she looks familiar. In fact, I've had a crush on her since I was a kid.

Line 3 seizes the moment because I don't want her to slip away or leave, letting time go to waste. While time is certainly important on a blind date or any date, I hope she can be patient with me. I need to be confident that she is truly the girl from my childhood.

Suddenly, I flirtatiously and boldly say to her these proceeding lines:

Chorus

Babe you got me blinded ***(Line 1)***
I can't see ***(Line 2)***
Kiss me, so I can tell ***(Line 3)***
Touch my body, so I can tell ***(Line 4)***
Don't worry, I don't kiss and tell ***(Line 5)***

The first word that comes to mind when I think of the theme "blind date" is the title of the song "Blinded." As I gaze at her beautiful face, I struggle to jog my memory, I realize that her immaculate beauty is not helping; only adds to my confusion. Since it has been years—perhaps even two decades—since our last encounter, I can't confirm her true identity, and her beauty has left me feeling blinded. As the song progresses, the story takes on a more adventurous, flirtatious, and intimate tone, featuring pickup lines. Lines 3 and 4 suggest that the only way for her to persuade me is through a kiss and touch. Line 5, my favorite from the chorus, not only rhymes with the preceding lines but also champions women's privacy with the line "don't worry, I don't kiss and tell." While blind dating is perfectly legal, it does not grant anyone the license to violate someone's privacy.

In Line 5, the phrase "kiss and tell" came to mind as I played with words from the chorus, particularly using the first word from Line 2, "Kiss," and the last word from Line 2, "Tell." there you have it. Ultimately, this message is designed to reassure her that she can trust me to be honest, have a good time on our blind date, and allow herself to be blinded by the experience. That's all.

Verse II

You might be wondering why I don't decode every line of every song. The answer is simple: sometimes less is more. I also want to maintain a sense of suspense—who doesn't enjoy a little mystery? Additionally, I prefer for my readers to interpret my lyrics thoughtfully, analyzing them closely and taking notes. This particular verse evokes a cozy and romantic scene in which I attempt to get more comfortable and closer to her without being disrespectful.

You look so good in daylight **(Line 1)**
I got to see you at night **(Line 2)**
Come a little closer so you and I **(Line 3)**
Can see an eye for an eye **(Line 4)**

Line 1 seems like a perfect pickup line. Would you agree? I believe it is. The last three lines were added to further express myself in a clever and smooth way by incorporating more catchy lines. I'm not sure if she will appreciate them or pick up on the pickup lines, so I keep the momentum going with the following lines.

But babe I ain't trying to be blind **(Line 4)**
Let's go in the dark **(Line 6)**
And close the blinds **(Line 7)**

If my memory serves me correctly, after writing Line 4, I felt like I was running out of pickup lines and my game was losing momentum, as if I would never reach the finish line. I had to redeem myself, so Lines 5 through 7 would be my last chance to break the ice. I aimed to use keywords related to eyesight to guide her attention to a place where she would feel comfortable. At the same time, I wanted to create an engaging atmosphere by incorporating strong imagery along with wordplay and rhymes inspired by phrases like "an eye for an eye" and "close the blinds." Things would get even more interesting later on; we can cross that bridge when we get there. And here we are.

Bridge

They say love is blind **(Line 1)**
But I'm not **(Line 2)**
Not sure if you're the one for me, but **(Line 3)**

As reality sinks in and the day comes to a close, I start to look at her through a different lens to determine if she truly is the right companion and partner for me. I express to her that I am not superficial; love is founded on more than just beauty and outward appearances. However, as our conversation progresses, her beauty continues to distract me. Once again, I find myself blinded and unable to see her flaws.

Track 05♪♪♪Dreaming

Verse I

Our dreams were shattered
But I still have dreams
I've been chasing for years
So many years make me wonder
Where do dreams come from?
Do they come thru the window at night?
Do they fall from the sky at night?
I don't know

Pre-Chorus

But, I know
I'm gonna wait by the window for you
Gonna keep looking up to the sky for you

Chorus

'Cause life is nothing but a dream
So keep on dreamin, keep on dreamin'
Yeah, yeah keep on dreamin'
Yeah , yeah keep on dreamin'
Cause life is nothing but a dream

Verse II

Our dreams were to travel the world
But I still have dreams
I've been traveling for years
So many years make me wonder
Where do dreams come from?
Do they come when you have no one left?
Do they come when you lose hope?
I don't know

Pre-Chorus

But, I know
I'm gonna stay hopeful til' I see you
Gonna keep living life through you

Track 05♪♪Dreaming

Chorus

'Cause life is nothing but a dream
So keep on dreamin', keep on dreamin'
Yeah, yeah keep on dreamin'
Yeah, yeah keep on dreamin'
Cause life is nothing but a dream

Behind the Lyrics

This song is dedicated to anyone mourning the loss of a loved one or someone special to their heart. In this song, the griever feels they have lost everything except for one essential aspect of life: hope. As a result, the mourner has been patiently waiting by the window, gazing at the sky and reminiscing about the dreams and memories they once shared. Every night, the mourner dreams of a miraculous reunion, imagining that the person returns home as if they had never left. That was the vision I had in mind, but for weeks, I struggled to write down the verses, not even the opening line, until one twilight.

On a calm summer night, while staring out the window, my heart overflowed with sadness and loneliness. In that moment, I began to sing these lines in my mind to help me get through the rest of the night, wishing for a reunion with those I had lost.

Verse I

Our dreams were shattered **(Line 1)**
But I still have dreams **(Line 2)**
I've been chasing for years **(Line 3)**
So many years make me wonder **(Line 4)**

Line 1: I remember my late cousin. We would often dream together about his goal of building an academic institution, where he would be the founder and I would be named the president.

Line 2: Although my cousin passed away over two decades ago, I still find myself dreaming of seeing him again and making him proud, as mentioned in Line 3. Line 4: I added the line "so many years make me wonder" to emphasize that time has not healed all my feelings of mourning and grief.

As a result, I have included more context in Verse I and posed the following questions:

Where do dreams come from? **(Line 5)**
Do they come through the window at night? **(Line 6)**
Do they fall from the sky? **(Line 7)**

The text compels listeners to engage and allows them to truly feel the message being conveyed. As I mentioned earlier, it's important to never leave questions unanswered. In the worst-case scenario, one should provide listeners with subtle hints, so the same principle applies here. Albeit I initially intended to wait until the pre-chorus to address the questions, I ultimately decided to answer them right away, as I felt the listeners might lose patience.

Pre-Chorus
By now, you should be an expert in identifying lyrical musical twists. Did you notice a twist in the pre-chorus? If you didn't, I replaced the last two lines (Lines 2 and 3) with new lyrics, while keeping Line 1 unchanged. Always expect the unexpected; after all, I'm an Aries.

Pre-chorus (after Verse I)
But, I know
I'm gonna wait by the window for you
Gonna keep looking up to the sky for you

Pre-Chorus (after Verse II)
But, I know
I'm gonna stay hopeful til' I see you
Gonna keep living life through you

Line 1 begins with "But, I know," indicating that the mourner is willing to wait impatiently for the person to return, uncertain if tomorrow will arrive. One thing is certain: the mourner will keep looking up at the sky and waiting by the window, as mentioned in Lines 2 and 3. In Line 3, the sky serves as a spiritual reference to heaven, suggesting that the deceased are watching and smiling down while the mourner gazes upward.

Chorus
I wanted to stay close to the song's title, which led to the repetition of the word "dreaming" throughout.

'Cause life is nothing but a dream **(Line 1)**
So keep on dreamin, keep on dreamin' **(Line 2)**
Yeah, yeah keep on dreamin' **(Line 3)**
Yeah , yeah keep on dreamin' **(Line 4)**

In Line 1, the mourner has been waiting for a miraculous return. However, as reality sinks in, they come to realize that the person is dead and gone. Nevertheless, the mourner concludes with a powerful message: we should not let death disrupt the audacity of hope, stating, "Life is nothing but a dream."

In Lines 2, 3, and 4, the word "dreaming" is repeated throughout the lyrics. This repetition makes the song catchy and creates coherence, ultimately conveying the central idea and driving the song forward. I chose to repeat "dreaming" to remind listeners of the title, encouraging them to keep dreaming.

Verse II

Our dreams was to travel the world	***(Line 1)***
But I still have dreams	***(Line 2)***
I 've been traveling for years	***(Line 3)***
So many years make me wonder	***(Line 4)***
Where do dreams come from?	***(Line 5)***

Initially, I considered repeating every line from Verse I in Verse II, but I realized that it might become tedious. As a conscientious lyricist, I understand how much I could enervate my listeners, who might fall asleep listening to a lengthy verse before reaching the chorus. After further thought, I decided to go for it and see what would happen.

I ended up copying and pasting lines 2 through 5 of Verse I. Historically, this isn't a technique I often use, but when applied correctly, it can add cohesion and a unique element to the song as a whole. Did I get lazy with this song? The answer is no; I did not simply get lazy by copying and pasting previous lines of an earlier verse. However, as a lyricist, I believe that your creative process can take you on unexpected journeys, allowing the song to write itself magically, both structurally and musically. That's exactly what happened here—using those four lines wasn't my initial intention, but like a shadow, I followed my creative instincts and allowed my pen to guide me, acknowledging that I had lost lyrical control.

Do they come when you have no one left?	***(Line 6)***
Do they come when you lose hope?	***(Line 7)***

Lastly, Lines 6 and 7 of Verse II are somewhat similar to Verse I in that they pose questions. The endings of these questions are not identical; I used different keywords to convey a sense of uncertainty and sorrow: "No one left" and "lose hope." This variation helps ensure that my listeners do not find the song completely draining.

In conclusion, this song is one of the few I've chosen not to include a bridge. I felt that breaking the repetition of the verses, especially since there are two embedded questions, would not serve a purpose.

Additionally, I believe the artist I envision singing this song would convey the message effectively without needing a bridge to lead the listeners to believe that life is nothing but a dream.

Track 06♪♪♪♪♪♪♪♪♪♪♪♪♪♪♪♪♪♪♪♪♪♪♪♪♪♪♪♪♪♪♪♪♪♪♪♪♪♪Forever Hold Your Peace

Verse I

You promise me
Once you've the key to my heart
You would make me happy
Like a kid in a candy store
How come when you open the door
You don't call me sweetie
And kiss my lips like before

Pre-chorus

I am tired of running after you
Let's cut to the chase
'Cause I can't do this anymore

Chorus

If you gonna break my heart
Drop it now
Don't sugar coat it
Just say your piece
Or forever hold your peace
If you gonna break my heart
Drop it now
Don't sugar coat it
Just say your piece
Or forever hold your peace

Verse II

You come and go unseen
In a matter of minutes
It seems like your love is losing steam
You ain't hitting the sweet spot
Am I still the girl of your dreams?
Please tell me, tell me you still love me
Then I'll stay calm and won't scream

Pre-chorus

I am tired of running after you
Let's cut to the chase
'Cause I can't do this anymore

Track 06♪♪♪♪♪♪♪♪♪♪♪♪♪♪♪♪♪♪♪♪♪♪♪♪♪♪♪♪♪♪♪♪♪♪♪♪Forever Hold Your Peace

Chorus

If you gonna break my heart
Drop it now
Don't sugar coat it
Just say your piece
Or forever hold your peace
If you gonna break my heart
Drop it now
Don't sugar coat it
Just say your piece
Or forever hold your peace

Bridge

Drop it now, drop it now
Drop it now, drop it now
Drop it, drop it right now
I'm ready to pick up the pieces

Chorus

If you gonna break my heart
Drop it now
Don't sugar coat it
Just say your piece
Or forever hold your peace
If you gonna break my heart
Drop it now
Don't sugar coat it
Just say your piece
Or forever hold your peace

Behind the Lyrics

For this particular edition of "Behind the Lyrics," I recorded a five-minute explanation on my phone while sitting in traffic on my way to my nine-to-five job in Burlington, Massachusetts, on Tuesday, February 27, 2024. I remember thinking how hard it was to believe that February was coming to an end; packing its frigid self, especially after experiencing quite a few bitterly cold weeks. Over the past couple of months, I've been recording my thoughts to make this section of the book, "Behind the Lyrics," more efficient, utilizing my idle time in traffic.

Now, let's dive into the meaning behind "Forever Hold Your Peace." This song explores a relationship that lacks commitment and communication, filled with confrontation and frustration. It is influenced by a female perspective, inspired by a conversation I overheard between two women discussing how their partners were not fully committed to the relationship. Despite this, they were determined to fight for their relationships, hoping for a long-term commitment in the future.

Verse I

You promise me **(Line 1)**
Once you've the key to my heart **(Line 2)**
You would make me happy **(Line 3)**

The opening line begins with her lover's promise to bring happiness into their relationship. Line 3 establishes the current status of the relationship. However, as the story unfolds, she begins to notice that her partner is neglecting the little things—he's no longer calling her "sweetie," using her first name instead, and he doesn't greet her with a kiss when he comes home.

While there is no ambiguity in Line 3, as it directly references happiness, I wanted to strengthen the verse with metaphor and wordplay inspired by the earlier lines. This led me to the idea of a "candy store," which represents the joy I associate with seeing children happily indulging in sweets. I then added the following lines.

Like a kid in a candy store **(Line 4)**
How come when you open the door **(Line 5)**
You don't call me sweetie **(Line 6)**

I have noticed that when kids enter local stores, they often shout "candy" to their parents as soon as they walk in. Even better, they head straight to the candy aisle, grab their favorite treats, and try to persuade their parents to buy them.

The phrase "You don't call me sweetie" cleverly plays on words related to the sweetness of candy. More importantly, referring to someone as "sweetie" conveys a sense of romantic or affectionate interest.

Pre-Chorus

I am tired of running after you **(Line 1)**
Let's cut to the chase **(Line 2)**
'Cause I can't do this anymore **(Line 3)**

The pre-chorus sets the expectation that the relationship is ending, as each line points in that direction. However, my intention was not to end the relationship—at least not yet. Instead, I wanted to create a pre-chorus that represented a turning point in the relationship, where the girlfriend confronts the boyfriend and ultimately gives him an ultimatum. More importantly, I aimed to build perfect anticipation before the chorus. As I have consistently mentioned, the pre-chorus is meant to heighten the emotional tension, so I thought it would be effective to initiate a nonviolent confrontation or argument within the song using just words. In this scenario, the girlfriend is infuriated and tired of broken promises, so she begins with:

Chorus

As expected, the chorus details the girlfriend's choice of words as she confronts her partner.

Drop it now **(Line 2)**
Don't sugar coat it **(Line 3)**
Just say your piece **(Line 4)**
Or forever hold your peace **(Line 5)**

Line 1 essentially states, "If you are going to break up with me, do it now and tell me the truth." However, in this context, the word "do" is replaced with "drop," which serves as a metaphor for breaking someone's heart.

Line 3, "don't sugarcoat it," references Line 4 of Verse I, "like a kid in a candy store." I didn't expect Line 3 to come to mind, but when it did, I felt a sense of accomplishment. It may sound boastful, but I genuinely enjoy this part of songwriting: linking and referencing words throughout a song.

Furthermore, Line 4 essentially reiterates, "Say it now." In this instance, the word "piece" symbolizes the broken pieces of the heart. Lastly, Line 5 is often heard in Christian wedding ceremonies, suggesting that if he, meaning the boyfriend, remains silent, it would lead to an eternity of uncertainty as she envisions a future without him.

Lyrically, Line 4 rhymes perfectly with the previous line (Line 3), utilizing the words "peace" and "piece" in succession. Lines 6 through 10 are repeated lines, so I won't go into detail about them. However, I realize I should have repeated the title, “Forever Hold Your Peace,” one last time before closing the chorus to make it more memorable and catchier. This is important, but I didn’t do it. It’s not the end of the world, as any artist or producer interested in pitching the song will likely refine the lyrics during the editing and arrangement phase. For instance, a producer might recommend moving a chorus or line to enhance the song’s coherence.

Verse II

Verse II perpetuates the girlfriend's frustration and highlights the behaviors her boyfriend has stopped displaying

You come and go unseen	***(Line 1)***
In a matter of minutes	***(Line 2)***
It seems like your love is losing steam	***(Line 3)***
You ain't hitting the sweet spot	***(Line 4)***

Line 1, “You come and go unseen,” implicitly suggests that he comes home and stays in his own bubble, ignoring the fact that she is even there. While writing this section, I thought about how some couples stop putting effort into making love once the honeymoon phase is over; there is no foreplay, no emotions, no connection, and no chemistry. One partner seems to be racing like a squirrel trying to get a nut, seeking an orgasm as quickly as possible. Meanwhile, the other partner, often the girlfriend, desires time—romantic time—both before and after intimacy.

In lines 2 through 4, she outlines the issues that have been piercing her heart up to this point. The final two lines (lines 5 and 6) need no explanation or justification; she is clearly presenting her case and unapologetically expressing her feelings, unlike her boyfriend, who has remained silent. She repeatedly asks him to let it go now, as she has reached her tipping point and is losing patience waiting for him to commit. Using the bridge below, she eloquently reiterates her message, ready to pick up the pieces of her broken heart and move on.

Bridge

Drop it now, drop it now **(Line 2)**
Drop it, drop it right now **(Line 3)**
I'm ready to pick up the pieces **(Line 4)**

This bridge represents her final warning or ultimatum, providing him with one last opportunity to reassure her that their relationship is still strong and that he still loves her. In the end, however, her boyfriend remains silent and unwilling to commit. As a result, she decides to forsake him and walk away from the relationship.

Track 07♪♪♪He Can't

Verse I

The angels above
Must be looking down on me
Used to date bad guys for fancy things
Now I buy them everything
Cars they see in movie scenes
And diamond watches of their dream
This guy is so ungrateful, wait a minute
All can be taken away in a split second
'Cause I don't have time

Pre-chorus

If he thinks I'm gonna let him
Call the shots
Boy, keep on drinking

Chorus

My car he can't drive it
My phone he can't touch it
My money he can't waste it
My heart he can't break it
(I repeat)
My heart he can't break it
That's right, he can't

Verse II

If he's tripping, I'm a trip, so girls' trip
He ain't the one, bounce like Spalding
Cause they're ballers and players
Not to brag, the jag his braggin' about
You guessed it, I bought it
Girls night out, he ain't coming
I might have more issues than Digest's
But I ain't buying Kleenex
Crying over no exes, still the sexiest

Pre-chorus

If he thinks I'm gonna let him
Call the shots
Boy, keep on drinking

Track 07♪♪He Can't

Chorus

My car he can't drive it
My phone he can't touch it
My money he can't waste it
My heart he can't break it
(I repeat)
My heart he can't break it
That's right, he can't

Bridge

I'm bossy and freaky
Anything that I want, he gotta do it
Otherwise I'll get rid of him

Pre-chorus

If he thinks I'm gonna let him
Call the shots
Boy, keep on drinking

Chorus

My car he can't drive it
My phone he can't touch it
My money he can't waste it
My heart he can't break it
(I repeat)
My heart he can't break it
That's right, he can't

Behind the Lyrics

How did this song come to fruition? Well, on a chilly night in the early Winter of 2019, I was in a nightclub in South Boston Waterfront, situated in Boston, Massachusetts, as I was shuffling through a packed crowd, trying to squeeze my broad shoulder through the crowd so I could get somewhat or to the proximity closer to the bartender to ask for a drink; suddenly the DJ dropped the beat to 7 Rings by Ariana Grande, the dance floor went bananas, my thirst was ebbing away.

I stood there emotionless, listening to the beat and the instrumental while watching the girls mouth every word of the chorus. I realized the chorus was dope—so dope it moved me lyrically. The whole song felt powerful enough to make a DJ's needle jump, if he'd had a turntable in front of him.

Curious, I immediately pulled out my phone and checked the credits for "7 Rings" to see who wrote it. That's when I discovered it had ten songwriters and lyricists behind it, including Ariana Grande. I felt jealous and inspired at the same time. The way the beat connected so effortlessly to the chorus was beautiful, and I couldn't help myself—I went from tapping my feet and nodding my head to quietly singing along.

As the DJ prepared to play the next track, I told myself I could use the "7 Rings" instrumental as the foundation for my next song. The following day, the beat was still pulsing inside me, louder than my own heartbeat. It kept ringing in my ears as I sat down, unsure of what I wanted to write about or who I wanted to write for. But eventually, the inspiration took shape, and I ended up penning
"He Can't"—a story about women's empowerment, independence, and successful women calling the shots.

Verse I

The angels above	***(Line 1)***
Must be looking down on me	***(Line 2)***
Used to date bad guys for fancy things	***(Line 3)***
Now I buy them everything	***(Line 4)***

The two opening lines provide a history of a woman's early life, her past relationships, and her economic status before achieving success. It took her years of hard work to reach her current elevated position and independence.

She is portrayed as a "superwoman," symbolized by an "S" on her chest. As mentioned in Line 2, she once pursued men for material gains.

Lines 3 and 4 describe her current status as she begins to accumulate wealth. Rather than seeking gifts from men, she starts to give them material things. However, when they behave poorly or show ingratitude, she quickly reminds them that she is the one in charge and the boss. She warns them to take it easy; otherwise, everything she has given them could be taken back in an instant.

In Line 9, the phrase "'cause I don't have time" may seem unnecessary, but I was open to including it. I had already used words like "minutes" and "seconds" in the previous lines, so this line, which ends with the word "time," fit perfectly to conclude the first verse.

Pre-chorus

If he thinks I'm gonna let him **(Line 1)**
Call the shots **(Line 2)**
Boy, keep on drinking **(Line 3)**

This pre-chorus accurately captures the atmosphere of the soiree at the nightclub in Seaport. Can you identify the reference to the nighttime gathering in the pre-chorus? Do you notice any similarities between the pre-chorus and the story I shared about my experience at the nightclub that inspired this song? If you do, you might just be a lyricist too.

Regarding Lines 2 and 3, do you remember the story about my time at the nightclub? If so, you would understand the meaning behind "call the shots," which refers to actually getting a "shot" glass from the bartender and drinking it. This was my intention as I squeezed through the crowd to reach the bar. Additionally, the concept of this pre-chorus was designed to mirror the ambiance of a real nightclub. Using keywords such as "shots" and "drinking" elevates the song, making it a potential summer pop club banger—perfect for getting people on the dance floor.

Chorus

My car he can't drive it **(Line 1)**
My phone he can't touch it **(Line 2)**
My money he can't waste it **(Line 3)**

The chorus is straightforward, as the concept is sweet, simple, and repetitive. As her wealth increases, she becomes more established, independent, and assertive; she begins to implement rules that her partner should follow. More importantly, she feels her heart is unbreakable, as she views herself as being in complete control with extraordinary confidence. Lyrically, I've maintained consistency in each line, using end rhyme schemes.

Let's pause for a moment. End rhyme schemes are the most common form of rhyming in songwriting, where two or more lines end with the same sound. If you had asked me to explain end rhyme schemes at the beginning of this journey, I would have struggled. However, after years of writing, I can now articulate and describe these important rhyming techniques clearly. Additionally, each line ends with the word "it."

My heart he can't break it **(Line 4)**
(I repeat) **(Line 5)**
My heart he can't break it **(Line 6)**
That's right, he can't **(Line 7)**

Although in Lines 5 and 7, I intentionally included an adlib—"(I repeat)"—to give the audience a break and prevent fatigue.

Furthermore, I took the opportunity to incorporate internal rhymes within the song, titled "He Can't." These internal rhymes are seamlessly woven into the middle of each line, demonstrating that rhymes do not always have to occur at the end of phrases.

I also employed open or beginning rhyme schemes with the word "My" throughout the chorus. This choice enhances memorability and creates a beautiful lyrical flow. There are many types of rhyming schemes (such as slant rhymes, alliteration, AABCCB, and AABBAA), but as a lyricist and author, my primary goal is to maintain consistency within the song. This consistency helps to keep the audience engaged and ensures the song flows smoothly. Lastly, the chorus is short and features catchy lyrics that are enjoyable rather than boring.

Verse II
If he's tripping, I'm a trip, so girls' trip **(Line 1)**
He ain't the one, bounce like spalding **(Line 2)**
'Cause they all ballers and players **(Line 3)**

Initially, the opening line was written as "Everywhere I go, I'm tripping." However, I found it too vague, so I decided to revise it and incorporate more wordplay. I used the informal expression "someone is a trip," which refers to someone acting wild, strange, or exciting—a term my sister Addjany often uses.

Line 2 is a play on words, using terms related to a "player" (commonly understood as a man who has multiple romantic partners), such as "bouncing" and "Spalding," which was once the official basketball manufacturer of the NBA (National Basketball Association). This line reflects the idea that some men can be dishonest and play games in relationships.

Line 3 continues the theme from Line 2. Despite being wealthy and powerful, I wanted to include a moment where the character offers advice to her female audience. I didn't want her to be seen as an intimidating powerful woman who feels unrelatable to her fans. By sharing this caring message, she becomes even more powerful in my eyes as I penned this line, as she provides valuable advice to women and girls navigating the dating scene to be prudent. That's the essence of it.

Not to brag, the jag his braggin' about **(Line 4)**
You guessed it, I bought it **(Line 5)**
Girls night out, he ain't coming **(Line 6)**

These lines are clear. Again, she brags about her wealth while calling out others who boast about the material things she has given him.

Might have more issues than Digest's **(Line 7)**
But I ain't buying Kleenex **(Line 8)**
Crying over no exes, still the sexiest **(Line 9)**

In lines 7 through 9, she reflects on her success while also acknowledging her personal struggles. I aimed to convey a sense of vulnerability through wordplay and references, such as using "Kleenex" instead of "tissues" to symbolize drying her tears. However, it's important to note that she is not actually buying Kleenex to deal with the drama caused by men.

Bridge
The chorus of the song is quite repetitive, featuring both end rhymes and open rhymes. I thought that building a bridge—no pun intended—would add to the song's appeal.

I'm bossy and freaky **(Line 1)**
Anything that I want, he gotta do it **(Line 2)**
Otherwise I'll get rid of him **(Line 3)**

Line 1 introduces her sex appeal with the phrase "I'm bossy and freaky." In this context, "bossy" isn't meant literally; it refers to her desire for control in a sexual sense. She prefers to take charge. This song was a lot of fun to write, from the introduction to the story development. That's all for now—on to the next song!

Track 08♪♪♪Heart of a Champion

Intro

Really? You wanna know the truth?

Verse I

Honestly, you ain't the tallest
Even the strongest
But somehow, someway
Knocked gravity down in a forceful way
Found a way to reach my heart
Can't believe after all these years
You are still holding on to me
Like your grandparents' souvenirs

Pre-chorus

Honestly, with all my heart
You deserve a trophy
A metal , even the purple heart

Chorus

'Cause you got a heart of a champion
Heart of a champion, of a champion
Lion king, even Tiger in the woods
Ain't got nothing on you
'Cause you got a heart of a champion
Heart of a champion, of a champion

Verse II

Sadly, thank you for putting up with me
Showing me what love should be
We've gone thru tough times and fights
But you put them in the past like history
You couldn't write a better love story
It took me awhile to write this, I'm sorry

Pre-chorus

Honestly, with all my heart
You deserve a trophy
A metal, even the purple heart

Track 08♪♪Heart of a Champion

Chorus

'Cause you got a heart of a champion
Heart of a champion, of a champion
Lion king, even Tiger in the woods
Ain't got nothing on you
'Cause you got a heart of a champion
Heart of a champion, of a champion

Bridge

The truth is, before we get old with gray hair
Sitting on lies and regrets in a rocking chair
I wanna thank you now
For loving me and always being there

Pre-chorus

Honestly, with all my heart
You deserve a trophy
A metal, even the purple heart

Chorus

Cause you got a heart of a champion
Heart of a champion, of a champion
Lion king, even Tiger in the woods
Ain't got nothing on you
Cause you got a heart of a champion
Heart of a champion, of a champion

Outro

Forever a champion, forever a champion

Behind the Lyrics

The purpose of this song is to express appreciation and seek forgiveness. Thanking someone who continuously accepts your flaws, past mistakes, unacceptable behaviors, and even lies.

Intro

Really? You want to know the truth?

It didn't take long for me to come up with this introduction. Initially, all I had to work with was the title "Heart of a Champion" and the opening lines. I aimed to create an intro that would set the groove for the song. As you can see, the intro lacks proper lyrics, which is common; many intros include vocal riffing or instrumental sections. Historically, I've strived to ensure that every intro contains some conversational element and remains brief and concise. That's why I started with the question, "Really?" as if I were directly speaking to someone. I followed that up with, "You want to know the truth?" Again, my goal was to engage the audience in a conversation. The intro doesn't confirm whether the other person answers "Yes" or "No," but it does imply that they want to know the truth. In songwriting 101, every question should be answered, and I try to address every question in my songs with the best of my lyrical ability. Since I hadn't written any verses at that point, I thought it would be clever and informative to answer the question posed in the intro within the context of the song. By now, you should be familiar that I'm referring to Verse I.

Verse I

I typically wouldn't cover every line of every verse, but this song resonates deeply with me. Each line reminds me of my late grandmother, Amalia Forgue, who had the heart of a champion. She accepted all my flaws, my destructive behaviors, and my lies, even during my difficult, belligerent, and disobedient adolescent years. I wish I had the chance to tell her face to face how grateful I am and, more importantly, to apologize. I hope the angels can read this story to her. Sorry, I lost my train of thought while reminiscing for a moment. I didn't expect this to happen while writing this book, but since it did, I wanted to document the mood I was in as I narrated this section. After all, I like to write authentically, as if I were using a typewriter.

Honestly, you ain't the tallest **(Line 1)**
Even the strongest **(Line 2)**

These two lines had one purpose: to answer the question posed in the introduction. I believe they accomplished their goal.

The truth always hurts, especially when it involves someone you love dearly. That's why I had to start with the word "Honestly," reassuring this person that I no longer want to cause harm. From this moment forward, there would be no more lies or wrongful behaviors. Telling someone they are not the tallest or the strongest could spark a family feud, but it's essential to remember that true love wouldn't feel as gratifying without a bit of tough love.

As painful or harsh as the first two lines might seem, Lines 3, 4, and 5 take the song in a completely different direction, with a more positive tone.

But somehow, someway	***(Line 3)***
Knocked gravity down in a forceful way	***(Line 4)***
Found a way to reach my heart	***(Line 5)***

Despite a person's physical characteristics, they can still find a way to touch your heart. I envision that physical traits are insignificant when true love or unconditional love is the foundation of a relationship. In fact, even gravity cannot pull love down or knock love down.

Can't believe after all these years	***(Line 6)***
You're still holding on to me	***(Line 7)***
like your grandparents' souvenirs	***(Line 8)***

These three lines capture the essence of the relationship, revealing a sense of gratitude that I intended to express as the verse progressed. I thought incorporating conditional words related to longevity—like years and souvenirs, as well as references to grandparents—would resonate well. Grandparents, in particular, often hold on to souvenirs for many years, which aligns with my intent, especially in Line 8. This imagery serves to highlight the enduring nature of the relationship.

The reference to "grandparents' souvenirs" aims to reinforce the idea that this love is something to be cherished and preserved over time, even during difficult days or when issues arise, and even when there could be trouble in paradise. It reflects the choice of one person to remain by your side out of a sense of loyalty and gratitude. This is how you can recognize someone with a "Heart of a Champion."

Do you have a heart of a champion? If so, you'll likely relate to the rest of the song and its lyrics.

Pre-Chorus
Honestly, with all my heart **(Line 1)**
You deserve a trophy **(Line 2)**
A metal, even the purple heart **(Line 3)**

I must confess that it was not too hard to come up with this concept. As a sports fanatic, when I think of a champion, the first thing that comes to mind is a trophy—such as the Vince Lombardi Trophy awarded to the winning team of each season's Super Bowl, or the Larry O'Brien Trophy awarded annually by the NBA to the championship team. Therefore, giving this person flowers while they are still alive is imperative; in this case, a trophy is more appropriate, as they have a champion's heart. This individual has won your heart, and most importantly, your love.

In Line 3, I metaphorically reference sports, particularly the Olympics, as I envision a winning Olympian biting their medal on the podium after their courageous and extraordinary efforts. In addition, this line was added to build texture before the chorus and to pay homage to all the fallen soldiers. My goal was to broaden the reach of this song so it could resonate with a wider audience.

Chorus
'Cause you got a heart of a champion **(Line 1)**
Heart of a champion, of a champion **(Line 2)**

Up to this point, I hadn't provided a reason for why this incredible person is so deserving of recognition. I felt it was important to give listeners a logical explanation or justification. To do this, I started the opening line with a critical conjunction: "'cause" or "because." I also emphasized the song's title by repeating the word "champion" three times in the first two lines. While repetition can create a strong rhythm and consistency in music, I didn't want to be seen as a dull writer. Therefore, I skillfully avoided repeating the same two lines, giving thc listeners — and the singer — a brief break. This set the stage for the two subsequent lines:

Lion king, even Tiger in the woods **(Line 3)**
Ain't got nothing on you **(Line 4)**
'Cause you got a heart of a champion **(Line 5)**
Heart of a champion, of a champion **(Line 6)**

Consequently, I wanted to showcase my lyrical skills in this piece. The references to "The Lion King" highlight the American animated musical coming-of-age film, while "Tiger in the woods" nods to one of the greatest golfers of all time, Tiger Woods. I thought both references would align well with the central theme of "Heart of a Champion."

In lines 5 and 6, I mirrored the first two lines to maintain the same melody, flow, and tempo, ensuring that listeners have an easier time following the song's structure. Overall, I believe the chorus features a strong repetitive pattern. Repeating the idea of the champion's heart emphasizes that this appreciation isn't a one-time feeling; it represents a recurring emotion. The person perpetually embodies the spirit of a champion, expressing their unconditional love for someone who may not fully appreciate it.

Verse II

Before we dive into the lyrics of "Heart of a Champion," I want to point out that Verse II contains six lines, while Verse I has eight. This lack of structural alignment bothers me since I prefer each verse to have the same number of lines. I generally dislike deviating from any standard, especially in songwriting, as it suggests a lack of commitment. When I don't adhere to the process, I feel stagnant. Now that I have gotten this out of my championed hear, let's proceed to decode Verse II in full.

Sadly, thank you for puttin' up with me ***(Line 1)***
Showing me what love should be ***(Line 2)***
We've gone thru tough times and fights ***(Line 3)***

I opened the verse with new lyrics that provide additional background to the song, highlighting the turmoil within the relationship. This champion, who possesses a true champion's heart, refuses to let go of not just the rope of love, but also the rope of hope. In the second line, I emphasize this person's unmatched acceptance and patience, as they consistently display nothing but "One Love," reminiscent of the great Bob Marley's chant. Speaking of love, there is a heart reference in the first line of the chorus: "One Love, one heart."

The third line is straightforward and relatable, as it applies to most relationships, if not all. While many relationships experience fights and struggles, I want to underscore that there are no relationships that are completely free of challenges or that "walk on water." If yours does, all glory to you and your partner—count your blessings! However, that is not the reality for many, and this line encourages listeners to reflect on their own relationships. Thus, this line serves to create a connection, as it is certainly relatable.

But you put them in the past like history **(Line 4)**
You couldn't write a better love story **(Line 5)**
It took me awhile to write this, I'm sorry **(Line 6)**

Line 4: "Don't Let It Fester; Don't Hold a Grudge." I wrote this line to indicate that this person does not hold grudges; in fact, they are very forgiving. They champion the idea of not allowing difficult times to ruin or destroy relationships. Instead, they work through challenges and leave them in the past, using history as a metaphor. The phrase "to forgive and to forget" is metaphorically expressed here.Line 5: This specific line was added to create a good rhythm, which is why I used words like "story."

Line 6: This is a powerful line that highlights both regret and remorse. The truth is that we often express our appreciation for others only when they are no longer alive. Don't be a late florist; if you want to thank someone special in your life, time is of the essence. Tell them thank you so they can enjoy those flowers. If you need to apologize or say sorry, please don't delay; let them know you are "sorry." Overall, the ending rhymes with words like history, story, and sorry, which reinforces the song's rhythm.

Bridge

What can you learn from this bridge? First, you should do everything in your power to avoid sitting in a rocking chair, reflecting on your past mistakes, unacceptable behaviors, regrets, and lies during the final phase of your life.

The truth is, before we get old with gray hair **(Line 1)**
Sitting on lies and regrets in a rocking chair **(Line 2)**
I wanna thank you now **(Line 3)**
For loving me and always being there **(Line 4)**

The first line bridges the choruses and uses vivid imagery to help paint the scene and bring the song to life. For example, I imagine myself growing old. As I age, my hair will likely not just be salt and pepper; the gray will spread throughout. I also picture myself sitting in a rocking chair, as mentioned in Line 2.

In Lines 3 and 4, there is no surprise. After all this, the song expresses gratitude for someone who deserves admiration after all these years. I prefer to be specific, so Line 3 clearly indicates the reason for my thanks: I love this person from the bottom of my heart because they have shown me what it means to have the heartbeat of a champion.

Outro

I did not believe that this particular song required an outro; however, before concluding, I strongly felt that the artist I had in mind for this song should deliver an empowerment message. As they looked into the audience, they would say, "Forever champion."

Track 09♪♪♪♪♪♪♪♪♪♪♪♪♪♪♪♪♪♪♪♪♪♪♪♪♪♪♪♪♪I'll Be Fine (With A Bottle Wine)

Verse I

Don't wanna lose you
But every time I dream
I see you with someone else
Tell me it's only a nightmare
You ain't having an affair
Then I'd stay sitting on my chair
Otherwise I'd scream like I'm scared

Chorus

If you gonna break up with me
Don't play me
Like a game of chess
Just get it off your chest
I know it will hurt at first
But I'll be fine (with a bottle of wine)
I'll be fine (with a bottle of wine)
Oh yes, I will

Verse II

Who do you think I am?
I ain't a 24-hour store, staying up all night
Tired of waiting for you until 4 AM
I have stayed optimistic my dear
Hoping you would change
But its clear, the end is near

Chorus

If you gonna break up with me
Don't play me
Like a game of chess
Just get it off your chest
I know it will hurt at first
But I'll be fine (with a bottle of wine)
I'll be fine (with a bottle of wine)

Track 09♪♪♪♪♪♪♪♪♪♪♪♪♪♪♪♪♪♪♪♪♪♪♪♪♪♪♪♪♪♪I'll Be Fine (With A Bottle Wine)

Verse III
You don't have to lie
I can see a broken heart in your eyes
Please tell me it's not mine
Just look me in my eyes
Tell me its over then I'll leave
Like the autumn leaves

Chorus
If you gonna break up with me
Don't play me
Like a game of chess
Just get it off your chest
I know it will hurt at first
But I'll be fine (with a bottle of wine)
I'll be fine (with a bottle of wine)
Oh yes, I will

Bridge
I'm trying to make it easier for you
I don't know why
You are making it hard on yourself
Oh sweetie, don't sugar coat it

Chorus
If you gonna break up with me
Don't play me
Like a game of chess
Just get it off your chest
I know it will hurt at first
But I'll be fine (with a bottle of wine)
I'll be fine (with a bottle of wine)
Oh yes, I will
Oh yes, I will

Behind the Lyrics

Does the song "I'll Be Fine (With A Bottle of Wine)" remind you of a previous song I discussed and decoded? If you guessed "Forever Hold Your Peace," you are unquestionably on point, just like a straight arrow. "I'll Be Fine (With A Bottle of Wine)" serves as my redemption song, a do-over for "Forever Hold Your Peace." I was unhappy and dissatisfied with how the lyrics were written and structured in "Forever Hold Your Peace." I believed that some lines should have been reorganized, the verses could have had better rhymes, improved wordplay, and a more concise storyline. Overall, I felt I could have done better, so I decided to start over. What do I have to lose? Maybe a bottle of wine—just kidding! Nothing at all.

I saw this as an opportunity not only to challenge myself but also to enhance my lyrical skills. As cliché as it may sound, there is always room for improvement, even in songwriting. So, I put my head down and my fingers on the keyboard, searching for perfection, a different vibe, and various word schemes, as if I were playing Scrabble, unsure if my second attempt would be successful or not.

I'm constantly looking for the next hit record that meets the music industry's expectations for sales and, more importantly, commercial success. No one wants to release music that flops or features mediocre lyrics.

Despite my determination and motivation to rewrite the song, I didn't know how to start. Oddly enough, the idiomatic phrase "fine like wine" popped into my head, so I decided to incorporate it into the title. I titled it "I'll Be Fine (With A Bottle of Wine)," which is longer than my previous song titles, but it works. This version of the song addresses themes like insecurity, infidelity, abandonment, and honesty.

Verse I

Don't wanna lose you **(Line 1)**
But every time I dream **(Line 2)**
I see you with someone else **(Line 3)**

The opening line begins with the fear of losing someone, which I included to heighten the drama in the first verse. Who doesn't enjoy a touch of drama in modern times, right? However, I felt it was important for this verse to clearly convey the current state of the relationship as it navigates through a challenging period. The relationship is in a questionable state, for lack of better words.

In Line 2, I explore a different scenario filled with self-doubt and superstition. One partner has been questioning the other based on unfounded suspicions that they may be having an affair. The relationship is clearly in turmoil.

In Line 3, the wife shares a dream she had in which she sees her partner with someone else. She follows up with, "Tell me it's only a nightmare." The response from her partner is left unclear or unarticulated in the verse, which I intentionally chose not to address. As she moves on to the next line, one might assume that the husband did not answer her question.

Tell me it's only a nightmare **(Line 4)**
You ain't having an affair **(Line 5)**
Then I'd stay sitting on my chair **(Line 6)**
Otherwise I'd scream like I'm scared **(Line 7)**

Once again, I relied on end-rhyme patterns to strengthen the close of the chorus, especially since the opening lines don't follow a strong rhyming structure. As she continues confronting him, I intentionally layered in additional end rhymes toward the conclusion. Lines 6 and 7 stand out to me in particular; they flow naturally with the word *"nightmare"* introduced in Line 4. That connection reinforces the rhyme scheme established in the previous lines and helps the chorus land with a more cohesive and satisfying rhythm.

Since this song does not contain a pre-chorus, let's swim into decoding the newly rewritten chorus, shall we?

Chorus
If you gonna break up with me **(Line 1)**
Don't play me **(Line 2)**
Like a game of chess **(Line 3)**
Just get it off your chest **(Line 4)**

This is the breakthrough line, focusing on stipulation; she sets certain conditions before the relationship can end in heartbreak. Lines 2 through 4 allow her to express herself clearly while giving him the opportunity to speak nothing but the truth. At this point, she is fed up with his games.

I know it will hurt at first **(Line 5)**
But I'll be fine (with a bottle of wine) **(Line 6)**
I'll be fine (with a bottle of wine) **(Line 7)**
Oh, yes will **(Line 8)**

Lines 5 and 6 suggest that she will initially feel pain and heartbreak, but she will be okay if she sips on wine, as mentioned earlier. What type of wine will she be sipping? Only she knows. If I had to guess, I would envision her enjoying a glass of smooth Pinot Grigio or Pinot Noir.

After the first verse and chorus, the second verse should follow. However, before I proceed, please pour yourself a glass of fine wine and allow me to compare the two choruses side by side, as illustrated below.

I'll Be Fine (With a bottle of Wine)
If you gonna break up with me
Don't play me
Like a game of chess
Just get it off your chest
I know it will hurt at first
But I'll be fine with a bottle of wine
I'll be fine with a bottle of wine
Oh, yes I will

Forever Hold Your Peace
If you gonna break my heart
Drop it now
Don't sugar coat it
Just say your piece
Or forever hold your peace
If you gonna break my heart
Drop it now
Don't sugar coat it
Just say your piece
Or forever hold your peace

Which chorus do you prefer? Please be honest, as I appreciate constructive feedback more than positive feedback because it encourages me to improve my craft.

If I had to choose, I'd pick the first chorus—the one shown at the top—because its wordplay and rhymes land so cleverly. The line "with a bottle of wine" really elevates the whole section. I still hope that one day it reaches the top of the Billboard 200. After all, who can resist a bottle of fine wine? Unless, of course, you prefer to eat your grapes instead.

As a lyricist, my goal is to keep persevering, no matter how long it takes. I have been bold and unafraid to revisit my work in order to improve my lyrics. I genuinely believe that I achieved this with this version of the song. Had I not taken the time to review and reevaluate the original version, I might never have discovered this new form of expression in my mind.

One important lesson we can learn from this experience—and from life in general—is that we should be courageous enough to go backward and take risks, even if it means facing failure. Going backward doesn't mean the race is over or that we have lost; rather, it's a period of growth, change, adaptation, and ultimately rejuvenation before reaching the finish line and claiming the checkered flag that lies ahead.

Conversely, some individuals are unable to go backward because they have never taken a step forward or embraced any risks. They tend to follow in the footsteps of others, traveling well-worn paths. As a result, they leave no footprints or marks of their own and miss the vital lessons of success and excellence that come from experiencing failure and setbacks.

So, be grateful for both the ups and downs. Bottle them all up, and one day you'll have the opportunity to pour yourself a glass of fine wine, make a toast, and say, "Bottoms up."

Enough of my rambling—it's time to decode Verse II!

Verse II

This verse gives a detailed account of her frustrations and his current behaviors.

Who do you think I am? **(Line 1)**
Not a 24-hour store, staying up all night **(Line 2)**
Tired of waiting for you until 4 AM **(Line 3)**

As I was developing this verse, I felt that opening with a question would re-engage the audience, especially as she continues to unleash her emotions—feeling disrespected, sensing a lack of commitment, and never knowing whether her partner would come home at a reasonable hour or offer even the basic decency of an apology with a valid explanation.

Lines 2 and 3: These lines shift the tone just enough to give her more space to speak her mind. They allow her to voice the questions she's been carrying since Verse I, pushing for the answers she still hasn't received.

I have stayed optimistic my dear **(Line 4)**
Hoping you would change **(Line 5)**
But it's clear, the end is near **(Line 6)**

In Line 6, she concludes that the relationship is not worth fighting for without solid evidence. This line is crucial, allowing the singer to transition into Verse III.

Verse III
Until now, the audience has been left puzzled by the idea of a breakup attributed to infidelity, despite the fact that the root cause has not been confirmed. I believe there should be some kind of evidence to support this claim, so I used Verse III as my validation for these assertions.

You don't have to lie **(Line 1)**
I can see a broken heart in your eyes **(Line 2)**
Please tell me it's not mine **(Line 3)**

The opening line conveys nothing but frustration and speculation, as she has yet to obtain concrete evidence from her partner. However, Line 2 serves as the turning point, revealing what feels like the smoking gun. For the first time, she sees signs of a broken heart reflected in his eyes, confirming that he has broken his vows and is mentally checked out. In Line 3, although she recognizes the brokenness in him, she remains unconvinced. Her plea, "Please tell me it's not mine," underscores her desire to hear the truth directly from him. She follows this with, "I'll be fine (with a bottle of wine)," pressing him a little harder in the subsequent line.

Just look me in my eyes **(Line 4)**
Tell me it's over then I'll leave **(Line 5)**
Like the autumn leaves **(Line 6)**

As he is unwilling to tell her the truth, she proceeds with two bold and powerful lines, Lines 5 and 6, embedded with wordplay such as "I'll leave, like the autumn leaves."

Bridge
I'm trying to make it easier for you **(Line 1)**
I don't know why **(Line 2)**
You are making it hard on yourself **(Line 3)**
Oh sweetie, don't sugar coat it **(Line 4)**

Verse III could have effectively served as a bridge to break up the repetitive chorus. However, this section stands out on its own due to its explicit language and clear statements, particularly as noted in line 4. The narrator offers her partner an opportunity to leave, but ultimately, he decides to stay. As a result, she chooses to move on.

Track 10.♪♪♪In Your Bedroom

Intro

Oh nah, Oh nah

Verse I

It wasn't love at first sight
Remember when we first met by the bar
You were yelling at me, ready to fight
'Cause you thought I'd grabbed you
I tried my best to avoid you, right?
Little did I know
We came to hang out with the same crew

Pre-chorus

That night, I remember sitting next to you
Saying to myself, I wish I never met you
But thinking, damn, you kinda cute

Chorus

Thank God I met you
'Cause I've been looking
For a cutie just like you
But who knew? (ew)
One day, we'd be in the same room
Let alone naked in your bedroom
Naked in your bedroom
Thank God, I'm naked in your bedroom

Verse II

Remember when we'd argue
About the stupidest things alive
I was never good enough for you
Always at the bottom, I think number 45
You hurt my feelings more than a few
But I kept it calm on my way home
Even though I couldn't stand you

Pre-chorus

That night, I remember sitting next to you
Saying to myself, I wish I never met you
But thinking, damn, you kinda cute

Track 10♪♪In Your Bedroom

Chorus

Thank God I met you
'Cause I've been looking
For a cutie just like you
But who knew? (ew)
One day, we'd be in the same room
Let alone naked in your bedroom
Naked in your bedroom
Thank God I'm naked in your bedroom

Bridge

So babe lift me up from the ground
Hold me up against the wall
Like a picture in your bedroom
Make me feel new heights
Take me to the moon

Chorus

Thank God I met you
'Cause I've been looking
For a cutie just like you
But who knew? (ew)
One day we'd be in the same room
Let alone naked in your bedroom
Naked in your bedroom
Thank God, I'm naked in your bedroom

Outro

Ooh, yeah, in your bedroom

The Meaning Behind "In Your Bedroom"

The inspiration behind In Your Bedroom came from the idea of an unexpected encounter between two strangers in their early twenties. They meet up with friends at a sports bar for happy hour on a warm summer evening. A small incident occurs when he accidentally bumps into her, prompting her to yell at him, convinced he had grabbed her intentionally. In truth, he had simply stumbled in the crowded space.

As they talk, they realize they were both invited by mutual friends. Later that night, despite her initial irritation, they end up sharing a ride to a nearby beach with the group. Sitting together in the back seat, she finds herself developing an unexpected crush. Their connection deepens, and eventually they end up together in his bedroom, where the rest is left to the imagination.

Years later, they are a couple, and he reflects on the night they first met. As he begins telling his version of the story, she jumps in immediately, offering her own perspective and opening her retelling with a familiar introductory expression.

Intro
Oh Nah, Oh Nah

Although the introduction lacks proper lyrics, my goal was to capture a clear rejection of his claim. Her recollection of the situation does not align with his, which is why she objects. She emphasizes how difficult their journey has been to reach this point and how much they initially disliked each other. Ultimately, their experiences brought them to his bedroom. Now, she cannot believe she is in that space. Despite having a secret crush on him and finding him cute, she also cannot stand him.

Verse I
It wasn't love at first sight **(Line 1)**
Remember when we first met by the bar **(Line 2)**
You were yelling at me, ready to fight **(Line 3)**

These lines describe the scene and background of their initial encounter, which takes place in a sports bar. I really enjoy sports bars, but I dislike it when there's no room to navigate through the crowd. It forces you to carry your drink carefully, almost like a mother holding her infant. This situation is especially true if the bartender has already announced last call for alcohol.

Creating this scene was straightforward for me, as I have experienced crowded bars in my earlier years.

'Cause you thought I'd grabbed you **(Line 4)**
I tried my best to avoid you, right? **(Line 5)**

I wanted to create vivid imagery of the sports bar, so I drew from my own past experiences and the things I've witnessed—women calling out men for touching them inappropriately, whether intentionally or by accident. In crowded places like that, most women are understandably skeptical when someone claims the contact was "just an accident," especially because it often happens abruptly rather than gradually.

Pre-Chorus
That night, I remember sitting next to you **(Line 1)**
Saying to myself, I wish I never met you **(Line 2)**
But thinking, damn, you kinda cute **(Line 3)**

There's a saying—perhaps even a proverb—in Haiti that Danounou often quotes: "Rayi chen an, di dan'l blan." In English, it means, "You may dislike the dog, but you must still acknowledge its white teeth." Now, back to the story. She regrets ever meeting him, yet she can't deny that she finds him "kinda" cute.

When I reached this point in the songwriting process, I wasn't sure whether a pre-chorus was necessary. Still, I wanted to build more momentum before introducing the chorus. I had two choices: revise Verse I by adding another line, which would have expanded it to eight lines, or leave the verse as it was and insert a pre-chorus to make the song feel more dynamic. I chose the latter.

Chorus
Thank God I met you **(Line 1)**
'Cause I've been looking **(Line 2)**
For a cutie just like you **(Line 3)**
But who knew? (ew) **(Line 4)**

I wanted to shift the narrative of the story from a secret crush or fling to a love story. In the first two lines, she embraces him more and more, unable to deny or ignore her physical attraction to him. By lines three and four, the stark reality hits her: she never imagined that one day they would be sharing a room, let alone being naked in his bedroom.

One day we'd be in the same room **(Line 5)**
Let alone naked in your bedroom **(Line 6)**
Naked in your bedroom **(Line 6)**
Thank God, I'm naked in your bedroom **(Line 7)**

I really enjoyed writing the rest of the verse because the imagery felt adventurous and captured a summer vibe. The rhyming scheme is relatable, making it easy to imagine everyone at a sports bar holding their drinks and singing the last four lines together. So, let's sing it one more time!

One day we'd be in the same room **(Line 5)**
Let alone naked in your bedroom **(Line 6)**
Naked in your bedroom **(Line 6)**
Thank God, I am naked in your bedroom **(Line 7)**

Once again, I'm just kidding! Psych—one more time. One day we'll be in the same room. I hope you had fun, as I have had. Let's decode Verse II.

Verse II
Remember when we'd argue **(Line 1)**
About the stupidest things alive **(Line 2)**
I was never good enough for you **(Line 3)**

These lines focus on a conversation in their friend's car, driving to a remote location for fun.

Always at the bottom, I think number 45 **(Line 4)**
You hurt my feelings more than a few **(Line 5)**
But I kept it calm on my way home **(Line 6)**
Even though I couldn't stand you **(Line 7)**

In line 4, I referred to "number 45" to rhyme with "alive" and to indicate her low status on his preference list; nevertheless, they ended up making love in the bedroom. In line 5, she expresses how hurtful his behavior was that day, yet as the song progresses, she finds herself unable to resist.

Bridge
So babe lift me up from the ground **(Line 1)**
Hold me up against the wall **(Line 2)**
Like a picture in your bedroom **(Line 3)**
Make me feel new heights **(Line 4)**
Take me to the moon **(Line 5)**

Once again, the mood of the song shifts with lines like "Hold me up against the wall," which contribute to its sensual appeal in the bedroom, where everything is happening—if you know what I mean, figuratively speaking. I aimed to be as explicit as possible while making this section distinctive compared to Verses I and II. I also attempted to connect the ending of the chorus to the bridge for a smoother rhythm. The chorus concludes with the line, "I'm naked in your bedroom."

To begin the bridge, I used "so" as a conjunction to link the two sections, indicating a cause-and-effect relationship. I may not be an English major, but I suppose that's a minor lesson in English 101 for you, ha-ha!

In that space, you'll find the full story of how I wrote the song. While you may not relate to the entire piece, I believe you can understand at least the bridge—something you've likely crossed and experience in your life at one time or another, right?

Track 11♪♪♪Keep Going Back

Verse I

Lately, I've been standing by the window
You're the girl next door
That I admire, even when our views
Aint black and white
I'd be lying if I told you, you're just alright
That wouldn't be right
You're the neighborhood Christmas light
Everyone's dying to see

Pre-chorus

Part of me wanna invite you over
Part of me wanna push you away
To tell ya the truth, I'm scared to (fall in love)

Chorus

That's why
I keep running away from you
Like I'm running track
But every time, every time
I' m near the finish line
I can't get you out of my mind
I keep going back, keep going back
for you

Verse II

I've gotten lost looking for the right one
You seem like the one
I have been looking for
You hit me like a speeding bullet
Hitting my heart off my chest
But every time I dream about us
Something tells me dodge the bullet
And take my heart off my sleeve

Pre-chorus

Part of me wanna invite you over
Part of me wanna push you away
To tell ya the truth, I'm scared to (fall in love)

Track 11♪♪♪Keep Going Back

Chorus

That's why
I keep running away from you
Like I'm running track
But every time, every time
I' m near the finish line
I can't get you out of my mind
I keep going back, keep going back
for you

Bridge

Love had been unkind to me
I'm glad I found you
come with me
and leave all behind
There's no turning back from here

Pre-chorus

Part of me wanna invite you over
Part of me wanna push you away
To tell ya the truth, I'm scared to (fall in love)

Chorus

That's why
I keep running away from you
Like I'm running track
But every time, every time
I' m near the finish line
I can't get you out of my mind
I keep going back, keep going back
for you

Behind the Lyrics

This song explores the fear of falling in love and the hesitation to express what the heart truly desires, all while acknowledging that time is running out. If you admire someone, you should confront those fears and let them know how deeply you are attracted to them. However, it's easy to lack the courage to take the first step, like asking someone out or inviting them over. For now, the only option might be to admire that beautiful person from a distance, like a "window lover."

This song was one of the first that I actually had demoed, and there is so much to unpack in its meaning. Because of that, I might not be able to decode every nuance and line, so please keep that in mind if I overlook something.

Verse I

Unlike my previous songs, this one didn't need an introduction. I felt that a preview or opening tag wouldn't add any real texture to the first verse. Instead, I chose to dive straight in, letting the story unfold contemporaneously—right there in real time.

Lately, I've been standing by the window ***(Line 1)***
You're the girl next door ***(Line 2)***
That I admire, even when our views ***(Line 3)***
Aint black and white ***(Line 4)***

I wanted to express my deep admiration for a girl in my neighborhood. I often see her walking down the street, but from my window I can never get a clear view of her. That limitation—trying to appreciate someone from behind a barrier—is exactly what Line 3 captures. It highlights how difficult it is to truly admire or understand what's happening outside when you're looking from the inside. That's the intent behind the line.

I'd be lying if I told you, you're just alright ***(Line 5)***
That wouldn't be right ***(Line 6)***
You're the neighborhood Christmas light ***(Line 7)***

I wanted to highlight how her beauty illuminates the neighborhood every time she walks down the block—almost like a modern-day Jenny from the Block. I thought about events that communities traditionally celebrate, and the word *"lights"* came to mind. It fit perfectly with the existing rhyme scheme of *"alright"* and *"right."* As I reflected on it, the Christmas holiday was the perfect fit. Thus, I felt compelled to decorate and light up the verse, as her beauty is as captivating as the neighborhood Christmas lights. And there you have it.

Pre-Chorus

Part of me wanna invite you over (Line 1)
Part of me wanna push you away (Line 2)

I wanted to give the song a new direction and melody to capture the interaction between the two characters. What is she like when she's not being observed from the window? And who is he when he's outside, face-to-face rather than hidden behind the glass?

One Christmas night, he sees her and instinctively closes the curtain. Then he grabs a piece of paper and a pen and writes the two lines mentioned above. Later, he hands her the note as a way of explaining why he keeps running away.

Chorus

That 's why ***(Line 1)***
I keep running away from you ***(Line 2)***
Like I'm running track ***(Line 3)***

I penned the chorus using a football field as a metaphor. The goal is to reach the end zone, but lyrically, the ultimate aim isn't about scoring. Instead, the focus is on the idea that he's going backward, as if he doesn't want to score a touchdown. While writing these lyrics, I kept repeating that love is scary because, in reality, who genuinely wants to "fall" in love? Falling is one thing, but the impact of that fall is even more frightening and terrifying.

I' m near the finish line ***(Line 5)***
I can't get you out of my mind ***(Line 6)***
I keep going back, keep going back ***(Line 7)***

As he stands face to face with her near the finish line, he is on the verge of telling her something important. However, he hesitates and continually keeps going back or pulls back. He lacks the courage to express his feelings, and more importantly, he does not have the football, by "football" I mean the balls to say what he truly wants to say.

Verse II

I've gotten lost looking for the right one ***(Line 1)***
You seem like the one ***(Line 2)***

I have been looking for ***(Line 3)***

Lines 1 through 3 emphasize his admiration for his neighbor while also providing insight into his relationship history, as noted in Line 1: "Gotten lost looking for the right one." In the following lines, I aimed to provide additional context and strengthen the verse through clever wordplay, rhymes, and metaphors. I believe I achieved that with the subsequent lines.

You hit me like a speeding bullet ***(Line 4)***
Hitting my heart off my chest ***(Line 5)***
But every time I dream about us ***(Line 6)***
Something tells me dodge the bullet ***(Line 7)***

Do you concur? Honestly, what are your thoughts?

Lastly, let's evaluate the bridge. But before I do, I want to emphasize an important life lesson: try not to burn your bridges. You never know when you might find yourself in a situation where going back is the only way to move forward, as suggested by the title of the song, "Keep Going Back." That's my message. Now, on a different note, let's analyze the bridge I wrote.

Bridge
Come with me ***(Line 3)***
And leave all behind ***(Line 4)***
There's no turning back from here ***(Line 5)***

These lines suggest that he has found true love. As a result, he wants to move on from the past and present to start a future with her, without any intention of going back.

I spent several days trying to shorten the bridge; since both verses consist of eight lines, I ideally wanted the bridge to be half that length. In this case, I ended up with five lines instead of the desired four. I couldn't decide which line to exclude, so I kept all five. I'm confident that if I pitched this to an artist, it wouldn't be surprising if the bridge was shortened to four or even three lines. I suppose we can cross that bridge when we come to it. Until then, Until then, I will keep going back and debating whether this approach is appropriate.

Track 12♪♪The Way You Dance

Verse I

Hey girl, would you like to dance?
The look on your face, don't wanna dance
Its okay, I understand,
You think I'm trying to get into your pants
Girl, you got me all wrong
My mom taught me right from wrong
Never disrespect any woman
I know how to treat a girl right, like yourself

Pre-Chorus

If you don't believe me
Girl, just take my hand
Let's have this dance

Chorus

Two hands in the air
Feet moving nice and slow
Hips moving like a Shakira
Body is hotter than the Sahara
It's hard to focus in here
But I have to seize this chance
To dance, with you
'Cause I love the way you dance
I love the way you dance

Verse II

Listen, I might strike you as a lady's man
But I think just like a woman
I'm only here to have fun
And have a few drinks with my friends
Then I'll call it a night, that's the plan
Not into one-night stand
I got it, I completely understand
Where you stand

Pre-Chorus

If you don't believe me
Girl, just take my hand
Let's have this dance

Track 12♪♪The Way You Dance

Chorus
Two hands in the air
Feet moving nice and slow
Hips moving like a Shakira
Body is hotter than the Sahara
It's hard to focus in here
But I have to seize this chance
To dance, with you
'Cause I love the way you dance
I love the way you dance

Bridge
Later on
If you're looking for me
I'll be right here
Waiting on the dance floor

Pre-Chorus
If you don't believe me
Girl, just take my hand
Let's have this dance

Chorus
Two hands in the air
Feet moving nice and slow
Hips moving like a Shakira
Body is hotter than the Sahara
Its hard to focus in here
But I have to seize this chance
To dance, with you
'Cause I love the way you dance
I love the way you dance

Behind the Lyrics

This song portrays the nightlife scene during my early years as a regular clubgoer. In my late teens and twenties, I frequented nightclubs almost every weekend—Thursday through Sunday—and still managed to attend Sunday services. It was a time in my life when no distance was too far for my friends and me to drive for a night out. We would travel from Lowell to the heart of New Hampshire, exploring nightclubs in Manchester and Exeter.

Some friends had more free time and deeper pockets than I did, so they often ventured further to Maine for a night of fun. Notably, many of us used the nightclub scene as a dating environment, socializing and meeting potential girlfriends or one-night stands. Some of these encounters extended beyond just one night, even if it meant enduring the frigid cold in their old, unreliable cars while driving from Lowell Connector (American Legion Connector Highway) to Interstate 95 North.

My favorite nightclubs were The Underground in Manchester, NH; Ozone in Hampton, NH; and The Palace in Saugus, MA.

Verse I

Hey girl, would you like to dance? **(Line 1)**
The look on your face, don't wanna dance **(Line 2)**
Its okay, I understand **(Line 3)**
You think I'm trying to get into your pants **(Line 4)**

First and foremost, my favorite part of clubbing has always been dancing on the dance floor, whether I was vibing solo or dancing the tango—no preference. Most nights, I would start the conversation with one of my favorite lines: "Would you like to dance?" Historically, I often faced rejection during my first couple of attempts, which I kindly accepted by walking away. Before leaving, though, I would typically utter a few parting words:

Girl, you got me all wrong **(Line 5)**
My mom taught me right from wrong **(Line 6)**
Never disrespect any woman **(Line 7)**

These lines emanate from my relationship with my mother, whom I deeply respect. Because of this, I treat every woman with the same respect I give to my mother—never with disrespect. It's a principle I stand by, "word to my momma." Even the slightest thought of disrespecting a woman dissipates when I hear the marvelous voice of Aretha Franklin singing the lyrics written by Otis Redding:

R-E-S-P-E-C-T, find out what it means to me
R-E-S-P-E-CT, take care of T-C-B

It would stop me because it is not in my nature to disrespect any woman or any human being. Regarding the lyrics mentioned earlier, I have understood the meaning of respect since I was a child. Line 8 is particularly important for breaking the ice: "I know how to treat a girl right, like yourself." More importantly, this line reflects what I would often whisper or murmur if I had another chance to ask her to dance with me.

Pre-Chorus

Having the best pickup lines, a fresh haircut with sharp lines, and a stylish outfit doesn't guarantee that you'll find a dance partner to share a drink with. At the nightclub, you have to put in some effort to find someone to dance with, but some nights it's easier to find a partner than others.

If you don't believe me	***(Line 1)***
Girl, just take my hand	***(Line 2)***
Let's have this dance	***(Line 3)***

I wrote these lines to build anticipation for the song before we proceed to the chorus. The aim is to create an exciting atmosphere on the dance floor in case she stumbles or responds to one of my pickup lines.

Chorus

Two hands in the air	***(Line 1)***
Feet moving nice and slow	***(Line 2)***
Hips moving like a Shakira	***(Line 3)***
Body is hotter than the Sahara	***(Line 4)***
Its hard to focus in here	***(Line 5)***

My pick-up lines obviously work, so I wanted to impress my dancing partner even more by creating vivid imagery that would allow my audience to feel the sexiness, fun, passion, love, and movement on the dance floor.

In Line 3, I referenced the hit song "Hips Don't Lie" by Colombian singer-songwriter Shakira, featuring Wyclef Jean. As I considered which body parts to describe—hands and feet—Shakira's hips caught my attention. After completing Line 4, "Body is hotter than the Sahara," I thought about changing the reference from Shakira to Rihanna, as it would have better aligned with the preceding line, "Hips moving like a Rihanna."

Verse II

Listen, I might strike you as a lady's man **(Line 1)**
But I think just like a woman **(Line 2)**
I'm only here to have fun **(Line 3)**
And have a few drinks with my friends **(Line 4)**

As the atmosphere heated up on the dance floor, I felt it was the perfect moment to express my desire to dance with her because I truly admire her dancing. Moreover, the last two lines (Lines 3 and 4) reflect the typical responses I receive from my dance partners.

Then I'll call it a night, that's the plan **(Line 5)**
Not into one night stand **(Line 6)**
I got it, I completely understand **(Line 7)**
Where you stand **(Line 8)**

Lines 5 through 7 convey a subtle psychological technique aimed at easing her mind, ensuring she doesn't entertain thoughts beyond the dancefloor. However, if anything were to happen outside of that setting, I wouldn't be averse to it; after all, I tend to think like a man naturally. In the last five lines, I primarily employ end rhyme schemes.

Bridge

Later on **(Line 1)**
If you're looking for me **(Line 2)**
I'll be right here **(Line 3)**
Waiting on the dance floor **(Line 4)**

I wanted to avoid crossing the bridge with lengthy lines, so I kept the scenario simple and unchanged. While I could have expanded the setting to include a moment where she gives out her phone number, that would have been too easy. Instead, at the end of the song, she leaves the dance floor, and he tells her that he will be waiting for her there, as mentioned in Line 4. Will she return for another dance? That remains to be written.

In early 2020, I completed the *Peaceful* album, though I wasn't entirely at peace when it came to promoting my songs. I found myself torn between demoing another track to diversify my portfolio or focusing on writing new lyrics for my upcoming project, *Looking Ahead.*

I ultimately chose the former. But then came the real challenge: which song—and from which album? After days of reviewing and reevaluating everything I had written so far, and with Rachel's help, "Let Him Go" and "The Way You Dance" rose to the top. Their storylines and their ability to immediately capture a listener's attention made them strong contenders. Still, I had to be realistic. Demoing both would have been ideal, but financially, it wasn't the right moment.

So I decided to move forward with a single track. I entrusted the recording company in Nashville—where Rachel worked as a Writer Relations Coordinator—to produce my second demo, "The Way You Dance." I also agreed to sign a recording contract authorizing the company to pitch the song to potential artists and musicians. If my calculations are correct, the demo was recorded on Friday, July 10, 2020—approximately one year, one month, and twenty days after "Addicted" was completed.

With two demos now under my belt, I felt energized to create more music. But after hearing the final versions of "Addicted" and "The Way You Dance," I sensed it was time for a shift. I wanted to explore a new direction—perhaps collaborate with a different studio or company that could bring a fresh sound and a new creative spark to my next project. It felt like the right moment for a change in both scenery and sonic identity.

I understood that a demo is only a demo, and the true magic depends on the artist who eventually brings the song to life. Still, I longed for a demo that would captivate me from the very first note—a track that would make my eardrums pop and have me tapping my feet the moment the producer dropped the beat.

Naturally, I didn't struggle with this decision because I've never considered myself a complacent person. I've always embraced change, as change is inexorable and a byproduct of improvement and growth. In the end, change challenges us to test the very skills and talents we believe we possess.

Luckily, after extensive online research and searching for a new outlet or company to either record my songs or review them, I came across a recording company in Troy, Kansas. Yes—Kansas. This particular company specializes in music distribution and publishing services. I've never traveled to that part of the Midwest, let alone Troy, but something about the discovery made me realize my lyrics were "ain't in Kansas anymore."

I formally introduced myself via email, and a few days later, a representative named Christine agreed to have a phone conversation with me. During our conversation, I provided a brief yet concise biography of myself and explained my work as a lyricist. I felt comfortable partnering with this recording company based in Troy, KS.

I submitted the complete tracklist of my third album, **Seize the Moment,** which comprises tracks or records such as: Seasonal Love (Part I) , Seasonal Love (Part II), and Fame, just to name a few.

Truthfully, I've never set high expectations when the outcome depends heavily on someone else; in this case, the final approval rested with the recording company. As a perfectionist, I hold myself to high standards. I constantly remind myself that the effort I put in—the input—shapes the output, the outcome, and ultimately the results. Because of that, I never take my work lightly. The final product, at least on my end, is always my responsibility.

I can't control whether a company accepts, approves, or rejects my work. But I do know, deeply and without question, that I can always rely on myself. As long as I give my best, work with intention, and do my part wholeheartedly, then—win or lose—I can live with the outcome without regret.

This philosophy has been a part of me since I was a boy: no excuses—do your part and live with the results. That's the bottom line, embedded in every line I write. I strive to create the best lines, verses, pre-choruses, choruses, bridges, and rhymes, painting the clearest and most vivid imagery. These are my standards—my prerequisites—for great song lyrics.

After eleven days had passed, I sent a follow-up email on Tuesday, August 27th, while I was waiting to hear back from the recording company. In response, I received my first report card, so to speak.

Not bad, right? It was only the second recording company—and the first in Nashville—to open its doors to me, and I felt a genuine sense of gratitude. I made sure to express that to Christine, the person guiding me through the process.

Before moving into contract discussions, the company took several preliminary steps, including registering and entering my song information with BMI and the Harry Fox Agency, a leading provider of licensing and royalty services for physical products and permanent downloads in the U.S. music industry.

Soon after, the recording company sent over the contract, which I forwarded to my lawyer for review. After multiple rounds of edits, revisions, and negotiations, my lawyer concluded that certain clauses would give the company too much leverage—particularly one clause that raised significant concern. Although we agreed on adding some of my songs to their library, we ultimately couldn't reach a final agreement on the contract terms and decided to part ways amicably.

On Thu, Oct 10, 2019 at 5:22 PM [redacted] wrote:

I completely understand. Unfortunately, that is a standard publishing contract and another attorney in the industry would probably write one similar in content.

Who knows what the future holds. Continue to write. You're very good.

How would you like me to refund your money?

I was refunded the registration fees I had previously paid.

Then, as always, you win some, you lose some, and you move on. I wasn't shaken by the situation. I kept my eyes fixed on the prize and held my head higher than a giraffe, knowing I had gained something—not lyrically, but from a business standpoint. I understood exactly where I stood.

The music industry is dicey. You can pour your heart into the work—writing tirelessly, with no publishing or recording agent beside you, no one witnessing the struggle, the labor, the dedication—yet a company can still have the audacity to demand fifty percent of everything you've created. No way, Jack. They didn't do jack.

As daunting as the contract seemed, the truth is that this is corporate America in its rawest form. I quickly learned the importance of educating myself and staying vigilant when it comes to the music industry, record deals, and contracts. Show even a drop of vulnerability or desperation, and they'll eat you alive the way a shark devours its prey.

And it doesn't stop there. Not only would they trample over you, but they would also compromise your integrity as a person. That realization made it clear that I needed to set my standards high—to protect my work, my integrity, and my identity as an artist and lyricist. I could only imagine the pain some of my contemporaries had endured on their way to the top, trying to become stars while the sharks of the music industry preyed on people like me—dream chasers, whether legally or illegally.

That is why I wrote "Winner," the third track from the "Happiness "album, which features uplifting lyrics:

I ain't no quitter, I am a winner (winner)
I ain't no quitter, I am a winner (winner)

I wrote it for those who have had to walk away from unfair recording or music deals—for the individuals who chose self-respect over exploitation.

The following year, in 2020, amidst the Coronavirus (COVID-19) pandemic, we faced one of the most devastating crises in modern history. Every neighborhood felt its impact, whether directly or indirectly. Some people survived, others were healing, and many were grieving. I found myself in a state of isolation. The truth is, who wasn't affected?

In that isolation—caught between confusion and reflection—I had a change of heart. I reconsidered and reached out again to the recording company in Troy. We eventually found common ground, a place of partnership, and signed a deal to include some of my songs in their library. I suppose you could say I broke my own rule: "You win some, you lose some, and you move on."

During that time, I also discovered another recording studio in California that was willing to record "Alive." If memory serves, this was at the end of 2019, when the world was blissfully unaware of the storm that was coming. The virus had not yet reached the U.S. in any significant way, and life still felt normal. Socially, we were close—friends, colleagues, families. We hugged freely, kissed on the cheek, and half-hearted, distanced embraces were unheard of.

But as the pandemic progressed, everything changed. The new normal became fist bumps instead of warm embraces. Masks became commonplace, almost as if we were reenacting the 1994 film *The Mask,* starring Jim Carrey. If you haven't seen it, it's a classic—funny, lighthearted. But this time, the world wasn't laughing; we were dying.

As a survivor and a writer, I felt compelled to capture this moment in humanity—a moment that was consuming people from every corner, every block of America, and across the world. I realized that the song I had drafted a year earlier could paint the picture I carried in my mind, using a unique brush to portray not only the pandemic but also the darker, divided side of America: Black lives pinned under knees, bodies tased, riots erupting, protests rising, demonstrations filling the streets. The Black Lives Matter movement fought to stop the darkened blood—literal and symbolic—from flooding the streets of America.

I believed that *Alive* would be a powerful song—one capable of capturing the stories of those in America who had been deprived of hope, especially families grieving the loss of loved ones. It speaks to the narratives of fallen Black men

RECORDING AGREEMENT

This Agreement is between Manley Petit (the "Songwriter") and
[redacted] "Producer");
The Songwriter hereby warrants that he is the author and owner of the song listed below: **"Alive "** ©
2020 Manley Petit

and the heartache carried by their families, who were unable to give them a proper burial.

"Alive" also represents those who are still living and have overcome personal challenges and life difficulties. I didn't want the lyrics to go unnoticed, unheard, or unrecorded; the story needed to be told. I wanted to hear the song and feel every word resonate with the heartbeat of these events, both lyrically and musically, for years to come.

I was fortunate to be involved in the recording of *Alive* from the very beginning through the final stages of production. The producer was collaborative—sending samples, discussing the process, and sharing edits. Although I never traveled to California to be in the studio with the producer and the hired singers, most of our conversations took place over Zoom, and I still felt deeply connected to the team. I was included in every part of the process: the samples, the edits, the sound, and the final mix.

As COVID-19 ravaged the nation, every industry felt the impact—including the music industry. Recording Alive became a slow, drawn-out process. I tried to keep my patience intact, but it wasn't easy. I was dying to hear the finished version. It wasn't until late 2020 that the song was finally completed.

The final version of *Alive* lived up to its expectations—but, as always, there is a "but." I wasn't pleased with the singers. Their voices didn't do the song justice. Still, the demo was satisfactory, and the heart of the song remained intact.

In 2020, I was surprised to receive an email from a music publishing company that read:

> From [redacted]
> Date [redacted] AM (GMT-05:00)
> To Manley Petit [redacted]
> Subject AIN'T GIVIN' UP, FAME and KEEP GOING BACK
>
> Manley, you originally sent your songs AIN'T GIVIN' UP, FAME, RED LIGHT, RUNNING BY MY SIDE and KEEP GOING BACK to Sun Music Group in Nashville and apparently that didn't work out so they referred you to us. We are a 57-year-old music publisher with more than 50 commercial songs and 17 #1 hits to our credit.
>
> My team and I reviewed them this morning and everyone on our staff enjoyed the songs very much, especially AIN'T GIVIN' UP, FAME and KEEP GOING BACK. They are full of emotions and are very true-to-life. We feel a lot of people feel the same way, and will be able to relate to these songs if properly presented.
>
> We have an offer for you. We would like to set AIN'T GIVIN' UP, FAME and KEEP GOING BACK to unique commercial music and create professional recordings. When the recordings are finished, the attached agreement allows us to pitch the songs to singers in Nashville with the intent of getting them placed on the market. If we can get your songs on the market within 24 months we earn the right to act as your publisher for the songs.
>
> We only use professional Nashville studio musicians and singers so that our recordings are ready for any use, including radio or television. We usually spend between $1,000 and $1,200 on each song, however we only ask you the writer to contribute $390.00 a song towards those costs. We pay everything else. We will never ask you for another penny.
>
> It is customary for songwriters and publishers to share in the recording costs like this. Of course, you will have your recordings forever.

I was adamant about recording another demo at the time; paying recording fees, navigating contract negotiations, and dealing with all that jazz felt overwhelming while I was also managing family responsibilities, job-related projects, and writing song lyrics. After a few days of contemplation, I finally gave the recording company the green light to record "Keep Going Back" as a promotional demo.

Four long weeks later, *Keep Going Back* was finished. I was pleased with the record. It wasn't a hit by any stretch, but it kept the momentum—and the dream—alive. The lyrics felt brilliant to me, or at least perfectly aligned with the song's purpose. I received two CD copies and a digital file. I shared the digital version with a few close friends, and I must have played that single for a week straight while sitting in traffic on my way home from work. One of the CD copies is shown below.

Pretty cool, isn't it? I have to admit, I kept going back—no pun intended—to that record, just to enjoy it and relive nostalgic moments listening to the words I wrote. Not bad, huh? For an immigrant from Lakou Kokoye? I know I'm getting ahead of myself, but who's judging? At this point, these four tracks I had written and demoed stood as my witnesses, testifying that patience, consistency, and perseverance do pay off.

They weren't paying my bills, putting food on the table, or feeding my family, but they gave me something to chew on. In the meantime, I returned to my regular life and continued working on my craft—writing song lyrics. I spent the next two

years, from 2021 to 2022, focused solely on that work. It was during this stretch of quiet dedication that the idea of writing this memoir first appeared on my writing radar.

Stop the record, I said. Let's stop the record for a second. We've been listening to so many tracks, yet there's still so much left to unpack. Let's take a mental break—a little breather—so pour yourself another glass of wine or a shot of cognac before we proceed.

Well, I hope you enjoyed the break. Now, where were we?

I was reflecting on the past two years, and as 2023 began to wind down, my focus remained unchanged. But as the days of that year grew numbered and waved their quiet goodbyes—the sky darkening before five o'clock as daylight saving had already settled in, the cold air reminding me to bundle up as winter crept in—I found myself on Sunday, November 26, 2023, gazing out the window. I watched the last autumn leaves drift down onto the pile that had gathered on the partially landscaped front yard, and I found myself asking the same questions I had asked eighteen years earlier in that basement:

How skilled am I as a lyricist? Will I ever be recognized as a writer—specifically as a ghostwriter? Is songwriting just a distant dream for me? Will I ever be honored with induction into the Songwriters Hall of Fame, even if only in my imagination? And will I ever be content with how far I've taken this aptitude for songwriting?

These questions were deflating because I couldn't answer them confidently—not even with the infinitesimal audacity of hope.

For one, I still hadn't received any meaningful recognition as a writer. I had never seen my first and last name, or *Patience the Ghostwriter*, printed in the song-credits section of any recognized artist's album—let alone attached to a single track.

In the book's introduction, I echoed the phrase, *"Life is nothing but music in my eardrums."* I should have taken it a step further by adding that life is nothing but a dream; yet at this point in my odyssey, that dream felt like a *cauchemar*—a nightmare—one I hoped someone, somewhere, would be kind enough to wake me from. Where is Aloe Blacc when you need him, so he could sing the chorus of "Wake Me Up" to me? (Rest in peace, Avicii.)

Wake me up when it's all over
When I'm wiser and I'm older
All this time I was finding myself
And I did not know I was lost

After years of writing—over fifty completed songs, plus countless unfinished ones—my track record extends far beyond what can be neatly listed here. Still, it's worth noting some of the songs I've penned, in no particular order:

The Good with the Bad. Addicted. Be Careful What You Wish For. Despite Everything. Best Believe. Fame (A Gift and a Curse). I Don't Forgive & Forget. In Thin Air. Never Too Late. Seasonal Love (Part I). Seasonal Love (Part II). Alive. Keep Going Back. Broken Record. Let Him Go. Déjà Vu. Seasonal Love.

Despite having four demos in my portfolio—admittedly a modest number for promotion—I remain a ghost, unseen in the eyes of the music world. I don't believe in ghosts, but I do believe ghostwriters are the heartbeat of every song you hear on the radio or on a streaming platform. We are everywhere, in every genre, shaping the world of music. Yet no one believes in ghosts. Is that why we don't receive our accolades?

I am still undiscovered among music-industry writers. And although I'm not hard to find—you don't have to travel to Lakou Kokoye—I am right here, patiently waiting to ghost-write for any musician or artist who believes in ghosts.

Hence, there were moments when I thought about quitting—about exiting this world of lyricism altogether. I imagined packing up my pen and notepad, stepping away from the journey, and disappearing without anyone noticing.

After all, I am a ghost: a writer whose stories have yet to catch the attention of legitimate, recognizable artists—male or female—whose voices could bring them to life.

And here I am, writing a book about song lyrics when, in another universe, I should be writing songs for some of today's finest artists—those who have collected the world's most prestigious awards. I'm talking about the Grammys, the Billboard Music Awards, the People's Choice Awards—especially the Best Songwriter category. I've imagined being nominated, hearing my name called as the presenter walks slowly onto the stage, unseals the envelope, and announces, "The Grammy Award for Best R&B or Pop Songwriter goes to… Manley Petit, also known as Patience the Ghostwriter." But then again, my name wouldn't be mentioned. Why would it? After all, I am a ghost who happens to be a writer.

As I've always said, "You win some, you lose some, then you move on." By that logic, I should have moved on already—no breakthrough, no recognition, no spotlight. But this time, I didn't. I refused to. Not yet. Because throughout this never-ending odyssey, I've learned valuable lessons—lessons I will carry with me today, tomorrow, and until the day I finally wake up from this dream.

And in the background of my mind, like a broken record spinning endlessly, these words continue to play in my eardrums:

Patience, Consistency, Perseverance. Perseverance, Patience, Consistency. Patience, Consistency, Perseverance. Consistency, Patience, Perseverance. Perseverance, Patience, Consistency.

Over and over, the same trio of virtues—looping, repeating, reminding me why I'm still here.

ALBUM XII
CONSISTENCY

Consistency can only be established with self-discipline and the ability to identify, control, or eradicate inconsistencies derived from extrinsic factors — Manley Petit

I want to take it a few steps further, so allow me to go farther. It is not that it was defined incorrectly; it is far from the truth. My original definition of consistency does not do it justice. So, allow me to go harder. Isn't that why you purchased this book? If not, why bother? Some people are very consistent when it is required. For instance, if their jobs require them to, they put the extra effort and energy to it, but when it comes to their personal life they are all over the place, struggling with inconsistency leading to more Bad Habits than Ed Sheeran's song.

Consistency comes with an inexpensive price tag, yet some struggle to afford it, and others cannot afford it at all. As a lyricist, I try to be repetitive or repeat everything I do routinely, which ultimately induces consistency. Once I have found a method that works for me, I stick to it like crazy glue; that is the bottom line and the reason that every line I ever pen is freshly crafted like a fresh hairline. For instance, my evening routine includes a few minutes spent titillating every line of written songs. I have been doing that on a regular nightly basis for years. Admittedly, I find the process boring and tedious some nights, yet I never stop.

Because of my early experience with consistency. I grew up observing my mother performing house chores tirelessly and consistently, may I add, no matter the weather—cyclones, hurricanes, and rain. She never cheated the process or wavered:

1. Waking up every single day at the crack of dawn to sweep the house floor
2. Mopping floors if required
3. Ironing our school uniforms with a charcoal iron the night prior
4. Getting me and my brothers ready for school
5. Cooking spaghetti early in the morning, yes, spaghetti for breakfast. Then, I would add a few drops of ketchup on top and mix it with laughing cow cheese to enhance the flavor.

During my adolescent years, these activities simply looked like the life of a hard-working single mother — a parent doing what needed to be done. But as I grew older and began reflecting on those years, I realized she was instilling something far deeper in me: responsibility, yes, but more importantly, consistency. Whether she knew that or not remains a mystery. What I do know is that those routines spread into my own life like a quiet virus, settling into the front mat of my household and refusing to leave.

Even now, whenever she visits, she slips right back into those same habits — sweeping, straightening, making sure the house is clean and welcoming. Every guest who stepped foot in our home understood the unspoken rule: leave your trash outside. My mother didn't just talk about consistency; she lived it. And consistency, I've learned, is contagious. It inspires people who struggle with prioritization, with discipline, with competing responsibilities. It inspired me then, and it inspires me now. I'm simply carrying the legacy forward.

Consistency also brings a sense of stability to my stories and to my personal life. I don't need to wander around like a nomad searching for the tools I need every time I sit down to write. Everything has its place. My laptop and headphones are always pre-staged. I follow the same writing process every single day — even on the days when I can't find a single thing to write about for the life of me.

I'm well aware that the distance between me and greatness stretches miles — figuratively speaking — from the dirt and rocky roads of Lakou Kokoye all the way to the ocean-blue sky. And I know I'm far from being recognized in the same atmosphere as the people I idolized: Jay-Z, Eminem, André 3000, Tom Brady, LeBron, Giannis, Serena, Tiger Woods. But the audacity of hope inside me runs like a speeding bullet, powerful enough to strengthen and reinforce my belief that I could become one of the greatest lyricists of all time. As for the genre — that part is still unfolding.

Writing song lyrics does not happen overnight — never mind exceptional lyrics — even if you had a tremendous and rested night of sleep; they just do not. Writing lyrics entails planning, brainstorming, memorizing, drafting, reading, reviewing, listening, editing, and deleting. The process is continuous, as one is consistently trying to improve and find ways to keep the same patterns, the same routine, and the same passion alive every single time; that is one of the reasons I lay my pen on the paper to this day. I firmly believe it is one of the critical elements to greatness. I do not believe an individual could be great in every sense of the word while being inconsistent and inconsistently performing at the highest level, where the stakes are high; that would be considered a failure or a bust. There are levels to greatness, and each level demands its own discipline, its own logic, its own consistency. In my pursuit of accuracy and the discipline required to reach a specific goal, I've held myself to these same principles as a wannabe writer.

Making your bed every morning may seem like a tedious chore. Some people shrug and say, "Why make your bed when you're just going to sleep in it later?" But the most successful people see this uncomplicated task differently. To them, it's not about the bed — it's about self-discipline, one of the foundational building blocks of consistency.

The great ones — the true GOATs — carry this discipline in their DNA. It's coded into them, sequenced into their habits, reflected in the techniques, regimens, and principles they follow on their path to greatness. Their greatness comes with high expectations, and with high expectations comes high demand — from the masses, from die-hard fans, from anyone who believes in them. These greats put the world on notice. And the commitment of their supporters never wavers. Fans crave results — hit records after hit records — and that kind of output requires consistency. They expect the artist to deliver the same level of excellence every time, without deviation.

Consistency creates believers. It turns skeptics into supporters because the formula keeps proving itself, whether things are going smoothly or falling apart behind the scenes. Artists who stay true to their craft give their supporters a reason to hold on, to stay focused, to keep rooting. Their consistency becomes a promise — a silent contract — that expectations will be met.

The same rule applies in sports, especially in one of my favorites: basketball. Take Anthony Davis (AD) from the Los Angeles Lakers. He is one of the most talented and skillful athletes in the NBA. Yet, as gifted as he is, he remains one of the most inconsistent players I've watched. You never know if he will perform at the highest level from game to game. Ironically, he is so consistent at being inconsistent that you could bet on it and win by double digits. I don't hate AD — far from it — but his inconsistency has been documented and debated by analysts, commentators, and fans for years. I'm not saying anything new; I'm simply acknowledging what has been visible all along.

And every time he underperforms, every time his output fails to match his ability, it forces me to think deeper about the essence of consistency — what it means, why it matters, and how it separates the great from the merely talented.

Inconsistency is detrimental to songwriting and music, especially when it comes to song structure. If a song isn't built with a clear structure, listeners become puzzled and disengaged. They lose the rhythm, the flow, the ability to sing along. And lyrically, the words must align with the song's theme; otherwise, the entire piece becomes difficult to decode or interpret. Consistency is the key that unlocks dependability within your fanbase. When you release marvelous music again and again, something powerful happens: the relationship between you and your listeners strengthens. They become loyal — unwavering even — relying on your music not just for entertainment, but as a way of life.

Because of that, I have no choice but to keep employing the same rudimentary method: early writing sessions before the world awakens, timing my creativity with the quiet hours, intentionally anti-social in the mornings to keep my mind sharp. I avoid unnecessary conversations that could distract my lyrical mind or dictate how the first line or verse unfolds. I steer clear of pointless tasks — like taking out the trash for no real reason — and I stay away from my phone. No distractions. Nothing that could impede or influence the creative process.

Once I'm fully locked into my lyrical zone, I always ask myself two questions: "Who am I writing for?" and "Who am I writing to?" These questions are simple, but they are essential. Without them, I'd be writing just to write — with no accuracy, no intention, no logic.

I wouldn't feel right ignoring this unorthodox step. I don't know if every lyricist uses a method like this, but I've been relying on it for the last two, maybe three years. It works for me, and I expect it to keep working.

Before I implemented this technique, I often struggled to identify my target audience. And this principle doesn't apply only to lyricists — authors, novelists, anyone who creates for others faces the same challenge.

I genuinely believe that if someone isn't relentlessly using their talent and skill set — consistently, repeatedly, with intention — they're cheating the art. They're cheating their audience. That's why every time I put my head down and write on a piece of paper, my goal is to be as consistent as possible. I wake up in the early hours between 5:00 and 7:30 AM, knowing deep in my heart that those quiet moments will positively impact my creativity. Call me

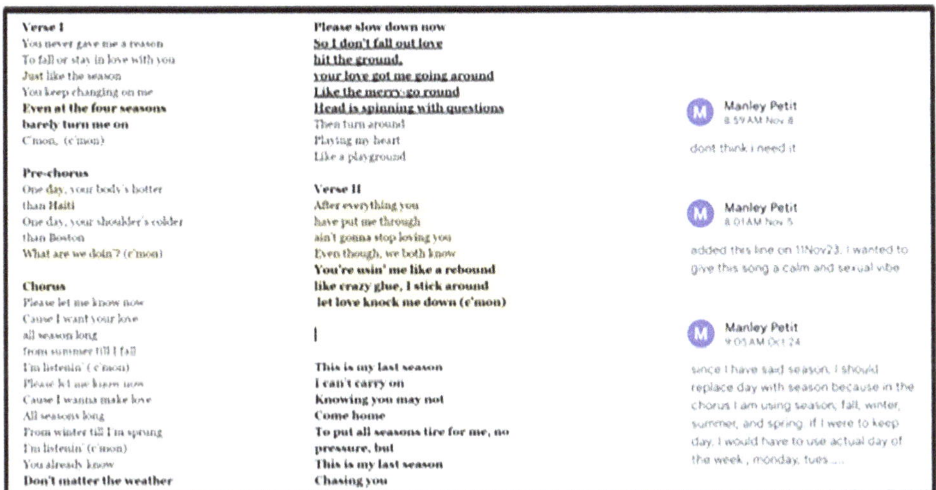

Verse I
You never gave me a reason
To fall or stay in love with you
Just like the season
You keep changing on me
Even at the four seasons
barely turn me on
C'mon, (c'mon)

Pre-chorus
One day, your body's hotter
than Haiti
One day, your shoulder's colder
than Boston
What are we doin'? (c'mon)

Chorus
Please let me know now
Cause I want your love
all season long
from summer till I fall
I'm listenin' (c'mon)
Please let me know now
Cause I wanna make love
All seasons long
From winter till I'm sprung
I'm listenin' (c'mon)
You already know
Don't matter the weather

Please slow down now
So I don't fall out love
hit the ground,
your love got me going around
Like the merry-go round
Head is spinning with questions
Then turn around
Playing my heart
Like a playground

Verse II
After everything you
have put me through
ain't gonna stop loving you
Even though, we both know
You're usin' me like a rebound
like crazy glue, I stick around
let love knock me down (c'mon)

This is my last season
I can't carry on
Knowing you may not
Come home
To put all seasons tire for me, no
pressure, but
This is my last season
Chasing you

Manley Petit
8:59 AM Nov 8
dont think i need it

Manley Petit
8:01AM Nov 5
added this line on 11Nov23. I wanted to give this song a calm and sexual vibe

Manley Petit
9:05 AM Oct 24
since I have said season, I should replace day with season because in the chorus I am using season, fall, winter, summer, and spring. if I were to keep day, I would have to use actual day of the week , monday, tues ....

insane if you want; I wouldn't be offended. There's a thin line where insanity and consistency intersect — and I've learned to live right on that line.

Moreover, I am at my best in those early sessions, penning my strongest lyrics — intros, verses, lines, rhymes, wordplay, metaphors, flow, and everything in between. And on the days when I couldn't accomplish my goal or the writing session didn't unfold the way I anticipated, I would tell myself, *"So be it. At least it wasn't for lack of consistency."* Then I'd seize the moment, reset, and rise early again the next morning, devoting myself to the work and trying to concentrate as much as possible.

Sometimes I'd return to a song I hadn't finished, one that needed a few tweaks here and there. Other times, those early hours were unpredictable — I might revise lines from existing songs or end up deleting entire pieces I had been working on for months, even years. Those hours spent deleting lyrics you once believed had potential are never enjoyable. As a lyricist, I've always felt capable of bringing an idea to fruition, crafting great lyrics with the simplest words, and ultimately shaping them into a great song. So deleting is not my favorite task — but sometimes, it's necessary.

Over time, I've learned to make peace with that necessity. I've mentally reserved a specific time at the very end of the process for deleting and editing, a method I've consistently employed: I only delete once the song is completely done. For instance, I had two versions of "All Season." Let me take you behind the scenes. Below is the original version of "All Season" before I deleted and edited some of the redundant lines, words, and more.

As you can see, some of the text or words are intentionally bolded. This is a method I use consistently to keep track of lines and any part of the song that may not be needed, may be cut, or may need modification. The panel to the right captures side notes and comments. As I get older and my memory isn't as sharp as it once was, this feature has become essential for tracking and monitoring my progress — especially when a song is unfinished. This method doesn't apply to songs I complete in one take, because those rarely require further modifications.

As I devote my morning hours to writing lyrics, the setting matters less once I reach the midpoint of my process. By then, my mind is lyrically and musically committed — fully immersed in the art — whether I'm at home, at work, or even standing in front of a urinal. I mentally shut out everything else life offers, narrowing my focus like a laser beam locked onto a single point.

Here is another example: one of the first drafts of *Deja Vu*. Creatively and historically, my writing has always been at its peak at dawn — if I do say so myself. I'm not one to brag, but in those early hours, I'm in my lyrical bag, for lack of a better word.

During this period, I establish control over my surroundings — including the people in them. Which brings me to the second part of consistency: "the ability to identify, control, or eradicate inconsistencies derived from extrinsic factors." Some people aren't chasing greatness, so they can't fathom what it feels like to be consistent. They are inconsistent by nature. Therefore, as a consistent individual, one must break down one's inconsistencies in a specific order: identify them, control them, or eradicate them — all in pursuit of the ultimate goal: Greatness. There are myriad extrinsic factors that can interfere with consistency, but the most influential are the environment and the people around you — including relatives — who can unintentionally disrupt your rhythm.

When it comes to people, the first step is understanding their tendencies. What are their daily routines? When do they need your support? How does your schedule align with theirs? What are their priorities throughout the week? I've learned that most people are late sleepers. They don't rise at the crack of dawn, which makes it easier for me to seize those silent hours. While they're snoozing their alarms, I'm jotting lyrics. But once everyone wakes up, I would end the early writing session and swiftly tailor my focus back to my family — a little wordplay for you, in case you missed it — because family time is one of the most valuable parts of my life. Without it, I would feel incomplete.

I devote myself to them fully: indoor activities like cards, dominoes, and Scrabble; outdoor favorites like basketball, jogging, and playing catch. Afterward, I determine what house chores I'm responsible for so I can fit them into my schedule. Historically, my chores have been woven into my daily routine — each task performed at a specific time, every day and every week. Every aspect of my life is mapped out. No GPS required. Another wordplay for you.

Once I've identified everyone's schedule, I can plan mine — including my writing sessions. Even then, I double-check that I have the most up-to-date calendar so nothing catches me off guard. Still, life is full of surprises. I can't control when someone else's schedule changes, including my own. The goal is to control what you can and stay one step ahead, especially when you have children. Otherwise, you risk drifting away from your personal routines, and that drift is the enemy of consistency.

Furthermore, you must learn to say no — to be selfish at times — and protect your family time and your creative time, especially when the request isn't urgent. On the other hand, you must also learn when to say yes. Sometimes taking ownership of someone else's task isn't just being a team player; it's strategic. If a task takes them two hours and it would take you one, do it. Streamlining the process makes everything more efficient, and ultimately, it gives you an extra hour to focus on your craft. Time is of the essence. You cannot waste it and still expect to return to you for writing song lyrics — unless, of course, you're crafting them in your mind like the great Jay-Z.

The environment is an extrinsic factor that brings countless distractions and influences—especially if you have children who need babysitting and care. I'm not saying kids are a nuisance, but finding ways to focus on your craft can feel like a full-time job.

Luckily, I've discovered methods to block out the noise and keep my focus intact. Is it facile? Absolutely not. But I've built a mental fortress—a lyrical castle—with an OFF button that allows me to silence the world and concentrate on what truly matters.

What's the bottom line? Writing song lyrics. That's always been the goal. When I hit that OFF button, the environment fades, and I enter what I call the *Lyrical Fire Zone.* Anyone trying to put out this fire will get burned—at least lyrically. When I'm in my zone, even a firefighter couldn't extinguish the flames of my creativity.

Outside those sacred hours, my thought process suffers. Creativity dwindles. Motivation evaporates. I get frustrated with myself for waking up early without material, failing to write, and feeling drained all day.

Consistency, however, comes with its own prerequisites: practice and repetition.

Practice

Remember how your school teachers used to remind you, *"Practice makes perfect"?* What they rarely mentioned is that practice also makes consistency. Now you know.

To build consistency, you must be disciplined—repeating the same steps over and over while trusting the process is a rudimentary yet essential attribute. It sounds simple, but it's the foundation of mastery.

Take NBA superstar Steph Curry as an example. Those jaw-dropping long-range shots he makes during games? They're the same shots he practices relentlessly. Fans are amazed, but his teammates and coaches expect him to make them because he's one of the greatest shooters of all time. Why? Because he has perfected his craft—shot after shot, from every angle on the court. Missing is the exception, not the rule.

Writing lyrics works the same way. Whether good or mediocre, the act of writing—again and again—is what sharpens your skill. But here's the key: practice without external expectations. Curry's drive didn't come from applause; it came from an inner fire to improve. That same fire must fuel your writing.

In my case, Rachel became my unofficial coach. I started practicing more after receiving her feedback. As I chased this dream of becoming a recognized lyricist, I had to rely heavily on constructive criticism as a teaching tool—obeying the code and standards of songwriting, especially song structure.

For instance, I learned that the most common structure is:
Verse>Chorus>Verse>Chorus

Verse>Chorus>Verse>Chorus

I must admit, I wasn't always aware of such standards when I wrote my first lyrics. How would I have known? I had no mentor to teach me the do's and don'ts of songwriting. I was learning everything on my own—on the fly—like a butterfly spreading its wings freely with no sense of direction or rules.

But reality set in. I realized there are established requirements for songwriting, especially lyrics, and I had to adapt and adopt to reach the pinnacle of success—never mind greatness. I didn't want to be an outcast—unless, of course, you're André 3000 from Outkast, turning rules into art and making "Hey Ya!" a global anthem. But for me, staying disciplined meant adapting to the standards of songwriting rather than ignoring them. I didn't want to be the kind of outcast whose lyrics get tossed in the reject pile by A&R or record labels. So, I studied and incorporated proven song structures into my writing—without being coached or mentored—just to stay disciplined and stay the course.

Repetition

I discovered that writing the same line over and over, the same verse repeatedly—even if it doesn't result in a hit song—helps me memorize lyrics and builds a mental database of do's and don'ts. These experiences become invaluable for future songwriting sessions.

For example, after learning the most common song structure, I repeated and applied it in many songs. While doing so, I acquired and mastered other structures as well.

Verse>Chorus>Verse>Chorus> Bridge>Chorus

In other words, repetition makes it easier to pinpoint which lines work and which do not. By then, I have already tested every possibility. Yet the great ones never stop—they believe there is always another level to climb, another step waiting to be taken. So they repeat, repeat, repeat, expecting the second song to be better than the first, the third better than the second, and so on.

The great ones do not grow exhausted or bored from repeating a task over and over; they get even, even-keeled, as if there is always room for improvement, always space for perfection. For them, repetition becomes an addiction—without symptoms, without pain. In my case, carpal tunnel does not exist. Instead, I broaden my repertoire and expand my creative vision, finding new ways to structure songs. That is how new music is born—crafted and produced with intention.

One of my favorite song structures, with or without an outro, is:

Intro>Verse>Pre-Chorus>Chorus> Verse>Pre-Chorus>Chorus>Bridge>Chorus

I possess that drive. I am not sure where it originated, but it runs through me like a current—an insane force that accelerates to a hundred miles per hour when I write lyrics with precision and creativity. For me, good enough is never good enough. I repeat: good enough is never good enough. In fact, "good enough" does not exist in my vocabulary; it is a term I learned only from the dictionary. I still cannot understand how anyone can be content with being merely good, knowing there is a level of excellence waiting at the summit—a place where greatness is protected forever.

That is why, to this day, I toil for hours, writing on paper or typing on a Word document, unreluctantly willing to start from scratch if the original attempt falls short. I will repeat the entire process instantly, faster than Don Henley, Danny Kortchmar, and Jai Winding crafted *New York Minute.* If the first attempt does not translate into a satisfactory song, I begin again without hesitation.

Surprisingly, consistency can feel like a burden—or even a curse—when it comes to relationships. Immediate family and friends are often impacted when you rely on them to support any aspect of your regimented lifestyle. When you begin applying the same principles of discipline and repetition to personal interactions, some may not agree or appreciate such an approach. They may interpret your consistency as complacency, which can create tension.

For example, an inconsistent individual may not view daily routines as significant. They resist following the same schedule every day because their lifestyle shifts so frequently that their attention moves elsewhere. Plans change, priorities are ignored, and your carefully structured intentions are left behind. Therefore, you must be willing to sacrifice and compromise aspects of your lifestyle for theirs in order to maintain harmony. Without their support and investment, consistency becomes problematic, and focusing on your craft grows increasingly difficult. Balance is not optional—it is essential for sustaining both your art and your relationships.

As your level of consistency heightens, it can unintentionally repel others from interacting with you. They may become reluctant to share new information, perceiving your views as fixed and unchanging—as if you do not welcome fresh ideas, even when those ideas relate to your craft. This perception can create distance, not because of a lack of respect, but because your unwavering commitment to structure and routine feels immovable to those who thrive on flexibility.

Some individuals may support your consistency for a time. For example, if someone notices you need quiet to work on your craft, they may be considerate during your writing sessions—keeping noise to a minimum or avoiding it altogether. But reality cannot be ignored. No matter how hard they try, there will be moments when silence is impossible, especially in a confined space. Life happens—perhaps a new addition to the family, a newborn crying at the top of their lungs.

To survive and keep your level of consistency afloat, you must implement a new approach. For instance, figuring out when the child naps, which can be learned through a brief conversation with the caregiver or parent. All this information must be factored in; otherwise, your routine may fail, and your songwriting will suffer. If they hire a caregiver, that person might offer ideas or a plan to support your schedule. Otherwise, you may have to devise other alternatives to protect your creative time before inconsistency—the enemy of a consistent mind—drives you crazy.

On the other hand, consistency can build trust within your inner circle. People begin to rely on you because you've earned their confidence through reliability and discipline. They believe you will deliver on time—just like Amazon Prime—because you've proven it repeatedly, not only through your efficiency but through the sense of ease you provide, time and time again. That kind of trust cannot be duplicated by others.

Ultimately, once you realize not everyone possesses this dominant trait—consistency—you must learn to account for their inconsistency while remaining efficient. This may require a difficult but necessary skill: learning how to say no, as previously suggested.

Sometimes, I take a breather because consistency can be exhausting—but I return to the basics quickly, perfecting my songwriting skills. For instance, have you ever forgotten to brush your teeth first thing in the morning? You would know something was missing, right? The same applies to writing lyrics. If I miss a day without writing, I feel incomplete, as if a required step has been skipped.

The goal is not to deviate from your daily routine or intentionally do something unusual that derails your thought process. Once you have mastered the art of consistency, some people—though not everyone—may notice even the slightest trace of discrepancy. They become accustomed to your routine and expect it from you.

Is that all it takes to be consistent? The answer is no. This is only the tip of the pen—the tip of the iceberg. I hate to sound like a broken record, but it takes a village to build the ability to be consistent. Establishing your standards, requirements, and regiment is key. Writing lyrics is something I am deeply passionate about, but passion alone can only take you so far. I cannot take this God-given gift for granted. It would be detrimental to the process if, one day, I wrote the best lyrics, and the next day, I wrote a mediocre song just for the sake of writing—because I chose not to put my heart into it. That is not in my nature, nor in my DNA. Penning lyrics without substance or purpose would never sit well with me, even if I fastened my seat belt while seated.

I know every day brings new challenges as the world is constantly changing, advancing, and evolving. As you aim to build consistency, time becomes critical. You must prioritize your artistry, allocate hours wisely, and limit distractions like social media and your phone. Create time by any means necessary to do what's right. What is considered right? Doing everything in your power—and praying for help from above—to maintain control over life's interruptions. Once you establish and achieve that, you are closer to adopting true consistency. Then, concentrating on your art—whatever that may be—becomes second nature, like brushing your teeth every morning.

Once you find a system and process that works, you must maintain that same level of consistency—even when no one is watching.

I intentionally emphasize that people are not looking because, generally speaking, humans behave differently when isolated versus when surrounded by others. As it pertains to songwriting, this is something to consider—how will you behave when collaborating and co-writing with other artists and lyricists, especially when expectations are higher? You must be able to read the room and elevate your standards so you can write as if the environment has remained unchanged. In this instance, consistency gives you confidence. It allows you to feel comfortable and helps you craft the best lines and rhymes—words that others can feel deep in their spine.

As you age and become a well-seasoned lyricist, expectations remain the same, but you may struggle to maintain that same viscosity. When that happens, you can always fall back on the key routines that have carried you this far—writing night in and night out.

For example, I have written songs in one take, in one sitting. But sometimes, toward the last line of a verse, I catch myself thinking: *This is completely trash. What did I do wrong? Should I take the last line out? Should I continue?* I often contemplate whether to keep the verse, the line, or even the entire draft, while telling myself I could—and would—do better. Usually, I choose the latter so I can re-step on the ladder of improvement, which is part of the process. Sometimes, the best option is to revise verses or lines until they meet your expectations and resonate with your audience.

Eliminating parts that do not add value—unnecessary repetition, unmelodic rhymes, weak lines—requires tremendous heart and practice to determine a clear and logical path forward. In the end, a lyrical decision must be made in the best interest of the song. I am a law-abiding lyricist. I would never cheat the system or the songwriting process because I fear it would impact my overall performance, stop me from reaching the highest level of consistency, and ultimately cause my work to lose its viscosity. Whenever I have an idea, it doesn't always come to fruition. Nevertheless, I pour my soul into giving it life while asking myself: *Will it work? Is it an excellent idea for a song? Or is it too wild?*

I consistently ask myself these questions as I strive to perfect my art. Asking questions is a powerful way to define your scope, set priorities, and concentrate on the things that bring consistency to your craft—the same is true in life. The man in the mirror never lies, so you must face the mirror and look at yourself to ensure everything is intact. True consistency looks good—even in a broken mirror.

One of the things I have done historically—and consistently—is multitasking: working on two or three songs simultaneously to complete just one. I go back and forth, flipping through pages, navigating computer monitors, copying and pasting words and lines from one song into another, and vice versa.

It's not by design, but sometimes, as an avid lyricist, I crave a break—a pause. I call this a *lyrical break*. When I get tired of writing Song A, I open another tab with Song B. Navigating between two songs is not an art in itself, but if perfected, it can lead to multiple songs being completed in real time.

On the other hand, drafting three songs simultaneously can make or break a song. You need to time it right and stay focused because overwhelming thoughts can impair creativity. A lyrical break doesn't mean leaving the room; it means stepping away mentally while staying glued to my computer, laptop, or notepad. It's similar to a college student pulling an all-nighter to finish a paper—energy drinks nearby, refusing to leave the dorm room, pacing in circles but never exiting.

In my case, I spend hours in front of my computer with headphones on, lest I disturb anyone. Sometimes, I work on unfinished songs that I've been patiently waiting for *Patience, the Ghostwriter* to help me finish.

Other times, I revisit completed songs during breaks, hoping for inspiration—though that's rare. Still, this method has been my process for years, with no gimmicks.

Sometimes, I play one of my favorite records in the background so I can vibe to it—soothing, relaxing, and, more importantly, inspiring. It provides the lyrical helping hand I need to keep going. Consequently, some wonder: *"How can you write and listen to music simultaneously?"*

Well, I can block everything out—even writer's block. My thought process remains unhinged and unchanged, allowing me to create new work without slowing down. People may not understand that listening to songs while writing is part of my routine—a habit I've consistently maintained for ages. I don't want to age myself, but honestly, I've done it forever.

On the other hand, consistency can lead to complacency, which is dangerous for any craft. As a lyricist, you might feel cornered—stuck, with no evolution. But as humans, we are wired to evolve. I am a student of this art form, deeply studious in that sense—a scholarly lyricist who flows well. I keep my eardrums open to new sounds from every genre to ensure I never become the boy in the bubble, deprived of music.

To conclude, consistency is an excellent indicator for identifying the root cause of any issue. It allows you to pinpoint where a problem occurred in the process or system relying on historical routines and habits. While writing songs, I cannot count how many silly mistakes I've made. But the moment I identify an issue—say, the first verse doesn't provide enough background or fails to set the stage for the pre-chorus or chorus—I draft multiple alternatives, experimenting with different rhymes, words, and lines.

I have enough lyrics and verses to revise and improve. For example, when an opening line starts with a question, I know it will grab the audience's attention immediately. When determining whether I need five lines for a verse or a pre-chorus, I'm already thinking ahead—planning for balance. Sometimes, I even include a post-chorus, which I don't typically do, but it can prepare the audience for the next verse. This practice—a byproduct of consistency—may seem tedious to others, even to lyricists. It may not make sense to the masses, but deep down, you know you're staying true to your craft.

Consistency is challenging, especially when songwriting depends on others who are musically inconsistent. That can directly or indirectly impact your song. For instance, imagine working with a producer who is unexpectedly all over the place with the beat. You must ask yourself: *Is it because my lyrics are poorly written?*

In the end, always remember: consistency is infinite and leads to longevity. Never count out anyone who possesses this gene, because sooner or later, they will succeed and reach the level of excellence—simply because they never take days off.

They do not let extrinsic factors influence their goals. They control their intrinsic challenges—emotions, distractions—and external forces like people and environment. They maintain the same principles that have proven beneficial to their craft.

Furthermore, they do not make excuses; they simply keep working on every aspect of their art with self-discipline. Ultimately, they build a mental library filled with valuable resources, lifelong experiences, and stories to combat anything that could stand in their way—anything that threatens their success.

So here I am, about two decades later, still penning song lyrics regularly despite all the challenges, failures, setbacks, and distractions life has thrown at me. Today, I can confidently say: Mommy, the legacy of consistency lives on.

ALBUM XIII
PATIENCE

Patience can be defined in so many different ways. According to Oxford Learner's dictionaries, *"patience, noun. (1) (with somebody/something) the ability to stay calm and accept a delay or something annoying without complaining."*

More importantly, and religiously, I've learned that the Bible teaches us that suffering is patient. I remember holding on to these words during a season when waiting felt endless: *"Be patient, then, brothers and sisters, until the Lord's coming. See how the farmer waits patiently for the land to yield its valuable crop for the autumn and spring rains. You, too, be patient and stand steadfast."*

If you have time, read the entire chapter where this scripture is found. When I think of the word *patience*, I imagine a turtle—slowly moving, steady and deliberate, unconcerned about the final destination, focused only on the journey. A turtle that patiently takes its time to survey and study its surroundings, gaining knowledge and strength until it reaches the ultimate goal—never deviating from the process, regardless of how challenging the task ahead may appear, how far the road may seem, or how many others cruise by and leave it behind.

For years, I've been reminded that I possess a high level of patience. I've patiently achieved my goals, no matter how dicey the odyssey seemed. I've endured defeats, delays, and disappointments while staying calm and cool as a fan. Some people even joke, "You're so patient you could have been a doctor."

I'm not confident about how patience was instilled in me. I don't believe it came the same way consistency did. Maybe it was never ingrained at all. Perhaps somehow, I got gaga over patience, as if I was *Born This Way* like Lady Gaga. Honestly, I'm not quite sure.

But I do believe one thing: any personality characteristic that cannot be understood with the naked eye is heaven-sent and God-given.

Especially now, as I grow wiser, seeing life through different lenses and no longer suffering from spiritual blindness—even though I no longer have 2020—oops,

I mean 20/20—vision after undergoing one major surgery in my right eye in 2022 and a minor one in 2023.

This process—writing song lyrics and even writing this memoir—has reinforced my belief that patience is God-given.

Maintaining this level of focus and pursuing a dream for so long has yet to produce satisfactory results or harvest edible crops. If this is not considered a blessing, I do not know what else is. Patience is a unique seed of life and a way of living.

This journey has been a challenging one. I still struggle to come up with ideas for songs. There are times when completing a song feels like a waiting game—waiting for the last line, even the last word, to emerge in my head before I lose my mind. Yet, I have not given up on writing lyrics because I sincerely believe good things happen to those who wait; as cliché as it may echo and sound in your eardrums, I feel something good will come my way at the end of the day. I'm not sure if it will be in days or years, but I remain hopeful—one day.

Even if this long road I've been traveling ends up being the wrong way or doesn't lead to the anticipated destination, I will hit the road again and try a different route until I succeed.

That is one of the reasons I value quality over quantity. It's not about how many songs I write yearly or how fast I can write a verse. I focus solely on the bottom line. Knowing that the way I begin a song has a huge impact on the entire piece, I make sure I take my time and keep a steady pace to accurately pen every line.

Furthermore, I once thought patience was not just about the ability to wait—it's about how you behave while waiting. Do you get anxious or remain calm? Do you become impatient like a patient in a hospital waiting room? Do you get cranky and angry—so much that you need a Snickers bar? Are you able to tolerate the delays, the mistakes, and the missteps? Where do you place yourself in the patience sphere?

Today, I can finally testify that I was blessed with patience and I am forever grateful. Writing is highly time-consuming; it requires time, vigorous dedication, sacrifice, and strength to overcome and sustain—giving up valuable hobbies such as playing sports and video games, albeit I was never an avid gamer.

Visualize a load of laundry spinning in the dryer or washer, and you're standing in front of it waiting for the cycle to end. The process of writing lyrics is parallel to that—but the cycle never ends. It is continuous, involving repetition, editing, modification, deletions, copying, and pasting words, and lines, and verses. My mind is constantly awake, waiting for the next concept, rhyme, punchline, or wordplay to compose a hit record or successful song. Twenty-plus years later, that breakthrough has not arrived. I guess it's taking its sweet time.

It has been a long time coming—longer than Sam Cooke had envisioned when he sang, "It's been a long, long time coming, but a change is gonna come." In my case, I wonder if a change will ever come, because writing lyrics with no major breakthrough is exhausting, to put it bluntly. One verse may take hours, days, or even months to draft.

Speaking of time, I recall working on a song titled *"You Don't Have To."* At one point, I had three or four drafts. After reviewing the fourth, I realized the lyrics were poorly written—the verse didn't connect with the chorus, and there was no flow. So, I erased everything and started over. Eventually, I ended up with two more drafts, totaling six, none of which aligned with my original idea.

I spent the next few days thinking about a new concept for the song.

Finally, I decided the idea was too vague and unfounded to write about, so I shelved it in the back of my mind, hoping it would come in handy one day. Sadly, it never did. You could call that a step back, but I've learned the hard way that every mistake, every missed step, every erased verse or line is still a step toward achieving long-term results.

Hence, as I've coined over the years: *"You write some, you lose some, and you…"* I'll let you fill in the blank. Even though that idea consumed so much of my time, my only hope was to avoid a reprise with the next concept.

There have been times when I've gotten stuck on the first line of a verse—literally an unavoidable and unpredictable dead end, where the pen wouldn't move, as if suffering from carpal tunnel syndrome itself, and not a single drop of ink would fall for months. I would wait—wait until things started moving and flowing again.

Other times, I would stare at blank pages for hours, knowing what I wanted to write but not how to begin. It doesn't happen often, but when it does, it stings like a hornet. It drives me to a hopeless, barricaded road that makes me doubt myself even more and question my lyrical skills: *Am I good enough? Should it take this long? What is taking this long?* Obviously, my mind always says it shouldn't take such a long time to pen lyrics—I would angrily mumble to myself.

Writing lyrics is supposed to be fun, but sometimes frustration takes the fun out of fun. When that happens, I walk away. Sometimes I even leave the house and head to the local fitness center for a quick 30-minute workout.

Once I get there, I unpack my headphones, connect them to my phone, and select some of my favorite tunes—usually the same song I was listening to before going to the gym. I patiently wait for a way out of the slump.

Miraculously, as soon as I press play—nine out of ten times—my brain unfreezes. Instead of exercising and strengthening my aging muscles, I find myself immobilized on the equipment seat, writing lyrics rather than working out.

Sometimes, I lose track of time. I spend longer at the gym than planned, with little to show for it—hogging equipment without noticing if someone else needs it. Before leaving, I might lift a dumbbell or two, just so I have evidence of a workout. If anyone asks, "How was your workout? What did you work on?" I famously joke that I did "lyrical exercise," borrowing Jay-Z's phrase.

I've learned that sometimes walking away is the best immediate action when the writing process hits a roadblock and when dealing with writer's block.

How do you keep your patience? Quite frankly, I don't have the perfect remedy or cure. But if I could offer a dose of advice based on what this journey has taught me, it would be this: focus on what truly matters to you—what's right in front of you. Family. Passion. Mental, physical, and spiritual health. Build your tolerance for discomfort, so when things are delayed or don't go as planned, you remain composed. By then, you've already grown accustomed to being uncomfortable—waiting for a breakthrough, a miracle, a graduation ceremony, or whatever milestone you've been anxiously anticipating.

It's easier said than done. That's why I get on my knees every day, praying and asking God to bless me with patience. Patience is a gift of the present; without it, I wouldn't be present in the moment. I wouldn't have the ability to concentrate on the tasks at hand—tasks handed down by the heavens.

I would probably go insane if I focused solely on the destination and not the teachable journey. Humans have no control over the destination, which represents the future, which represents the future, which is not promised as it is unknown. Patience teaches us to have faith in the process—to trust it, to learn from delays and setbacks, and to see the present as the hope of the future

Even though I am blessed with patience, I hope I never lose it—even when it feels like I'm holding on by a single thread, the "P" in patience. In those moments, I remind myself: there's nothing to prove, no deadlines to meet, so why rush? I dig deep for inner strength and ask myself questions that keep me grounded: *Why do I write lyrics? Why do I accept these delays? Why am I not frustrated? What am I waiting for?*

If you've asked yourself similar questions, you're not alone. Answering them can reveal a deeper purpose in the waiting—a purpose of accepting the delays without being overwhelmed—a purpose that transforms delays into opportunities for growth, leading to a less stressful and more enjoyable life.

Furthermore, as you are nearing the finish line and start noticing the light of your dreams or goals flickering at the end of the tunnel, you must stay calm and silent and keep going at your own pace. Distraction, nuisance, and noise derived from extrinsic factors will be much stronger, faster, and louder; they will come from all angles with unprecedented speed, trying to either speed you up or derail you, so stay the course.

If someone had told me years ago that I'd write a book about song lyrics—let alone a memoir—I would have laughed and said, *"You lie like a rug."* Had I been impatient, rushing through life, or given up after my first album, *The Soundtrack of My Life,* or even that first mediocre song in the basement at 112 Methuen Street, I would have missed the gifts this journey offers. I would have overlooked the stones that held inspiration, the ones that led me here. With patience, no stone is left unturned.

The road ahead is always cloudy, but with patience, you can get a complete picture, view, or landscape of the entire road; that is the benefit of patience,

which is like a discovery channel where you discover your true self and calling. Additionally, having patience allows you to gather or pack necessities that would eventually be useful if tomorrow comes; by tomorrow, I mean the final destination, the future.

Was I wrong to believe this journey was about writing song lyrics? I used to think it was all about the craft—playing with words, crafting punchlines, weaving, wordplay, verses, and hooks. But as I near the end of this memoir, I begin to think otherwise. Perhaps the ultimate purpose of this dream was never about that. Maybe it was about writing a book all along. I had to find my way, remain calm, and endure the delays to discover the truth that validates my theory. I had to be patient enough to take the long ride and finally acknowledge the true meaning behind my lyrics. After all, it does not matter how late or how long; as long as I am where I was destined to be—in front of my computer, typing every word of this book to share this story with you—I do not mind being called a turtle.

Would you rather be a slow turtle or a fast-running hare? I have chosen the former for as long as I can remember—and look how far it has gotten me. I have fallen, I have tripped, and I have been rejected. I have paused along the way, but sure enough, I explored my environment while witnessing others speed through life, leaving me far behind, glancing at me in their rearview mirror. Yet, I am still moving at my own pace, taking my time, saving and reserving my energy so that when I reach my final destination, I have the strength to wave the checkered flag waiting at the finish line. This is not a rhyme; I genuinely and humbly mean it—both lyrically and figuratively.

Being impatient, you start creating bad habits—taking shortcuts, ignoring song structure and details—because your main focus becomes quantity rather than quality, aiming entirely at the destination instead of the journey, especially when deadlines loom. Still, I stayed the course, implementing verification steps to redeem myself and ensure every song was well-written. I used other artists' instrumental beats and tested my lyrics by singing them in my unorthodox voice in my car before completing a song.

The verification step encourages me to slow down—to double and triple-check my work: the number of lines, rhymes, word selection, and alignment. This step is like a speed bump or speed table, forcing me to pause and verify whether the song is well-written and meets the established requirements. Furthermore, once I am delighted with a song—well, somewhat satisfied—because satisfaction does not go hand in hand with greatness. Those chasing greatness, especially lyricists, are never truly happy; they always feel there is something they could have done better in retrospect.

Does the verification step take time? Absolutely—but it would take even longer if I sped through the process like a bullet, crashed, and had to start over. I would rather do it right the first time because rushing is exhausting; you never get a chance to breathe, enjoy, or seize the moment. I never wanted the writing process to be just a blur. I wanted to remember and understand my work for years to come.

As a lyricist, I constantly review other artists' lyrics—not to compete, but to analyze, benchmark, and evaluate their level of lyricism. Occasionally, I'm inspired by reading beautiful and unique song lyrics. Some songwriters are geniuses; they were born to write hit records, plain and simple.

On the contrary, I am far from being a genius. Still, the audacity of patience has kept me calmly poised, taking small steps—sometimes baby steps—without getting discouraged, so I don't prematurely exit this rollercoaster journey with regrets. I never want to be the regretful guy or lyricist sadly saying to himself, "What if, what if, or what had happened was."

So I refuse to let go of the rope of hope as I continue working toward this dream of mine, knowing that at the end of the day, one song, one lyric could be the defining moment where I, Patience the Ghostwriter, would no longer be a ghost. I would be visible in the music industry, no longer ghosted, but accredited as one of the world's exceptional lyricists—recognized for writing incredible songs and hit records charting at the top.

Billboards popping, people's eardrums buzzing, reuniting a divided America on the dance floor—because music is suffering from a state of depression. The current state of music feels unethical, un-sexy. I want my lyrics to not only bring sexy back—like the Tims, I mean like Justin Timberlake and Timbaland—but also make people party like it's 1999, where music becomes a release for stress in a society that has grown so depressed, it's depressing.

Until then, I am going to stay patient—more patient than a doctor—because success does not happen overnight. I am unbothered by those who have gotten a head start, as I am reminded every single day that each one of us has a mountain to climb to find our purpose. We all must climb patiently.

Some climb faster than others—whether they reach their final destination remains to be seen. The journey is like a movie, with so many scenes. So, I am still as patient today as I was in the early days, writing my first so-called rap song in the basement. And I do not believe that will ever change.

Along the way—even amid adversities and challenging times writing a song—I have always felt deep in my heart that something great would come to life; it was just a matter of time. An idea would turn into something beautiful, something unforeseen. But I had to stay the course to find out, because every song takes on a journey of its own.

If I had gotten angry and impatient, I would have never known the ending would lead me here. For art to exist, you must create something out of nothing. Writing a verse is one piece of the puzzle, but writing the chorus is another, so patience is *sine qua non*. Every letter, every word, and every line must be positioned in the correct section.

Sometimes, you can see the big picture and internalize how the pieces should fit together, but you cannot seem to get it right. That is when patience is tested—your mind tells you to quit, to go faster, or to take irrational shortcuts.

In those moments, I go back to where it all began—starting a song from scratch to move forward. It's a disappointing phase of the writing process, completely erasing lyrics that took months, even years, to write, just to create something better. It's scary because you may not come up with something as good—or worse, you may forget the initial idea. As I've alluded to throughout this book and journey, the writing process is a road; sometimes, making a U-turn feels right. Does it necessarily lead to a better path? No. It does not guarantee you'll find your way or go the right way.

So, as you come to a complete stop at a pivotal intersection in life—or in your craft, in my case—the writing process, you wait. You wait for the light to turn green, knowing that if you accelerate and run through that red light, you may see your life flash before your eyes. Waiting for the red light to turn green, as painful as it may seem, keeps your craft alive. Had I not patiently waited for ideas to flow, songs like *I Ain't Give Up, Winner,* and *Alive* would have never seen the light of day. They would have never been penned because I would have walked away halfway—especially when patience was rapidly fading. These songs represent the fruits of my long-awaited labor: delicious fruits harvested, although patience itself is sour.

As you wait for a breakthrough or for the light to turn green, you must adapt to the climate and your surroundings, accepting the reality that waiting is the safest choice to reach your destination. Once you make peace with this intersection—the so-called red light—your creativity will change, your mindset will change, and you will become a rejuvenated artist with new ideas, better than what you had before. That is the power of patience: obeying and accepting the delays, the tardies, and the challenges, knowing ultimately nothing—absolutely nothing—will start until you arrive.

In reality, one always arrives on time at their destination because, with the blessing of the Lord, you dictate when, how, and where the story ends—and when the verse ends. So why rush as if you're playing football, trying to rack up rushing yards? It's not worth it. The waiting is worth more. Trust the process, because the grind is part of the ultimate prize. The most important thing I've discovered during this odyssey is that the journey is the present—a gift to you. So take great care of it, most notably with patience. If you rush through life—or through your craft, whatever you've devoted yourself to—you may never fully embrace everything it has to offer.

To conclude, I am not sure how many stones you'll have to collect and turn while waiting for a breakthrough, or how many roads you'll have to travel, nor do I know how many red lights you'll encounter before reaching greatness. I am not sure how beautiful your stones will be either. But it is wise to remain calm and not leave any stones unturned. Take your time to assess and enjoy the journey you're on; you might be surprised where one stone will lead. I went from a wannabe lyricist to an author. You could say no destination is set in stone—unless you're a rolling stone.

ALBUM XIV
PERSEVERANCE

"Blessed is the one who perseveres under trial because, having stood the test, that person will receive the crown of life that the Lord has promised to those who love him."

-James 1:12 (NIV)

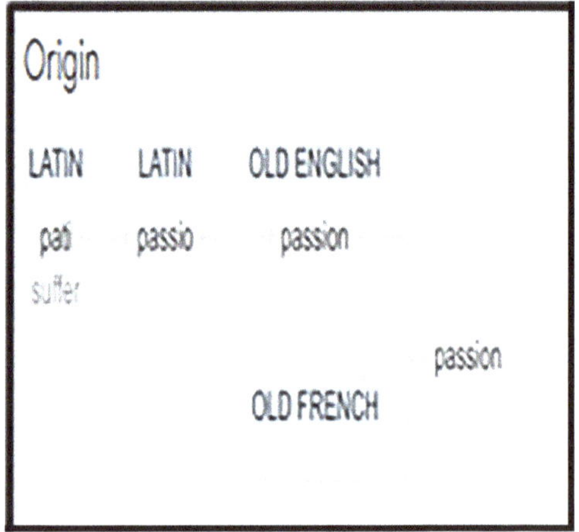

What is keeping my dream afloat? The most obvious and simplest answer is another word starting with the letter P. Not Petit—that would be too facile. Not Patience—that would be too monotonous. If you guessed perseverance, you are absolutely correct, as hinted on the book cover. However, you don't know the half of it—respectfully so. The other half consists of Passion, People, and Prayers: what I call the three Ps, representing the building blocks of perseverance, like amino acids are to protein—essential to the human body.

As I begin to fully grasp how far I've come and who I've become, I realize patience and consistency alone did not get me here. Perseverance is the driving force that carried me to this destination. Without it, I would have broken down on the side of the road long before this book was written. There were times I had nothing left in the tank—I was gassed out, out of words, with no energy or motivation to keep going. I had already exhausted all my strength patiently waiting for a breakthrough. Somehow, I managed to proceed because of these essential building blocks—the three Ps.

Where do they come from? Well, lean back and take another sip as I narrate.

Passion

Passion is a powerful emotion that can—and will—make you lose yourself, even sacrifice invaluable things, to focus on what truly matters to your heart. It is a personal trait driven by unseen, uncontrollable forces. You cannot rely on anyone to give you passion; it must be cultivated and accumulated within your core.Passion is a delicious fruit—just like a passion fruit. You have to hold on to it and squeeze every tiny seed, savoring the juice through difficult times. In life, it forces you to reflect and look at yourself in the mirror, facing it head-on and asking: Why do I dedicate my life and time to this? Is it a hobby or a passion? Does it fulfill a need? Do I love it? Do I crave the reward? Do I do it for fame?

As for me, I love writing because it is—and has always been—therapeutic. It gives me a platform to socialize internally with myself, especially since I'm not on social media. I love writing with a passion. Had it been just a hobby, I would have given up years ago.

As much as I have an appetite for writing and a knack for it, some days I may not seem as enthusiastic. Every day brings new challenges, and life often pulls me in different directions. So I do my best to find any creative space—a writing setting—to focus solely on writing because it is essential to have that sanctuary. An Uber driver once told me, "A clean space is a clear mind." After I complimented him on how clean and fresh the interior of his car was, I couldn't agree more. I saw the similarities with my writing—purging unhealthy thoughts from a cluttered mind.

Some days, I struggle with so many moving pieces—ideas and daily personal activities—but knowing I can overcome that nuisance with a pen stroke, I find my true self again. Writing restores my sanity. The bottom line is that writing has been my sanctuary. It took me a while to digest and comprehend this in the beginning. Still, with over two decades of writing, the excitement, the joy, the mystery, and the suspense in writing lyrics is something I would never trade for money or fame. I firmly believe the next verse, line, chorus, or hook I write could bring me happiness and peace. So why would I ever quit? When I am still profoundly moved by wordplay and rhymes? In the words of MC Hammer, "I am too legit to quit." Or should I say, I am too passionate to quit? Either way, you get the message.

That is one of the reasons why, even without a breakthrough, my knack for writing has helped me persevere—celebrating small wins and learning from constant setbacks that come with the writing process. As a lyricist, I often go through moments where I feel hopeless and think about giving up this dream. I replay this cliché in my head: "When you have everything, you have everything to lose. When you don't have anything, you have nothing to lose." So you go despite the odds. You become a cavalier, a maverick. I have so many ideas and writing material I

There were times I thought about quitting this dream because of someone's feedback or comment. But I've realized this journey was never—and will never—be about anyone but me, Patience The Ghostwriter. No one told me to grab a pen and start writing. No one injected words or lyrics into my veins. This passion didn't come from outside—it chose me, for reasons I may never understand.

So as I continue to contribute to the art of lyricism, I refuse to fear anyone's opinion, positive or negative. I must write—joyfully, religiously, and passionately—because I love to write. This is not about chasing fame or becoming a shooting star like Stephen Curry. It's about the love of the art. And I believe if I keep writing, one day I will go far, because my ceiling is limitless.

If you love something, never let judgment or criticism derail your passion. Whatever you put your mind to will eventually come to pass. That's why I've taken the "pass" out of "passion"—because I have a free pass to write whatever I want, whenever I want, to please myself and heal myself. I will never be dissuaded by anyone—not even a recording or publishing company. That doesn't mean I won't need their support; it means my passion isn't driven by outside forces.

Without passion, setbacks don't just slow you down—they destroy your dreams and drain your energy. Without passion, you don't enter this mysterious, uncertain world, let alone travel its infinite road. Some may try, but when the road gets dicey, how long will they last? Not long—their days will be numbered.

However, with passion, you can redeem yourself and confidently say "No" to that persistent voice in your head—the one playing tricks and whispering, "Give up! Give up!" in the face of adversity. Passion silences that sound. No matter what you do, no matter the challenges, even if you take a hiatus, something will always pull you back and push you forward until you reach your destination.

With passion, we break the standard rules. We strive and persevere because our belief in ourselves is undeniably—and unshakably—unbreakable.

Most of the time, it wasn't people fueling me when I couldn't write the next verse or line—it was the passion inside me. That passion has paved the way and kept me going against all odds. When you put your heart into something, passion will always prevail. It's stronger than the voices telling you to give up. That's why I won't quit anytime soon, even if I never break through, because I have one of the building blocks of perseverance always at my disposal.

People.
How can you achieve your dream without a support system? Better yet, how can anyone persevere without a helping hand? What strategies do you use to push through challenges? For years, I failed miserably to answer these questions—until now. So bear with me as I explain.

When passion went AWOL during this journey, I had to lean on others for support. Many individuals stood in my corner during difficult times. Whether or not they realize how impactful their support was—and still is—is another story.

I truly believe no dream is achievable without a support system or cast. Every player needs teammates. Even if someone reaches greatness alone, without help along the way, the victory may feel sweet—but not as sweet as your grandmother's Kool-Aid when no one is there to toast with you, raise a glass, or wave the checkered flag at the finish line. Loneliness can overshadow accomplishments so much that it rains on your parade.

That's why I've surrounded myself with believers, dreamers, and hardworking people—those who believe in themselves and, in turn, believe in me. They share my dreams selflessly, without jealousy or envy. My mother was the first to teach me that life is nothing but a dream. She often reminded me to be brave, bold, and fearless. Had it not been for the wisdom she imparted early on, I might not have had the strength to get this far—writing lyrics, let alone this memoir.

The tenacity to keep pursuing a dream requires understanding and commitment from others. They must believe in the most fundamental, unwritten rule of support: *"If you make it, they all make it."* Without that belief, their commitment may be short-lived, leaving you stranded and struggling to take the next step toward finishing what you commenced.

Moreover, I would not be writing this book—or continuing to write lyrics—if it were not for some incredible people in my life. Most notably, I want to thank Danounou, Ebenezer, Ms. Drayton (alias Verizon), Nicolas, my father, Valerie, Nerly, Takaya, Reggie, my sister Natalie, AJ, A&R, Rachel, and last but certainly not least, MJ, who has been the most influential of all. They consistently provide unwavering support that reignites my lyrical mind, helping me reach for lines and verses that would otherwise remain far beyond my radar.

All of them have urged me: *Keep writing! Keep writing!* Even on days when I feel like I've developed tunnel vision—or carpal tunnel—from years of effort without a breakthrough, these individuals remind me, both directly and indirectly, that there is a light at the end of the tunnel waiting for me. They help me fight the voices that whisper I will never become a recognized lyricist—sometimes through uplifting words and actions, and sometimes through tough love and constructive feedback.

For instance, they have read and critiqued most of my lyrics—if not all. I would email them each completed song, and they would reply with honest feedback, both positive and constructive. No matter how harsh their critiques were, I was never offended, knowing their honesty came from a place of love and respect. Each time, I returned to the drawing board, approaching my lyrics from new angles to satisfy them—and myself.

To my firstborn, Marcell—the youngest of all my supporters—you once said, *"Daddy, I have never seen you cry."* I must confess that when I wrote "HSH," dedicated to you, I cried like a baby because you have brought so much joy into my life. Even with a broken heart, I will love you eternally. You may not know it yet, and you're probably too young to fully understand, but those trips to New Jersey—where we chatted about life and silly topics to make the long journey from Massachusetts to Grandma's house in Linden engaging—are moments I cherish deeply. On one particular trip, we even came up with lyrics on the fly while stuck in traffic, inspired by *"Mad About You"* by Son Little. I can't quite remember whether it was on I-95 in Connecticut or New York, but I'll never forget Sunday, December 17, 2023. You were seated behind the passenger seat when we created the following lines together:

Verse I
They called me lazy
But when I start loving you, baby
They called me crazy **(Inspired by Marcell)**
'Cause I am hazy **(Inspired by Marcell)**
I am gonna drive you crazy
Like me Miss Daisy **(Inspired by Marcell)**

Chorus
And I know you gonna love me baby
And I know you gonna love me baby

And I know you gonna love me baby
'Cause I go crazy
For you
Cause I am like Ms. Daisy **(Inspired by Marcell)**
(hey,hey, hey)

Although this is not a complete song, moments like this remind me why I persevere—they bring me joy beyond what I could have imagined.

Whenever I'm at my computer writing song lyrics and you come by the desk, quietly reading through my lines, your presence inspires me to create my best work. You enthusiastically praise my writing and rhyming abilities, which encourages me tremendously. Even when you come to interrupt me, asking if you can have more playtime with the Nintendo Switch, just hearing your footsteps approaching gets my lyrical mind moving. For that, I am forever appreciative and grateful for your priceless support. You have shown immense

appreciation for what I love to do. If I ever fall short of fulfilling my dream as a lyricist, I know you will be nearby to lift me up, just as the saying goes: the apple never falls far from the tree. Speaking of apple trees, it's important to choose your supporters wisely, much like picking fruit and separating the good from the bad. Let's focus on the bad apples first. I believe it's best to identify and set aside the bad ones before picking the good ones, as you might be surprised at how many good apples are left.

The bad ones are non-dreamers, non-achievers, and non-believers—essentially, *quitters*. These are the people, including acquaintances, who can deflate your spirit, making you feel small and reminding you that your dreams are unattainable. Some will go even further, projecting their fears onto you, which can lead you to abandon your journey prematurely and never reach your goal of greatness.

To protect my dreams, I've chosen to be secretive and selective about whom I share my ideas and visions with. Otherwise, the fear, jealousy, and envy of others can derail your progress. Until you reach your goal and accomplish your dream, I strongly advise you to keep your thoughts to yourself—like a church mouse. It can be very challenging to persevere when people are lurking around like a cat sneaking through the house, undermining your dreams. Therefore, be prudent!

On the other hand, there are those who truly support you—your dream chasers and believers. They have your best interests at heart, whether things are going well or not. These individuals stay the course through thick and thin, cheering for you and uplifting you with encouraging words.

However, there were times I questioned the authenticity of their feedback. Were they being too kind? After all, they are part of my inner circle and might hesitate to express their true feelings about my work. Yet, they have only spoken the truth, which has helped me grow and build confidence. I am forever grateful for their honesty because, too often, loved ones unintentionally harm your dreams by offering only conditional love that overlooks your weaknesses. You may believe you're as great as they say, but if they only highlight your strengths, you miss out on crucial areas for improvement.

These amazing people have kept it real, calling a spade a spade. Their unfiltered criticism has strengthened our relationships and made me a better lyricist. I've worked harder on every aspect of my craft, especially during challenging writing sessions, striving to address their concerns and feedback. Ultimately, their influence has brought out the best in me, sharpening my skills and helping me improve my weaknesses.

For example, the best producers and directors don't collaborate with mediocre artists; they seek out the best—the greatest lyricists and singers. They aim to challenge these artists, enhance their skills, and elevate them to the next level because there are various levels to greatness. They want to work with peers who thrive, who are uniquely talented, and who share a vision of excellence—where their complete skills can shine.

These are the people I want around me—the ones who will look me in the eye and say, "These lyrics suck," instead of telling me what I want to hear. Their candid feedback is invaluable because it prevents false hope and pushes me to grow. For that, I am deeply grateful.

However, there's always a "but." I cannot conclude without acknowledging the artists who have motivated me—even though I've never met them and likely never will. I found inspiration in their lyrics: Jay-Z, Eminem, Talib Kweli, André 3000, and Lil Wayne. They are among the reasons I continue to write. Even if my work were to surpass theirs, I would never have the audacity to consider myself their rival; they are my idols. In my book, they belong on the Mount Rushmore of greatness—the true GOATs.

There were times when writing felt painful, yet their music always inspired me to keep going. They consistently deliver the best verses, hooks, stories, wordplay, rhymes, metaphors, and similes—all with perfect cadence and flow. Their artistry has shaped my lyrical aspirations and even certain aspects of my personal life.

I recall the summer of 2008—a particularly dark time for me academically. After discovering my unsatisfactory GPA, I was placed on academic suspension with two options: drop out or appeal. I chose to appeal, and my request was granted under probationary conditions. During the following semester, I walked through campus with tears in my eyes, uncertain how to improve my grades. I was listening to Kanye West's *Graduation*—a classic album—but I couldn't envision myself graduating while hearing it. Nevertheless, the lyrics of my musical idols inspired me.

Ultimately, I walked across the stage at the 2010 graduation ceremony with pride, thanks in part to songs like "Lose Yourself" by Eminem, "Around My Way" by Talib Kweli, "Moment of Clarity" by Jay-Z, "Best Rapper Alive" by Lil Wayne, and "Da Art of Storytellin'" (Parts 1 and 2) by André 3000 and Big Boi of Outkast. Their songs capture the zeitgeist of my lyrical journey to this day.

Prayers

How do you persevere when the first two Ps—passion and people—prove insufficient? What steps do you take when your dream starts to feel more like a nightmare? What happens when passion and support are nowhere to be found? For a long time, I searched for solutions elsewhere, hoping for a helping hand, but I consistently came up empty. Then I realized this journey had always been part of God's plan. That's when I began to rely on the most essential building block of perseverance: prayer. I pray to Almighty God to help me push through difficult times so that I never abandon this journey, trusting that my life is in His hands. I praise Him because my ability to persevere is a gift from Him, and He knows why the breakthrough has not yet come. I thank God for strengthening me—physically, spiritually, mentally, and lyrically—so I can continue chasing my dream despite the challenges I face.

I believe every person is born with a God-given talent, though some are blessed with multiple gifts. Growing up, I thought talent was simply embedded in our DNA, but I've learned it runs much deeper—it is a divine gift. When we value and cherish this gift, it can transform not only our lives but also make a meaningful contribution to our communities, society, and the world.

Take Rapper Jay-Z, for example—undeniably one of the greatest lyricists of all time. Even though he no longer writes down his lyrics, had he not showcased his talent beyond the Marcy Projects where he grew up, the world might never have known how gifted he truly is. His gift has inspired countless lyricists like me, helping us persevere and beat the odds. The purpose of a gift is to share it with others and the world; otherwise, it remains hidden and invaluable.

A gift provides a sense of contentment and purpose. It reflects who we are and shapes how others perceive us, allowing us to serve the greater good—even when it demands personal sacrifices and suffering. A gift cannot be acquired or learned, but it can be refined and enhanced to sustain us during difficult times, easing some of the pain that comes with pursuing dreams.

Writing song lyrics can be complex and challenging; imagine the difficulty if it weren't a gift I possessed. The process would be far more daunting, making it nearly impossible to compose even the opening line of a verse. Instead of sharing my songwriting talent with others, I would have been on the other end—relying heavily on someone to teach me the basics of songwriting, which would have come with its own set of sacrifices. The road to greatness is always long, but for someone with skills alone compared to someone who possesses a gift.A gifted individual may practice for a few hours each day on their craft, while someone relying solely on skill may need to invest nine or ten hours—or more—just to achieve satisfactory results. And by satisfactory, I mean an "A for effort." This is why perseverance is crucial; without it, the destination becomes distant, and the ability to overcome obstacles diminishes.

When talent is paired with skill, the impact can be extraordinary—shaping society and inspiring the world beyond imagination. This is why the talented and skilled continue to push boundaries, even when their endeavors are labeled as risky. A gift encourages us to keep serving and inspiring others despite challenges, teaching us to trust that higher powers guide us through the darkest times when we use our talents wisely and, most importantly, spiritually—while praising God for His glory.

Passion and people may fail us on the path to excellence—sometimes intentionally, sometimes unintentionally. But God will never fail us or forsake us. When the journey seems longer, riskier, and increasingly impossible, His presence becomes even stronger, blessing us with unwavering determination and courage to continue.

How much talent or gift were you blessed with? Regardless of its size, if I've learned anything, it is the wisdom of praying along the way and sharing your story so it can fulfill its purpose. You might be surprised at how your journey can inspire others and elevate your dreams to new heights of greatness.

Otherwise, how valuable is a gift if it remains unopened or sealed in its original package? It would be like giving a loved one a birthday present and instructing them not to open it. An unshared gift is akin to a hidden truth—concealing the power of the heavens and God's strength during difficult times.

There were moments when my pride and stubbornness urged me to continue this journey alone, but I chose not to, realizing that it wouldn't last. I would have become exhausted and never made it this far. The more time we spend traveling the road to greatness by ourselves, the more complex, longer, and riskier that journey becomes. However, when we surrender everything to God, the path ahead becomes easier, shorter, and safer.

Muhammad Ali once said, *"I knew I was the greatest before I even knew I was."* This powerful statement underscores his gift, strength, and ambition. However, I believe that without prayer, he may not have been able to demonstrate the tenacity needed to overcome the obstacles throughout his career—obstacles that ultimately propelled him to greatness and stardom.

I share similar beliefs, sometimes with great ambition, if I may say so myself. Honestly, I may not be the greatest, but if I keep praying, I believe I will eventually achieve my goals and see my name in the credits of a song. But what happens when you feel like God is not answering your prayers? Is it that God isn't responding? Perhaps He hasn't answered because He knows the journey is too difficult for you to bear right now. Maybe He has other priorities—like teaching us patience before perseverance. Or perhaps God simply takes His time. Who knows?

I would be lying if I said I have never felt that my prayers were going unanswered.

I have experienced moments of uncertainty and loneliness, especially when choosing the less-traveled path. At times, I felt that God would not take the wheel when I encountered roadblocks that seemed too hard to bear—including instances of writer's block. There were many days when I felt drained, with no ideas and not even the energy to hold a pen or press the keys on my keyboard to draft a single line, not even "Verse I."

However, when something is God-given, personal issues or crises cannot completely impede the thought process. I can affirm that God works mysteriously and spiritually in His own sweet time, with reasons too sacred or profound for us to comprehend. He always has a purpose. For instance, something unexpectedly miraculous always seems to come my way, providing me the strength to persevere and lifting me up spiritually.

It might be as simple as legendary NFL coach Bill Belichick chanting, *"No Days Off, No Days Off, No Days Off"* during the 2017 Super Bowl Parade after the New England Patriots made a remarkable comeback to beat the Atlanta Falcons and win Super Bowl LI. Hearing those words echoed in my ears like a chorus while I stood soaked, with frozen hands, in a flooded crowd of fans by Boston City Hall. At that moment, Belichick proudly delivered his memorable message from the balcony to Beantown. That experience rekindled my passion and reminded me that this gift cannot be taken for granted; it has an eternal purpose.

As I write this paragraph on Saturday, September 10, 2022, I have not taken a day off since then. All praise goes to the Almighty Lord, who has placed me on this incredible journey beyond my wildest dreams. During that time, I have written over fifty songs. While that may not seem like a lot, I have learned to value quality over quantity to ensure the best songs are created.

However, as Belichick's chants faded and the thought of giving up songwriting increased, I found myself at a church service where the pastor recited Psalm 118:14: *"The Lord is my strength and my song; he has become my salvation."* Initially, I considered this a coincidence, but after the service, as I headed to my car, I realized otherwise. I was deeply moved, feeling that God spoke to me and answered my prayers for perseverance and strength to continue my journey. I will forever praise the Lord as He is my song; therefore, I will continue this journey, reciting this verse like a broken record—especially through difficult circumstances, roadblocks, constructive feedback, and personal challenges.

Reaching this point in my life is nothing short of a miracle, especially for a kid from Lakou Kokoye and Lowell. If you count the unforgettable and marvelous years I've spent in Lowell, you'll see that I have never taken "no" for an answer. My entire life has been built on perseverance. From writing lyric hooks and verses to writing a book, I've defied expectations every step of the way.

So, who is going to doubt the next kid who looks like me, walks like me, talks like me, and writes like me? Never judge us by our appearance—this is not a fluke.

Sorry, as I was writing the sentence above, *"From writing lyric hooks to writing a book, who is going to doubt the next kid that looks like me, walks like me, talks like me, writes like me; so never judge us by the way we look. As this is not a fluke."* This surge—this itch of creativity—led me to feel an urge to rhyme. Sometimes, I can't help but drop a few bars. As a hip-hop enthusiast, here's how the verse goes:

Verse I

From writing hooks to writing a book
Don't judge us by the way we look
This is not a fluke, We couldn't read
'Cause they took away our books
Now we read between those lines
Correct them when they crossed the lines
Knowing our wrongs and civil rights
Now they are scared of us, right?
Killing us softly, kneeling on us, literally
Still, we persevere and fight all night
Even though, we know the system is right
All the time for the Whites
When it's all Black, it's not alright
For us, it's death or death, no life
Its time to wake up, turn on the light
Let's reunite this divided America, aight
Put our differences to bed, good nite!
Now you know why, I love to write

Sorry, where was I? I lost track—blame the blood of lyricism that runs through me like blood through veins. Anyway, as I was saying, my entire life is built on perseverance. But I've realized that without passion, people, and most importantly, prayer, even if you think you're moving forward—defeating the odds and overcoming obstacles—you might actually be standing still, like a stalled vehicle. The moment you give it all to the Lord in prayer, surround yourself with dream chasers and believers, and fully savor the juice of this delicious fruit called passion, you will reach the finish line—even if there are barricades or barriers in your way.

EPILOGUE

Well, well, well—look what we have here: the end. All good things must come to an end. This is not a farewell; rather, it marks the conclusion of an incredible journey not your typical fairytale. It all began with the birth of a child whose first dream was to become a dentist or dental hygienist. Little did I know that the heavens would take me on an unpredictable ride—a journey where only a few survive, filled with the pain of chasing greatness, and with a finish line that remains unclear, even if I'm the one to define it, even if the line is penned by me. The roads are treacherous, often clouded with obstacles and roadblocks.

Nevertheless, I chose to heed the signs from the heavens and took the fork in the road that led me to write song lyrics. Once I entered this musical world, I thought it would be smooth sailing—like cruising with Tom Cruise. However, I soon discovered it was more like a mission impossible. I imagined writing song lyrics and submitting them to record labels, particularly to A&R representatives, who would vet them and pitch them to artists. If selected, I would gain recognition and credit as a writer. Yet, finding acknowledgment as a lyricist in the music industry is no easy task; if anything, it often feels like a mission impossible.

I found myself at a crossroads: should I stop writing song lyrics or continue? I chose to continue because I believed that in life, *"you choose your own path; if you don't choose, then you snooze, you lose."* Consequently, I dedicated years to writing a multitude of songs, which I compiled into the following albums: *The Soundtrack Of My Life, The New Ending of My Life, Seize The Moment, Happiness, and Peaceful.* These albums reflect my lyrical imagination, not including my upcoming projects, *Looking Ahead and Back To Basics,* which are not part of this memoir.

I was on a mission to pour everything into my work—my soul, my heart, and my life—into every line and verse I wrote. Nearly two decades later, I am still writing without having achieved a breakthrough. This lack of success can be disheartening, as it threatens dreams and can take a toll on one's self-image and personality.

I kept my pen in my notebook, but when that approach wasn't yielding results, I changed my strategy and began typing my lyrics in Word documents. This shift saved me time later on, allowing me to focus solely on songwriting.

Additionally, I diligently reached out to record labels and local artists to pitch my lyrics directly, but still faced no breakthrough. I kept working on my craft, writing tirelessly. Unsure of how good or bad my songs were, I submitted them for review—and that's how I discovered Rachel, an A&R representative. During her review, she noted that I needed to improve my song structure and craft compelling, unique stories. Once again, I went back to the lab—the drawing board—to ameliorate and refine my skills.

Thereafter, I began receiving mixed reviews—more mixed than a biracial kid might encounter—with both praise and constructive criticism. I've never believed in "negative" feedback, so I took it on the chin and held tight to the rope of hope. Every song deemed poorly written or structured, I revised from top to bottom to meet Rachel's expectations. Yet, despite my efforts, no breakthrough came; no record label opened its doors.

Determined, I kept pushing forward, knocking on doors as if they were heaven's gates. Though I don't condone addiction, I became obsessed with submitting more lyrics to Rachel. The more I sent, the more feedback filled my inbox—and with it, more work. Despite my persistence, I struggled to fully address her comments.

Finally, a glimmer of hope arrived with a song titled *Addicted*, which earned encouraging feedback.

But as good as that break was, it wasn't enough to break the camel's back—it didn't change my situation. Still, it gave me the breath I needed to persevere.

Later, I learned that record labels wouldn't pay attention if I only had lyrics without a finished product. So, we demoed *Addicted*, but progress remained elusive. I then recorded demos for *Alive* and *Keep Going Back,* yet no artist showed interest. Once again, I shifted my approach, entering the "Only" lyrics contest with what I believed were my best songs—at least by my own vision. Meanwhile, I kept my fingers on the keyboard, writing writing more lyrics and waiting patiently for a breakthrough. Still, no progress to report.

In 2022, I faced a familiar question: should I stop writing song lyrics or keep going? This time, I chose to stop—a decision that led me here, writing a memoir, a destination I never imagined when my vision seemed so clear.

One reason I decided to write this book was to avoid sitting in a rocking chair years from now, gray-haired and full of regret, lamenting that life was unfair because I never saw my name in the credits. Instead, I'm putting everything aside to share a piece of my life that has been deeply rewarding. This book is my breakthrough—a reflection of the obstacles, roadblocks, and personal changes I encountered while chasing a dream that began in Lakou Kokoye.

My journey taught me that greatness—what I call "Black excellence"—demands hard work, sacrifice, consistency, patience, and perseverance. Consistency is the foundation of perseverance. It's about taking small steps, making incremental changes, and learning from mistakes. If you're fortunate, you'll learn from others' mistakes too, making the path easier.

My message is simple: *Consistency can only be built through self-discipline and the ability to identify, control, or eliminate external factors that cause inconsistency.* Once you establish consistency, perseverance becomes attainable. But without passion—the kind that finds meaning in suffering—you need people who believe in themselves and in you. Even then, perseverance remains distant until you kneel in prayer, seeking guidance from the Lord to walk with you, knowing your passion is a God-given gift that needs His blessing. Without that, you risk breaking down, taking detours, and losing sight of your goal.

To persevere, you need patience to endure obstacles and pain so you don't exit the path to greatness prematurely. Had I not cultivated consistency, patience, and perseverance, I would never have realized that my journey—from reading words in a dictionary to writing poems, crafting rhymes, and penning lyrics—would lead me to write a memoir.

Hence, I no longer believe in my theory: "You choose your own path; if you don't choose, you snooze, you lose." With the knowledge I have acquired, I now understand it's more accurate to say: *"You never lose anything in life, nor do you truly choose. Instead, you wake up and learn every day."*

I have learned so much, and that is one of the reasons I am here—reminding you never to give up and never fear failure, because failure fosters resilience. Stay on the journey, especially if you've taken the road less traveled. You may be surprised where it leads.

Continue with consistency, patience, and perseverance; in the end, you will leave your mark, making the path easier for others to follow—or your experience can serve as a blueprint. In my case, my son MJ can follow and pave an even better path for generations to come. Isn't that the ultimate dream and final destination? I believe it is—though if not, it is certainly one of them.

There is always a "but," right? Instead of "but," let's use "also," because I have other reasons worth sharing before the curtain call.

The other ultimate dream I have is to be recognized not only as a lyricist but as an artist—that is to say, without a country—an artist without borders who gives hope to the hopeless, dreams to the dreamers, and belief to the believers so we can pioneer the world together.

I took a small dream planted in Lakou Kokoye, nurtured it in the basement of 112 Methuen Street, and watered it every day. It may not have grown as much as I hoped, but I've squeezed every drop of juice from these lyrics and carried them to places they've never been. My hope is that one day, the next aspiring lyricist will use my story not just as a guide for songwriting but as a blueprint for embodying consistency, patience, and perseverance.

Life is a beautiful struggle; once you find your true calling, you will discover the beauty—*la beauté*—in the battle.

As a friendly reminder, I want to be remembered as a lyricist in every sense of the word—a lyricist who abides by the law. As for becoming a professional lyricist, I don't know how my story will be told or what the future holds. But whoever reads this journey should know that I poured my blood, heart, and tears into this work. Even if my lyrics never make it to your playlist, just know that I, Patience The Ghostwriter, tried so hard I might die from carpal tunnel syndrome.

I love getting lost in writing lyrics because I never know where I'll end up, what I'll do, who I'll become, which bridge I'll cross, or how my words will make an impact. It's thrilling. My passion for songwriting is rooted in joy and happiness. Even while writing this memoir, I couldn't resist the force pulling me back to lyrics. No matter how much I tried to ignore it to focus on this book, the urge grew stronger, pushing me to alternate between writing this memoir and crafting new songs—*Last Night, I Suck at Math, Mr. Bad Guy, Dance With Me, Nope,* and *IV.*

As for this book, I'm unsure whether it will be commercially successful—selling millions of copies or becoming a New York Times bestseller. I don't know if it will sell out. Still, in the end, I'll be fine—glass of wine in hand—because all I ever wanted was to illustrate how I cultivated my skills and God-given gifts, while acknowledging that every day, a star is born and a lyricist emerges.

Each story is unique, so let me tell you the difference between them and me: many die never understanding the significance of three key concepts—patience, perseverance, and consistency. That's why they never made it this far, far enough to write about it.

Until next time—and until further notice—thank you for listening. You could have chosen any book to read, but you chose this one, and for that, I am forever grateful.

But before you head out—LOL—I've got something cool to show you as a thank you. Just flip the page to see what it is!

How good is an album without bonus tracks?

Bonus Track♪♪Last Night

Intro

My last night in Haiti

Verse I

The year was 99, Oct 31st to be exact
Before it was 1999
We partied like Prince in 1999, fact
Life wasn't always beautiful
But with beautiful people
We called it the beautiful struggle
Even the poor were happy poor
At Mais Gate Airport, no lie
Tears falling down my eyes
Couldn't look mom in her eyes
If she cries, hand me a tissue
Brothers too young, so no issue
Friends become enemies, jealousy
'Cause I'm leaving them in poverty
To go where money grows on tree

Pre-chorus

Leaving Croix-Des-Missions
Coming to America was the mission
But,

Chorus

Wishing I could go back
Just to paint a different picture
W/o a Kodak, just like Kodak Black
My last night in Haiti
Full of memories, full of calamities
Full of sorrows, full of struggle
But, I wouldn't change a damn thing
As a matter of fact
Wishing I could go back
Just to paint a different picture
W/o a Kodak, just like Kodak Black
My last night in Haiti

Bonus Track♪♪♪Last Night

Verse II

I hate making a short story long
Please, bear with me
This ain't just your typical song
Last night I had a dream
I was back in Haiti, area code 509
Saw a young kid about 8 or 9
He looked just like mine
But was carrying a loaded 9
This could've been me every night
Hadn't I not flown in 99 in A. Airlines
If God had a plan for me years ago
God will show Haiti which way to go

Pre-chorus & Chorus (Repeat)

Verse III

Let's paint a perfect picture
I ain't talking about the picture
In your living room wall
Picture your back against the wall
Baby Jackson's crying, mom's starving
Tell me you wouldn't go off the wall
No PediaSure, Ensure, just dirt cookies
No government cheese , no nuts
Naturally I'm polite, but I'd go nuts
Knowing The haves are thrilled
Burgers and steak on the grill
Watching The have nots getting ill
From scurvy and swollen stomach
Something that I can't stomach

Pre-chorus & Chorus (Repeat)

Outro

Ooh oui, I'm craving that feeling back
Feeling that summer breeze on my back
Even if it means I have to watch my back
What doesn't kill you, makes you Haitian

Song Credits:

All lyrics written by
Patience the Ghostwriter.

END

www.ingramcontent.com/pod-product-compliance
Ingram Content Group UK Ltd.
Pitfield, Milton Keynes, MK11 3LW, UK
UKHW021831270726
14058UKWH00001B/96